Sydney

AN OXFORD ANTHOLOGY

For Meredith and Rhea

Sydney

An Oxford Anthology

Edited by Richard Hall

OXFORD

UNIVERSITY PRESS

OXFORD

UNIVERSITY PRESS

253 Normanby Road, South Melbourne, Victoria, Australia

Oxford University Press is a department of the University of Oxford.
It furthers the University's objective of excellence in research, scholarship,
and education by publishing worldwide in

Oxford New York

Athens Auckland Bangkok Bogotá Buenos Aires Calcutta
Cape Town Chennai Dar es Salaam Delhi Florence Hong Kong Istanbul
Karachi Kuala Lumpur Madrid Melbourne Mexico City Mumbai Nairobi
Paris Port Moresby São Paulo Singapore Taipei Tokyo Toronto Warsaw
and associated companies in Berlin Ibadan

OXFORD is a trade mark of Oxford University Press

National Library of Australia
Cataloguing-in-Publication data:

Sydney: an Oxford anthology

Includes index.
ISBN 0 19 550687 1.

1. Australian literature—New South Wales—Sydney. 2. Sydney (NSW)—Literary
collections. I. Hall, Richard. II. Title.

A820.803299441

Edited by Cathryn Game
Indexed by Richard Hall
Text designed by Derrick I. Stone Design
Cover designed by Karen Trump
Typeset by Desktop Concepts Pty Ltd, Melbourne
Printed by Kyodo Printing Co. Pte Ltd, Singapore

Contents

Introduction

When the Scotsman John Pringle wrote of the three winds of Sydney in 1958 he was seeing them as backdrop to a city, a stable community, with its own character and style, a place where most of the men in the city's centre wore blue serge suits, as they would have in John Kinsgmill's Sydney of the 1930s. The 1950s were the last years of the Anglo-Celtic city, the coalition of English, Scots, and Irish that had rubbed along from the beginning, although not without tensions. The new immigrants were coming, but they were still on the margins, put in their place by that patronising assimilationist tag 'New Australians'. In the early years of the decade writers of letters to the editor, the radio talkback callers of the time, worried that newspapers for the immigrant communities used their own languages: it was felt that this practice should rapidly die out. George Johnston in *Clean Straw for Nothing* has a revealing episode in which an old Sydney-sider can rebuke a newcomer for the offence of his accent. In those days the word *schnitzel* was a joke; spaghetti was something that came in tins with tomato sauce; Chinatown was a ghetto of a few mean streets. Some suburbs, certainly not all, had a token Chinese restaurant, the menus topped by sweet and sour pork, an unthreatening dish.

In 1954 when the Queen came the crowds did line the streets and cheer. The State Governor was a person of note, and the ABC sent a reporter out every Sunday to record the deep thoughts of that functionary as he moved from flower fête to RSL congress. Archbishops and their coadjutors were taken note of. Vicars and ministers were men of substance in their suburbs, influential beyond their congregations, while priests of the Catholic Church could expect two-thirds of their faith at mass every Sunday. It was a stable and secure world, or so it seemed.

But in 1958, the year Pringle's book *Australian Accent* came out, Sydney was on the cusp. The second age of the city was coming to a close. The first age, that of the colony, robust and pugnacious, ran from 1788 to the federation of 1901. The second age, an ordered Anglo-Celtic era, was very good at hiding away the unruly. It was a world of suburban respectability, and to be Australian was to be in the best of all worlds. Pangloss might have been the patron saint. However, as in Occupied Europe during World War II, there were resisters. Christina Stead and Jack Lindsay wrote about the outsiders, but it is significant that both writers had to flee.

Some would say the 1960s marked the end of that era, but then there are those people, like the not inconsiderable number who voted for One Nation in the late 1990s, who cannot accept that that era ever ended.

Pringle could see that change was coming but, shrewd observer though he was, he didn't grasp how far things would be changed. But then again some things have not changed. The best of his book is in his decription of what has not changed: the three winds of Sydney: the north-easterly, the soft, warm Pacific wind that brings the showers; the southerly buster, at any time of the year, sweeping in, jostled north by the front from the polar South, dumping the rain and dragging the temperature down; and then the westerlies of summer, dry, hot and nagging.

Both those who came to visit and those who stayed liked to exclaim at the extremes of the weather in Sydney. Arthur Bowes Smyth, a surgeon on one of the women's convict ships of the First Fleet, wrote in his diary about the events of 7 February 1788 when the female convicts were set ashore for the first time, provoking scenes of the utmost debauchery and riot, as the surgeon told it. He was the first but far from the last to deplore the morals of Sydney's inhabitants. But Bowes also recorded 'the most violent storm of thunder, lightning and rain that I have ever seen', which, although it killed five sheep and a pig struck by lightning, did nothing 'in the least respect' to damp down the debauchery. A few years later, in 1794, the painter Thomas Watling wrote of the westerly 'as a scorching wind so intolerable as to restrict respiration'. Charlotte Godley in 1851, while deploring the effect of the gold rush on servants' manners, took time to write of the menace of the brickfielders, those southerly busters so-called because they came in over the brickfields on the fringe of the city and raised the most fearful dust. A few years later an English journalist, Frank Fowler, invoked the Apocalypse to deplore the westerlies as being as 'hot and murky as the breath of an oven, as though the Last Seal was opened and the breath of the Destroying Angel came forth'. Visiting writers again and again took note of the extremes of the climate, so irregular compared to the order of the seasons at home.

Now in the concrete canyons of the Central Business District, the winds are lost, blocked, and tamed. For office workers in a high-rise building near a window, the rolling grey clouds of a southerly front sweeping towards the city are safe theatre. But in the suburbs things can be different, very different. The flat plains of western Sydney can be still stifled by days of westerlies, which brush aside any of the nor'easterly breezes that might have edged so far inland. The infamous hail storm of April 1999 played a trick of heading out to sea before veering back to shake the city by the scruff of the neck. Even the fastnesses of the high North Shore, proud of the huge eucalypts or their English gardens, are clawed every few years by fierce southerlies that strip the boughs and bring down trees. For those who sail in small boats on the harbour, a southerly is an ambush to be feared. Sometimes even the usually benign north-easterly can force the yachts to run before the wind. A week of southerlies can throw up great waves that can rip away beaches. The winds with all their capacity for extremes are very much actors in the drama of the city. But for all that the people of Sydney have adapted to the extremes, just as the men and women convicts did that night in February 1788, and got on with their lives. Watling seems almost frightened of winds and landscape, but at the same time someone was tending the vines and citruses in the Governor's garden.

Whereas many stayed, there were always some, even from the first days, who wanted to cut and run. The experiment of a penal colony at the end of the world was, as any scrutiny of the London press will show, regarded as an absurd act of folly. The officers of Captain Malaspina's Spanish fleet who visited Sydney in 1793 noted the widespread opinion that the colony would be closed down. Governor Phillip had gone home by then. Although the colony had that formidable patron Sir Joseph Banks, it can be judged that if Phillip had brought back a negative picture, the pessimists might well have been proved right. We are in debt to Phillip not only for those first days but also for what he said when he went back to London. It could have been a close run thing. Even so the bureaucrats of Whitehall were not envisaging the dream of Empire, merely a self-supporting penal colony, with perhaps a few strategic advantages on side. The Blue Mountains loomed to the west, but it would be twenty-four years before a party crossed them. The Cumberland Plain and the fertile Hawkesbury River flats could support the colony.

By 1802 François Péron, one of the scientists on a French expedition under Captain Baudin, found a solidly established settlement grown to more than 3,500 people. Government was enlightened, industry and agriculture thriving, and there was even 'a sort of coffee-house'.

Others saw things differently. Three years previously three missionaries driven from Tahiti by civil war and cannibalism found Sydney equally iniquitous: 'Adultery, fornication, theft, drunkenness, extortion, violence and uncleanness of every kind, the natural concomitants of Deism and infidelity.' This jaundiced view might have been influenced by the fate of a fourth colleague, who, while engaging in a spot of money-lending on the side, had tried to retrieve a debt from a sergeant. The sergeant killed him with an axe and was hanged the next day. But apart from that, the missionaries' horror should remind us that Fred Nile was not the first clergyman to despair of Sydney's morals.

Despite the fine vistas praised by Péron, it was still a settlement, and held together by violence; executions and floggings were hardly worth a comment. The savages might be quelled by providential smallpox and the musket, but the authorities could never be sure of the convicts. One threat was never very far from their minds: the prospect of a rising by the Irish convicts, augmented by prisoners from the failed 1798 rising. The Irish rebellion did come in 1804, botched in execution and then bloodily put down by the New South Wales Corps, who killed nineteen in the only skirmish. The next rising, in 1808 by the Rum Corps against the Governor, Captain Bligh, was more farcical than bloody, but it was an omen of Sydney's lasting mistrust of authority.

For the rest of that century the better classes and their newspaper leader-writers tended to pose the anguished question: what good could come of a colony so tainted by its origins? The querulousness was sharpened in the early decades by the competitiveness of the more successful emancipationists, ex-convicts, and, in later years, by a snobbish mistrust of colonial democracy. However, most of the locally born citizens of Sydney, the currency lads and lasses, were not much interested in the question. Charles Darwin, coming in 1836, was one of the earliest travellers to put Sydney in the book he wrote about his tour, and he was much struck by the extreme rancour between the emacipationists and the free middle class. (By the way, Darwin seems to have been the first to see Sydney as a future city of suburbs.)

John Hood, who visited in 1838, in his book deplored the number of hotels, 'dens of iniquity'. There was one for every 140 souls, men, women and children. He then expressed surprise that the streets of Sydney were safe to walk at night.

Whereas some ex-convicts did very well and others lived humble lives within the law, there was a vigorous underworld of old lags. The diary of the police Inspector Nugent, whose beat covered the Rocks and the city up to Druitt, Park, and Macquarie streets, records 107 'disorderly houses'—that is, brothels—as well thieves' kitchens, gambling dens, and bent publicans galore. The transportation of convicts did end, but then the gold rush brought a new class of plebeian immigrant, dangerously inclined to democracy.

The idea of the convict taint gained some fresh impetus among newspaper leader-writers in the 1870s with the rise of the larrikin pushes of the Sydney slums. In 1881 a new periodical, the *Bulletin*, exploited the popular fear of that underside of society with its report of a day at the Clontarf picnic grounds. By an unintended irony the same Clontarf a decade before had been the scene of riot by the more respectable members of society, who responded to an attempt on the life of Prince Alfred, one of Queen Victoria's sons, by attempting to lynch the assailant. But that was to look back, and in the early years of the 1880s the leader-writers returned to the larrikin threat again and again. Even a visiting actor, in memoirs published in New York, told Americans of this Australian horror. In 1885 a vicious Push rape of a girl at Mount Rennie led the city into an orgy of breast-beating sermons. The vengeance on the rapists seemed, to read the sermons and submissions of delegations, more important than the fate of the girl. The execution of four of the convicted, a shockingly bungled hanging, was the climax.

Politics in both Macquarie Street and the Sydney City Council was mostly petty and personal. On his visit to the colony in 1875 a rather priggish Havelock Ellis was, however, right when he characterised the Legislative Assembly as 'a body of businessmen, merchants, shop-keepers and the like'. Not very far below the surface in politics was the tension between Catholics and Protestants. In 1871 a boxing match—illegal, as they all were—was tagged an Orange v. Green match.

Sydney was never without slums, but the snowballing growth of the city in the second half of the nineteenth century meant that the old slums became worse and the new ones grew faster. There were only spasmodic qualms about health until the authorities were shaken by an outbreak of bubonic plague in 1900. In the slums there were no pensions for widows or the old, no unemployment benefits, only uncertain charity. The Chippendale slum streets walked by young H.M. Moran were a mile from the theatre where the visiting Melbourne artist Arthur Streeton would attend the At Home afternoon of Mrs Charrington, a leader of Society who was rich enough to hire the theatre and an orchestra as her social stage. After expressing his pleasure at Mrs Charrington's generous hospitality Streeton grumbled about the distractions of the Maritime Strike only a few streets away.

This anthology is not a gazetteer, a history, or a reference book. Readers will not find, to take one case, any account of the dull pompous charade played out in Centennial Park on January 1901 to institute the Commonwealth of Australia: the Governor-General in uniform with his cocked hat, the soldiers and sailors, the parade of drays decked with the produce of industry and farm, the inevitable artillery salute—all the sedate theatre of the British Empire, which might have been played out in many cities: Montreal or Ottawa, Dublin or Belfast, Edinburgh or Dunedin. Nor does the anthology record 'first' events, like aeroplanes, trains, and so on. That is not to say that a 'first' cannot tell us a great deal about the city, like the first election day of 1843, with the mob versus the quality.

The basis of selection has been to seek writing that says something about Sydney—writing with a sense of place, physical geography, Sydney's people, their manners, their passions and contradictions. Material has had to be either contemporary or written later from the memory of the observer or participant. No history from hindsight of a hundred years later, and no historical fiction. The boundaries were drawn to produce an anthology in which we hear the authentic voices from 1788 to the present day.

The witnesses don't have to come from the great and the good. We are only able to read about the old Van Diemen's Land man who boasts of his depravity and then crawls as an informant to Inspector Nugent in the 1840s because the inspector left behind his running diary when he was summarily sacked. The diary turned up in the archives 150 years later. There is, perhaps surprisingly given my interests, very little politics, largely because there has been a paucity of good writing about poltics and politicans, not only in Sydney but also in the rest of Australia. Alfred Deakin's razor-sharp portraits of Henry Parkes and George Reid, who really were giants, say as much about the Sydney society in which they flourished as it does about them. Perhaps it took a Melbourne man to write it. It is true that two of Sydney's twentieth-century politicians, Billy Hughes and Jack Lang, did leave memoirs, but they are rather too self-serving, too much concerned with themselves, or rather their fictions of themselves, than with the city.

Some witnesses have been hard to find. Watkin Tench's sensitive acount of first contacts with the Aborigines, rightly often anthologised, is generous and hopeful, but from that same year we can read a letter from one of the convicts, riddled with fear of and hostility towards the 'savages'. Then the smallpox came, and returned again in the 1830s, virtually wiping out the Sydney tribes. In 1845 Mahroot, the last male left of his tribe, gave evidence to a Select Committee of the Legislative Council. Its members spent a lot of time on theology, keen to ascertain the Aboriginal concepts of God and the Devil. When Mahroot, in the midst of their ramblings, burst out with 'Devil devil is its all over small pox like', his questioners took no notice and continued striving to establish that the annihilation of the tribes followed from drink and the men allowing their women to go with white men. Someone was to blame, but it wasn't the councillors or Providence.

In July 1890 the hubristic pride of the city and the colony of New South Wales was at its height (the discord of the Maritime Strike was a few months away). The press could celebrate with gross smugness an act of philanthrophy towards the surviving Aborigines by Quong Tart, the Chinese tea-shop proprietor and importer, who gave a banquet for the survivors of the Sydney tribes. A Christian, Mason, reciter of Robbie Burns, and wearer of kilts, Quong Tart was generous with banquets; asylums, orphanages, hospitals, and ragged schools, all at one time or another benefited from his largesse. A remnant of sixty Aborigines had been expected at the Zoological Gardens, but only forty came, to sit down to a feast laid out on baize cloth on the ground, watched by spectators who had paid 1s 6d, proceeds to a new Christian mission. One of the men gave a speech of thanks, surprisingly in good English. Then a hundred years later we have Elisabeth Wynhausen's account of life on the Block at Redfern.

Witnesses to immigrant life are also hard to find. The prosperity of the city in the last two generations has been built on the sweat and shoulders of the immigrant workers, but they have not been heard. There are some good poets, but little testimony of work or the way those people lived. The immigrants were too busy, too tired, to write accounts of their lives; many of the first generation survived hostility or indifference by silence. Older Australian writers have passed them by, Patrick White's Himmelfarb in *Riders in the Chariot* being a rare exception. The two voices in this anthology, Rosa Cappiello, an Italian, and George Papaellinas, of Greek parents, are brutally frank witnesses. She writes of female immigrant factory workers and their inner-city life in the mid 1960s. George Papaellinas creates the welder after thirty years on the same car assembly line, weary but unbowed.

Most writing about sport in Sydney has been ephemeral. There's nothing wrong with that; it's there to simply report. There has been nothing for Rugby League like the Englishman David Storey's *This Sporting Life*. Clive James's short, wry account of his life as a Rugby Union player says more about the game than a hundred match reports. Homebush Boy Tom Keneally's account of his 440-yard run glows with the passion of that high summer of schoolboy sport, the 1950s. Further back in 1843 the jolly reporter for the *Sydney Gazette* going along the Parramatta Road to see the Homebush Races went as much for the spectacle as for a wager. Then there is the anonymous reporter's account of Carbine's win in the 1879 Sydney Cup. Sometimes an anthologist can pick up a classic, a beautiful piece of writing, and this account from the *Sydney Mail* deserves all that praise. The description has all the rising rhythm, pounding pace, and tensions of the race, without stumbling once into a purple patch.

Selecting writing from the nineteenth century was in some ways easier than from the twentieth. There was a stream of English visitors, like Darwin, Trollope, Dilke, and Froude, who were good writers although primarily concerned to find chapters for their round-the-world books. The shock of the novel geography stimulated them, and they praised the harbour in appropriately respectful, even fulsome, terms, but thought themselves obliged to make social observations; in particular, they nagged at that question of the society with the convict taint. In time the genre did run down. Marcus Clarke, writing from Melbourne, savaged Trollope for using clichés.

The local press was vigorous. Journalists could write with originality and style, and were allowed to do so. A sports report could be a very polished piece of work, and even narrative reporting (for example, about the attempted assassination of the Duke of Edinburgh and about the Maritime Strike clash at Circular Quay) would give a striking, vibrant portrait of what was happening. But from around 1900, the second age of the city, the press quickly lost that nineteenth-century gusto. The *Bulletin* fizzled out, but when A.G. Stephens left to establish *The Bookfellow*, with some support from J.F. Archibald, it turned out to be dull and stodgy, despite the fact that they were two of the greatest writers of the *Bulletin*'s heyday. A scrutiny of all its issues found nothing worth using. The press reflected quickly the steep decline of the raffish side of Sydney in the years before World War I and the rise of suburban respectability. Politics had a lot to do with it. The non-Labor parties merged in response to the rising threat of the ALP and formed an alliance with the wowser Protestant churches, whose price was social control through a raft of anti-liquor, anti-gambling, and Sunday observance laws. These laws were unenforceable and turned many of the population, mostly working class, into offenders. From then on the laws fed and entrenched police corruption and created widespread public acceptance of corruption underneath the façade.

There were those who stood against the conventions, like the people in Jack Lindsay's memoirs and the characters in Christina Stead's novels, but (as noted already) significantly both those writers went into exile. The result is that for the twentieth century this selection relies more on literature and memoirs than on the press. Lennie Lower waging his endless war against the suburbs was a rare exception.

John Kingsmill's sketches of Sydney between the wars are a rich source, as also is Lydia Gill's story of Sargent's restaurants. Limited and insular as the society was, it was a good life, if you had a job. The King was on his throne, and all was right with the world. The city ran on networks of understood codes on dress and manners. Kingsmill delineates the vital hat and overcoat rules and the etiquette of a Bondi tram. They had their simple entertainments, such as Donald Horne's picture palaces, although never on Sunday. However, radio, which could be heard on Sunday, was the supreme popular entertainment, and Sumner Locke Elliott's virtuoso picture of 'the man with a thousand voices' freezes a long-lost world in a frame.

The society that had ridden out a depression was shaken by the new war. There was no wild enthusiasm for war, as Elizabeth Harrower's image of the soldiers marching to the ships shows. The coming of the Yanks brutally challenged the stolid old mores. After six years of war and seemingly unending shortages, the mood of the city was nervy and bad-tempered, as Johnston's returning war correspondent and his wife found.

The literary visitors of this century were not up to the standards of those of the nineteenth century, with the exception of Pringle, but then while he went home after *Australian Accent*, the Scotsman did return to live in Sydney. Usually, however, the visits were shorter, and it showed. Jan Morris came twice, once in 1961 to criticise and then later to praise. I had thought to use both, for a Pauline contrast, but when I read them, neither was up to the standard of her better writing.

In the wake of Pringle the pace of change has sometimes seemed giddying. Only the Opera House can be said to be safe from being pulled down, but then is it? One can hear the argument: 'It would be the same design of course, scaled up, but to do it again would solve the concert hall problem, the acoustics, sight-lines etc. Don't you want a bigger Opera House for the millennium?'

The world of the two battling immigrants in this anthology has gone. Christos worked as welder on a car assembly line; now there are no car assembly lines in Sydney and the Greeks are moving out of Marrickville to make way for the Vietnamese. Rosa Cappiello wrote of Paddington and Surry Hills being working class. No more. Even the seemingly impregnable world of the Roseville Chase Garden Club and the rest of Jessica Anderson's North Shore now lives with Chinese–Australian neighbours. Dorothy Hewett's side of Redfern is now the place to buy. The grotty inner-city terraces of Catt's haunting story 'Graffito spy' have been renovated, and the Devonshire Street tunnel has been cleaned up.

Some places cropped up again and again over the years. In 1802 Péron spoke of the charming habitation of Mr Palmer at Wallamoula, where he was shipbuilding on the edge of the bay. Then three generations later in 1878 Woolloomooloo had become a place of ill-repute. An unabashedly insalubrious journal *The Innocents* could give a lip-smacking account of some frolics in a brothel. In 1900 it is the depot from which the plague boats, under the yellow flag, depart for the North Head Quarantine Station. Then in 1920 Christina Stead provides a tough, unsentimental picture of the Woolloomooloo slums, in stark contrast to the Prince of Wales's frolics elsewhere in the city. Manly, one of the first seaside resorts, was flourishing in 1858, and in writing about Manly in 1935, Bruce Beaver tells how the seaside provided a distraction for Depression Sydney. Bondi, the *other* beach, was slow to develop: Jack Lindsay and John Kingsmill give accounts of a simple beach more for locals. Balmain crops up in the happy waterfront memoirs of James Tyrrell, and it appears under the name of 'Cockle Creek' in H.M. Moran's doctor's account of life in a robustly working-class suburb during World War I. David Foster reveals a changed Balmain world with its half-hippies, half-intellectuals mourning for Martin Luther King in 1968.

It would be possible to fill the pages of a book with Sydney–Melbourne rivalries and differences, some of them real, but most of them constructions. Frank Fowler in the 1850s told his English readers that Sydney was staid compared to Melbourne, but others would reverse that label quickly enough. Being born in Melbourne and having spent the first ten years of my life there, I always feel at ease; the streets of the city, the suburbs, the gardens, the beaches, and the railway routes, all have their resonances for me. Perhaps that is why I find myself so exasperated, or even angered, by those perennially boring beat-ups on Sydney v. Melbourne. On a football field, fine, but off the oval—get a life. So I have steered away from all those banalities, save for one exception that could not be resisted, and which is certainly not banal: Keith Murdoch's outburst of rage against Sydney in a letter in 1915 to Andrew Fisher, then still Prime Minister. It was the only time Keith Murdoch lived in Sydney and then only for a few months. A dour son of the manse, Murdoch found that Sydney, even in its middle classes, was not serious enough about the war. 'I don't think the Sydney spirit would prevail in a war against the native tribes of Papua. It is a pity the aborigines were not Prussianised,' he wrote. Presumably what he means when he wishes the Aborigines had been Prussianised was that they would have repelled, even wiped out, those first settlers. Where, one wonders, would Keith Murdoch have wanted to set the boundary of Prussianisation—the Murray?

Glen Tomasetti's story of a woman and her mother, remembering their lives in Sydney and Melbourne, shows a harmony not only between the two women but also between the two cities. Both women offer their memories of places, of people, of sorrow and joy. In their minds, the cities are not trite, jostling, barracking rivals. A citizen can have an abiding affection for their Sydney with all its glories, its beauty, its commonplaces, its failures, its flaws, and its faults. There are always its surprises, too. To be lost on a summer day amid the towers of the city, then suddenly to look north up Phillip Street from the Bent Street corner and catch the shimmering waters of Sydney Cove, always the same Sydney Cove, is a sweet surprise.

But a city is more than the sum of its setting, its landscapes, its buildings. It lives in its people, their conflicts and contradictions, their crudeness and their subtleties, their achievements and their failures, their virtues and their vices. It lives in this past and their present. The visitors come and go, but the authentic voices of the city, in the end, come from its people.

There is an old Negro spiritual about paradise:

> Twelve gates to the city,
> Three gates to the east,
> Three gates to the west,
> Three gates to the north,
> Three gates to the south.
> Oh, what a beautiful city!

(Some sing 'Oh! What a wonderful city'.) Sydney does not have the twelve gates; it is not paradise; but despite everything that has been done to disfigure it, it is still a beautiful city, a wonderful city.

Any anthologist is only as good as his friends, and mine have helped greatly in this task. Thanks to Nick Jose, Graham Pont, Ros Maguire, C.J. Lloyd (especially for the Keith Murdoch letter), John Ryan, Rosemary Cresswell, Paul Gardiner, George and Joan Masterman, Edmund Campion, Barry Porter, Chris Warren, Linda Funnell, Jim Crawford, Sally McInerney, Ann Turner, John Cross, John Ralston, and Sue Butler. As ever, the staff of the Mitchell Library were courteous and efficient.

The Sydney Scene 1788–1960, by Alan Birch and David S. Macmillan, while having a rather different focus, provided some good leads.

Arthur Bowes Smyth

Arthur Bowes Smyth, a surgeon on the *Lady Penrhyn*, a transport in the First Fleet, stayed until April 1788.

Dissipation ashore

Feb. 6th. At five o'clock this morning all things were got in order for landing the whole of the women and 3 of the Ships Longboats came alongside to receive them: previous to their quitting the Ship a strict search was made to try if any of the many things which they had stolen on board could be found, but their Artifice eluded the most strict search. At 6 o'clock p.m. we had the long wish'd for pleasure of seeing the last of them leave the ship. They were dressed in general very clean if some few amongst them might be said to be well dress'd. The men convicts got to them very soon after they landed, and it is beyond my abilities to give a just description of the Scene of Debauchery and Riot that ensued during the night. They had not been landed more than an hour before they had all got their Tents pitched or anything in order to receive them, but there came on the most violent storm of thunder, lightning and rain I ever saw. The lightning was incessant during the whole night and I never heard it rain faster—about 12 o'clock in the night one severe flash of lightning struck a very large tree in the centre of the Camp, under which some places were constructed to keep the Sheep and Hogs in: it split the tree from top to bottom; kill'd 5 Sheep belonging to Major Ross and a pig of one of the Lieutenants—The severity of the Lightning this and the 2 preceding nights leaves no room to doubt but many of the trees which appear burnt up to the tops of them were the Effect of Lightning—The Sailors in our Ship requested to have some Grog to make merry which upon the Women quitting the Ship indeed the Captain himself had no small reason to rejoice upon their being all safely landed and given into the Care of the Governor, as he was under the penalty of 40£ for every Convict missing—for which reason he complied to the Sailors' request, and about the time they became elevated, the Tempest came on—The Scene which presented itself at this time and during the greater part of the night beggars every description, some swearing, others quarrelling, others singing, not in the least regarding the Tempest, tho' so violent that the Thunder [that] shook the Ship exceeded any thing I ever before had a conception of. I never before experienced so uncomfortable a night expecting every moment the ship would be struck with the Lightning— The Sailors almost all drunk and incapable of rendering much assistance had an accident happened and the heat was almost suffocating.

> Lieutenant Arthur Bowes (also known as Bowes Smyth), diary,
> 6 February 1788, Mitchell Library, Sydney.

Watkin Tench

Watkin Tench (1758?–1833), captain-lieutenant of the Royal Marines, came with the First Fleet and stayed until December 1792. He was a well-read man, who knew the works of Gibbon and Voltaire.

· **Every delicacy was requisite**

We found the natives tolerably numerous as we advanced up the river, and even at the harbour's mouth we had reason to conclude the country more populous than Mr Cook thought it. For on the *Supply*'s arrival in the Bay on the 18th of the month, they were assembled on the beach of the south shore, to the number of not less than forty persons, shouting and making many uncouth signs and gestures. This appearance whetted curiosity to its utmost, but as prudence forbade a few people to venture wantonly among so great a number, and a party of six men was observed on the north shore, the Governor immediately proceeded to land on that side in order to take possession of his new territory, and bring about an intercourse between its old and new masters. The boat in which His Excellency was, rowed up the harbour close to the land for some distance: the Indians keeping pace with her on the beach. At last one officer in the boat made signs of a want of water, which it was judged would indicate his wish of landing. The natives directly comprehended what he wanted, and pointed to a spot where water could be procured; on which the boat was immediately pushed in, and a landing took place. As on the event of this meeting might depend so much of our future tranquillity, every delicacy on our side was requisite. The Indians, though timorous, showed no signs of resentment at the Governor's going on shore; an interview commenced, in which the conduct of both parties pleased each other so much that the strangers returned to their ships with a better opinion of the natives than they had landed with; and the latter seemed highly entertained with their new aquaintance, from whom they condescended to accept of a looking glass, some beads and other toys.

Owing to the lateness of our arrival, it was not my good fortune to go on shore until three days after this had happened, when I went with a party to the south side of the harbour and had scarcely landed five minutes when we were met by a dozen Indians, naked as at the moment of birth, walking along the beach. Eager to come to a conference, and yet afraid of giving offence, we advanced with caution towards them, nor would they, at first, approach nearer to us than the distance of some paces. Both parties were armed; yet an attack seemed as unlikely on their part as we knew it to be on our own.

I had at this time a little boy, of not more than seven years of age, in my hand. The child seemed to attract their attention very much, for they frequently pointed to him and spoke to each other; and as he was not frightened, I advanced with him towards them, at the same time baring his bosom and showing the whiteness of his skin. On the clothes being removed they gave a loud exclamation, and one of the party, an old man, with a long beard, hideously ugly, came close to us. I bade my little charge not to be afraid, and introduced him to the acquaintance of this uncouth personage. The Indian, with great gentleness, laid his hand on the child's hat and afterwards felt his clothes, muttering to himself all the while. I found it necessary, however, by this time to send away the child, as such a close connection rather alarmed him; and in this, as the conclusion verified, I gave no offence to the old gentleman. Indeed it was putting ourselves on a par with them, as I had observed from the first that some youths of their own, though considerably older than the one with us, were kept back by the grown people.

Several more now came up, to whom we made various presents, but our toys seemed not to be regarded as very valuable; nor would they for a long time make any returns to them, though before we parted a large club, with a head almost sufficient to fell an ox, was obtained in exchange for a looking glass. These people seemed at a loss to know (probably from our want of beards) of what sex we were, which having understood, they burst into the most immoderate fits of laughter, talking to each other at the same time with such rapidity and vociferation as I had never before heard. After nearly an hour's conversation by signs and gestures, they repeated several times the word *whurra*, which signifies 'begone', and walked away from us to the head of the bay.

> Watkin Tench, *Sydney's First Four Years*, Library of Australian History, Sydney, 1979.

Governor Phillip

Phillip's early optimism turned out to be misplaced. By the end of 1788 most of the vines had perished from a blight, accentuated by nearness to the sea air.

The Governor's vineyard

In the Governor's garden are excellent cauliflowers, and melons very fine of their kind. The orange trees flourish, and the fig trees and vines are improving still more rapidly. In a climate so favourable the cultivation of the vine may doubtless be carried to any degree of perfection; and should no other articles of commerce divert the attention of the settlers from this part, the wines of New South Wales may perhaps, here after be sought with civility and become an indispensable part of the luxury of European tables.

Governor Philip's diary (n.d.; c. 1788?), cited by Philip Norrie,
Vineyards of Sydney, Horowitz Grahame, Sydney, 1990.

A female convict

There are no clues as to the identity of this woman, although she was unusual in her fluent literacy.

Our kangaroo rats are like mutton

Port Jackson, 14th November, 1788.
I take the first opportunity that has been given us to acquaint you with our disconsolate situation in this solitary waste of the creation. Our passage, you may have heard by the first ships, was tolerably favourable; but the inconveniences since suffered for want of shelter, bedding &c., are not to be imagined by any stranger. However, we have now two streets, if four rows of the most miserable huts you can possibly conceive of deserve that name. Windows they have none, as from the Governor's house, &c., now nearly finished, no glass could be spared: so that latttices of twigs are made by our people to supply their places. At the extremity of the lines, where since our arrival the dead are buried, there is a place called the churchyard; but as hear, as soon as a sufficent quantity of bricks can be made, a church is to be built, and named St Phillip after the Governor. Notwithstanding all our presents, the savages still continue to do us all the injury they can, which makes the soldiers' duty very hard, and much dissatifaction among the officers. I know not how many of our people have been killed. As for the distresses of the women, they are past description, as they are deprived of tea and other things they were indulged in the voyage by the seamen, and as they are all totally unprovided with clothes, those who have young children are quite wretched. Besides this, though a number of marriages have taken place, several women, who became pregnant on the voyage, and are since left by their partners, who have returned to England, are not likely to form any fresh connections. We are comforted with hopes of a supply of tea from China, and flattered with getting riches when the settlement is complete, and the hemp which the place produces is brought to perfection. Our kangaroo rats are like mutton, but much leaner; and there is a kind of chickweed so much in taste like our spinach that no difference can be discerned. Something like ground ivy is used for tea; but a scarcity of salt and sugar makes our best meals insipid. The separation of several of

us to an uninhabited island was like a second transportation. In short, every one is so taken up with their own misfortunes that they have no pity to bestow on others. All our letters are examined by an officer, but a friend takes this for me privately. The ships sail tomorrow.

> Letter from a female convict, in *Historical Records of New South Wales*
> (ed. F.M. Bladen), Vol. 2, Lansdown Slattery & Co., Mona Vale,
> NSW, 1978.

A male convict

The writer, like his female fellow prisoner, cannot be identified.

The clothes are all wore out

To give a just description of the hardships that the meanest of us endure, and the anxieties suffered by the rest, is more than I can pretend to do. In all the Crusoe-like adventures I ever read or heard of, I do not recollect anything like it; for though you may be told of the quantity of salt meat that is allowed us, its quality in boiling does not make it above half as much, besides other inconveniences I cannot mention, and which I think make so many of the children very unhealthy. Of the same account, I believe few of the sick would recover if it was not for the kindness of the Rev. Mr Jackson, whose assistance out of his own stores makes him the physician both of soul and body. All out improvements, except our gardens, have lately been quite at a stand, neither do I think they will go on again till we have more assistance from England. God only knows what our Governor thinks of it, or what word he has sent home; but for my part, from the highest to the lowest, I see nobody that is so content as they were at first. We fear the troops, and they are not contented with seeing those who live better than themselves, nor with us who live worse; and I think if the savages knew that we were as short of powder as we are of provisions they would soon be more daring than they are. We have heard that some convicts at home, who might have been pardoned for capital crimes, have chosen their former sentence rather than come here; and which, though it was contradicted, we cannot help thinking is true. We cannot tell, if they have heard of our situation, how it could be, unless from the Cape or Norfolk Island, which we hear no more from than England. We have some Jews and Dutchmen from thence that would have settled if they thought it worth while. I should now be very glad of the things I refused to take with me when I came from London, and hope you will venture to send me some needles and blue thread; for, as the clothes are all wore out that we brought from home, we are mostly in our Woolwich dresses, and have so many disappointments about arrivals, etc., that the sullen reserve of superiority has only increased out apprehensions; and some of the most ignorant have no other idea than that they are to be left by the troops and the shipping to perish by themselves ! And really, if you was to see with what ardent expectations some of the poor wretches watch an opportunity of looking out to sea, or the tears that are often shed upon the infants at the breast, you might have feelings that otherwise you never could have any experience of.

A convict's letter, 9 April 1790, in *Historical Records of New South Wales* (ed. F.M. Bladen), Vol. 2, Lansdown Slattery & Co., Mona Vale, NSW, 1978.

Alessandro Malaspina

Alessandro Malaspina (1754–1809) was a captain of the Spanish navy whose expedition visited Sydney in 1793.

The climate is variable in the greatest degree

In the neighbourhood of Toongabbie and on the flats of the Parramatta River are cultivated with a good result Maize, Millet &ca, and even wheat; but this last, though large and clear, has concrete or smut in the ear itself, and besides is in short quantity compared with the requirement. It may only be called a not very encouraging attempt in my opinion, in spite of the common confidence.

The Climate, according to some, is healthy, temperate and beneficent, according to others hot and unhealthy. We can affirm that it is variable in the greatest degree, and that the dews, at least in this season, are little inferior to common showers. Dr White agrees that if one is exposed to these frequently they produce putrid rheumatic fevers and violent dysenteries.

Most believe that this part of New Holland will be abandoned, and that the colony, divided into 3 portions, will be transported, one to the North Coast to the place indicated by Captain Bligh, another to one of the Sandwich Isles, and the third to Nootka; but the better informed, or at least those who appear to and should be, affirm that Commodore Phillip went to England convinced of its usefulness and in accord with Dr Banks, that they are both pledged to sustain it, and that Mr Pitt, who views it with predilection, would with difficulty be persuaded to destroy his work.

Robert J. King, *The Secret History of the Convict Colony: Alexandro Malaspina's Report on the British Settlement in New South Wales*, Allen & Unwin, Sydney, 1990.

Thomas Watling

Thomas Watling (1762–?), a Scotsman who had trained as an artist, was transported for forgery in 1791.

Sympathetic glooms of twilight glimmering

The principal traits of the country are extensive woods, spread over a little-varied plain. I however confess, that were I to select and combine, I might avoid the sameness, and find engaging employment. Trees wreathing their old fantastic roots on high; dissimilar in tint and foliage; cumbent, upright, fallen, or shattered by lightning, may be found at every step; whilst sympathetic glooms of twilight glimmering groves, and the wildest nature lulled in sound repose, might much inspire the soul—all this I confess ... In the warmer season, the thunder very frequently rolls tremendous, accompanied by a scorching wind, so intolerable as almost to obstruct respiration;—whilst the surrounding horizon looks one entire sheet of uninterupted [sic] flame. The air, notwithstanding, is in general dry. Fifteen months have been known to elapse without a single shower; but though thus dry, the transitions of hot and cold are surprisingly quick and contrasted without any discernable [sic] injury to the human system. I have felt one hour as intensely warm as if immediately under the line, when the next has made me shiver with cold, yet have I not experienced any harm therefrom; owing, without a doubt to the dryness and salubrity of the atmosphere.

The vast number of green frogs, reptiles, and large insects, among the grass and on the trees, during the spring, summer, and fall, make an incessant noise and clamour. They cannot fail to surprise the stranger exceedingly, as he will hear their discordant croaking just by, and sometimes all around him, though he is unable to discover whence it proceeds:—nor can he perceive the animals from whence the sounds in the trees issue, they being most effectually hid among the leaves and branches.

Thomas Watling, *Letters from an Exile at Botany Bay*, Penrith, Scotland, c. 1794, cited by Bernard Smith, *Documents on Art and Taste in Australia*, Oxford University Press, Melbourne, 1975.

Governor Hunter

John Hunter (1737–1821), second captain of the First Fleet, left in 1792 but returned as Governor (1795–1800). In this passage he is condemning the officers of the New South Wales Corps.

Abandon'd and profligate manners

The introduction of this destructive trade, which took place since the departure of Gov'r Phillip, has done immense mischief, and, by the ruin of the oldest settlers, has retarded the progress of industry amongst that class of people, who were before sober and labour'd hard; but spirituous liquors, which has been a principal article of trade, has completed the ruin of many who might have been perfectly independent. This spirit for trade, which I must ever consider in the manner it is carried on here to be highly disgraceful to men who hold in their hand a Commission signed by his Majesty, has been carried so far that it has now reached all the inferior appointments, so that is has absorb'd all their time and attention, and the public duty of their respective offices are entirely neglected, to the no small injury of his Majesty's service; but although I may lose popularity amongst the traders, their recommendation, be assur'd, I am not covetous of. I have resolv'd to correct, as far as I can, many such abuses. I have not assistance sufficient; it is too much for any one man to manage in our extended state, and with our abandon'd and prolifigate manners and conduct to see and direct every little department ...

I will not fatigue you with an account of what steps I am pursuing for bringing back this turbulent and refractory colony to a proper obedience to the laws and regulations establish'd for the general welfare. You will see what I have thought it right to say in my public letters. I will, however, mention a circumstance which has just happen'd and which may serve to show how great a number of trusty people are necessary for looking after the worthless villains we have here to manage. Our windmill, which has been finished and is now at work, was the other day employ'd grinding some wheat for people who had some time past been oblig'd to pay almost one-half their grain to have the other ground. Whilst the miller was absent, and left these very people for whom the mill was then at work in care of it, during his absence they were clever enough to steal away some of the sails from the vanes or fans, and we have not been able yet to discover the thief. The mill, for want of its sails, was consequently stop'd.

> Governor Hunter to London, 1 June 1797, *Historical Records of Australia* (ed. F.M. Bladen), Vol. 4, Lansdown Slattery & Co., Mona Vale, NSW, 1979.

Three missionaries

Three evangelical missionaries who had been driven out of Tahiti by civil war and cannibalism found Sydney a wicked place.

Uncleanness stalks through the colony
Parramatta, New South Wales, 25th August, 1799.
Fathers, Brothers and Fellow-Labourers in the Gospel of our Lord Jesus Christ,—

His Majesty's ship the Buffalo, Capt. Kent, being on the eve of sailing from the colony for the Cape of Good Hope, we embrace the opportunity of confirming our letters to you of the 1st September, 1789, by the Barwell, duplicates of which we forwarded the beginning of December following, in

the Cornwallis, by way of Calcutta, in which we informed you of the circumstances which occasioned our removal from Otaheite to this colony, and
the prospect which presented itself to us of our being made useful in the
Ministry of the Word here, since which our views have been beclouded, our
expectations not so sanguine, the exercise of our minds various with respect
to the path of duty, whether we should persevere or not, as the belief of our
hearts at times was ready to suggest that the difficulties we had to encounter
were insurmountable—indeed, they are such to an arm of flesh—for here
we have to contend with the depravity and corruptions of the human heart,
heightened and confirmed in all its vicious habits by long and repeated
indulgences of inbred corruption, each one following the bent of his own
corrupt mind, and countenancing his neighbour in the pursuit of sensual
gratifications. Here iniquity abounds, and those outward gross sins which in
Europe could render a person contemptible in the public eye, and obnox-
ious to the civil law, are become fashionable and familiar. Adultery, fornication, theft, drunkenness, extortion, violence and uncleanness of every kind,
the natural concomitants of Deism and infidelity, which have boldly thrown
off the mask, and stalk thro' the colony in the open face of the sun, so that
it is no uncommon thing to hear a person say, 'When I was a Christian, I
thought so and so.' But our discouragements arise, not so much from these
things in themselves, as from their pernicious influence, which tends to con-
firm and strengthen the natural prejudices of the mind against the doctrines
of the Gospel, which are a sovereign remedy for all those deadly desires;
but, alas, they will not come into the Light, lest their evil deeds should be
reproved. This case may be justly compared to that of a person in the height
of fever, deprived of his reason, who refuses to have the means prescribed
for his recovery, and to this cause we may ascribe (in a certain sense) the
little success the labors of our brethren in the establishment here for these
several years past, sensible, however, that the choicest means will be inef-
fectual without the gracious concurrence of the Holy Spirit.

JAMES COVER
WILLIAM HENRY
ROWLAND HASSAL

Missionaries to the Directors of [London Missionary] Society, London,
1799, in *Historical Records of New South Wales*, Vol. 3 (ed. F.M.
Bladen), Lansdown Slattery & Co., Mona Vale, NSW, 1978.

François Péron

François Péron (1775–1810), a scientist with the French expedition led by
Captain Baudin, spent some months in Sydney in 1802.

♦

A sort of coffee house

In front of it is the armoury, where the garrison is drawn up every morning, accompanied by a numerous and well-composed band, belonging the New South Wales regiment. The whole western part of this spot is occupied by the house of the lieutenant-governor-general: behind which is a vast garden, which is worth the attention of both the philospher and the naturalist, on account of the great number of useful vegetables that are cultivated in it, and which have been procured from every part of the world, by its respectable possessor, Mr Paterson, a distinguished traveller, and a member of the Royal Society of London. Between the house and the magazine just mentioned, is the public school: here are educated in the principles of religion, morality and virtue, those young females, who are the hope of the rising colony; but whose parents are either too degenerate, or too poor, to give them proper instruction. In the public school, however, under respectable matrons, they are taught from their earliest years, all the duties of a good mother of a family. Such is one great advantage of the excellent colonial system established in these distant regions.

Behind the house of the lieutenant-governor-general, in a large magazine, are deposited all the dried pulse and corn, belonging to the state. It is a sort of public granary, intended for the support of the troops, and the people, who receive their subsistence from the government. The barracks occupy a considerable square, and have in front several field-pieces: the edifices for the accomodation of the officers form the lateral parts, or ends of the building; and the powder magazine is in the middle. Near this, in a small private house, the principal civil and miltary officers assemble. It is a sort of coffee-house, maintained by subscription, in which there are several amusements, but particularly billards; at which any person may play, free of expence. Behind the armoury is a large square tower, which serves as an observatory to those English officers who study astronomy: at the base of this tower, the foundation of a church has been laid, of which the building, just mentioned, is intended to form the steeple; but a structure of this kind, requiring time, labour, and expence, the governors have hitherto neglected to carry it into execution; preferring the formation of such establishments as are more immediately necessary for the preservation of the colony. While waiting, however, for the erection of a church, divine service is performed in one of the apartments of the great corn magazine. Two fine windmills terminate on this side the series of the principal public edifices. Over the rivulet that intersects the town, there was a wooden bridge, which, together with a strong causeway, may be said to occupy all the bottom of the valley. We passed over this bridge, in order to take a rapid view of the eastern part of Sydney Town. Before our departure the wooden bridge was destroyed to make way for one which they were about to build of stone; at the same time, a water-mill was built here by the government, and strong locks had been formed, either to keep in the water of the rivulet, or to stop that of the marshes, which runs to a considerable distance into the valley and which might be advantageously employed in turning the mill.

At the east point of the creek is a second battery, the fire of which crosses that of the signal station. The one of which I am speaking, was dismantled at the time of our arrival at Port Jackson, but it has been put in order since our departure. On the shore, as you approach the town is a small salt-pit, where the Americans, who were allowed to settle for the purpose at Port Jackson, in 1795, prepared most of the salt used in the colony. Further on, and towards the bottom of the harbour, is the part called Government Creek, because it is reserved for the agents, and vessels of the state. Between this creek and the salt-pit, is the place for the docking and careening of ships. The natural quays are so perpendicular, and well formed, that without any kind of labour or expence on the part of the English, the largest ships might be laid among them in perfect security. Near the Government Creek are three public magazines, one of them contains all the articles necessary for the various purposes of domestic life, such was earthenware, household furniture, culinary utensils, instruments of agriculture, etc. The number of these articles that is here amassed, is truly astonishing, and the mode in which they are delivered out, is wise and salutary. In this distant country the merchandises of Europe bear so high a price, that it would be next to impossible for the population to procure such as are indispensable to the common wants of life: the English government has therefore anticipated these wants, by filling large store-houses with every article that can be required, all of which are delivered to the colonists at fixed prices, that are extremely moderate; sometimes even below what they cost in Europe. But in order to prevent avaricious speculation, or waste, no one is admitted into these depots without a written order from the governor; in which are specified the articles that the bearer is in need of. In another house are preserved the different uniforms and clothing for the troops and convicts, as well as vast quantities of sail-cloth and cordage, for the government-ships. The last of the three buildings just mentioned is a kind of public manufactory: in which are employed female convicts. Behind these magazines is the governor's house, which is built in the Italian style, surrounded by a colonnade, as simple as it is elegant, and in front of which is a fine garden, which ascends to the sea-shore: already in this garden may be seen, the Norfolk Island pine, the superb Columbia, growing side by side with the bamboo of Asia; further on is the Portugal orange, and Canary fig, ripening beneath the shade of the French apple-tree: the cherry, peach, pear and apricot, are interspersed among the Banksia, Metrosideros, Correa, Melaleuca, Casuarina, Eucalyptus, and a great number of other indigenous trees: beyond the government garden, on the other side of the neighbouring hill, is the windmill, the bakehouse, and the state ovens, that are used for the making of ship biscuit; these are capable of furnishing from fifteen to eighteen hundred pounds per day. Not far from a contiguous creek, at a spot which the natives call Wallamoula, is the charming habitation of Mr Palmer, the commissary general; a rivulet of fresh water runs before it and empties itself into the creek, which forms a safe and convenient basin. Here, Mr Palmer has built several small vessels, which he employs in whale fishing, and catching Phocae, or sea Elephants, either at New Zealand or in Bass's Straits. The neighbouring brick-fields furnish a considerable quality of bricks and tiles, for the public and private buildings of the colony.

A short distance to the southwards of Sydney Town, to the left of the great road that leads to Parramatta, you observe the remains of the first gibbet that was erected on the continent of New Holland. The increase of habitations having caused it to be, as it were, surrounded, it has been succeeded by another further off, in the same direction and near the village of Brick-field. This village, which consists of about two score of houses, contains several manufactories of tiles, earthenware, crockery, etc., and its site is agreeable, and the soil, less sterile than that of Sydney, is better adapted to the different kinds of cultivation that have been introduced into these distant regions.

François Péron, *Voyage to the Southern Hemisphere*, 1807.

Sydney Gazette

The *Sydney Gazette* (1803–42) was Australia's first newspaper. It provides valuable evidence of the interests and habits of the colonists.

The amateurs of cricket

The late intense weather has been very favourable to the amateurs of Cricket, who have scarcely LOST a day for the last month. The frequent immoderate heats might have been considered inimical to the amusement, but very productive of the very opposite consequences, as the state of the atmosphere might always regulate the portion of exercise necessary towards this labourious diversion was originally intended to answer.

Sydney Gazette, 8 January 1804.

George Suttor

George Suttor (1774–1859) was one of the still-small number of free settlers. He wrote to Sir Joseph Banks after the Irish uprising of 1804. Despite his misgivings, Suttor became prosperous and died in self-governing New South Wales.

Horror and consternation

I hope you will not be offended by this intrusion, but from the state of things in this colony I am induced to trouble you with this letter, giving an account of the wretched state of my family and a most alarming disturbance which happened on Sunday night, the 4th of March, when between one hundred and two hundred convicts rushed out from the Government settlement at Castle Hill—which, indeed, had nothing to guard it but a few convict constables, the most of whom joined them. Having seized the muskets there, the whole body came armed upon the poor settlers, plundered them of what guns and ammunition they had, and threatened their lives if they made the least resistance. I had three muskets placed to my breast, and myself and my wife narrowly escaped being shot. Overpowered thus by numbers, we were obliged to submit to their mercy. In this manner they continued to storm and to plunder the settlers till, having possessed themselves of one hundred and eighty guns, swords, and pistols, they determined to take Parramatta, which was guarded by fifty soldiers. These they thought to overpower and to get their arms. Four hundred of them by this time had got together, and they expected in a little time to be fifteen hundred strong, but here, either from want of courage and a body of them not joining in time, they delayed their attack on Parramatta and retreated to Toongabbie Hill. They were led by two Irishmen, who had been soldiers. These and others of a like description were very busy drilling them and putting them in a military posture. In the meantime a company of soldiers was marched up from Sydney. Even these they thought themselves strong enough to engage, but as the soldiers approached them they retreated towards the Hawkesbury, where they expected numbers to join them in their retreat. They were overtaken by a party of soldiers under Major Johnson. He rode up to them and endeavoured to bring them back to a sense of duty, but in vain. Their cry was death or liberty, and a ship to take them Home. However, the Major, by a successful manoeuvre, cut off their two leaders, and the soldiers began to fire upon them. They made but little resistance. Seventeen were killed. They began to fly in all directions till the night, which was excessively dark, put an end to this pursuit ...

Nothing can equal the horror and consternation of the country, the women and children running from farm to farm, but could find no place of safety. For three days we continued in the most wretched condition of suspense, knowing we were surrounded by numbers of armed ruffians, as the fellows had at first surrounded all the passes to Parramatta. Many of them are now in the woods, and, being armed, the settlers will be constantly exposed to them. Plunder they must for subsistence. Dreadful indeed must be the state of a country when such villains are let loose upon it. Every insult, very injury, and every crime is to be expected from them that can be perpetrated by men so desperate, hardened and depraved. Indeed, so many are the crimes that have been committed by them for the last twelve months, that the bare recital is shocking to human nature—rapes, murders, robbery. Settlers' wives have been rushed in upon by seven or eight men, knocked down, treated in the most cruel manner and ravished in the sight of their families. No person in the colony is secure either in life or property, except the officers, civil and

military. Such is the state of things at present and has been for twelve months
past. About a twelve-month since, twelve men left the above settlement,
threatening the whole country, shot a man at a small distance from my farm.
At another farm, two of scoundrels broke into the house, seized the women,
and ravished a young woman, in sight of her mother ...

... When such is the state of the country what prospect is there for a set-
tler and his family? His business he cannot properly attend, for he never
lays down but in fear of being broken in upon by morning. Should he by
succesful industry get forward, his very property exposes him. Surrounded
by all these evils, no prospect for my wife and growing family but penury
and want, with spirits depressed and broken in mind ...

George Suttor to Sir Joseph Banks, *Historical Records of New South
Wales Wales* (ed. F.M. Bladen), Vol. 5, Lansdown Slattery & Co., Mona
Vale, NSW, 1979.

George Johnston

George Johnston (1764–1823) arrived on the First Fleet as a lieutenant of the
Marines. He transferred to the New South Wales Corps in 1790 and later
became a farmer.

How the rising was suppressed

Head-quarters, Sydney, 9th March, 1804

Sir,

I beg leave to acquaint you that about ½ past 1 o'clock on Monday morning last, I took command of the detachment marched from headquarters by
Lieut't Davies, consisting of 2 officers, 2 serjeants, and 52 rank and file of the
New South Wales Corps, and by his Excellency Governor King's Order, I proceeded immediately to Parramatta, where we arrived at the dawn of day. I
halted at the barracks about 20 minutes to refresh my party, and then
marched to Government House, and agreeable to His Excellency's orders
divided my detachment, giving Lieut't Davies the command of half, and
taking Quartermaster Laycock and the other half, with 1 trooper, with myself,
having the Governor's instructions to march in pursuit of the rebels along the
Toongabbee Road. I proceeeded that way, and directed Lieut't Davies to take
the road towards Castle Hill. On my arrival at Toongabbee, I was informed
the rebels, in number about 400, were on the summit of the hill. I immediately detached a corporal with 4 privates and about 6 inhabitants, armed with
musquets, to take them in the flank, whilst I proceeded with the rest up the
hill, when I found had marched on for the Hawkesbury, and after a pursuit of
anout 10 miles I got sight of them. I immediately rode forward, attended by
the trooper and Mr Dixon, the Roman Catholic priest, calling to them to halt,

that I wished to speak to them. They desired that I would come into the middle of them, as their captains were there, which I refused, observing to them that I was within pistol shot and that it was in their power to kill me, and that their captains must have very little spirit if they would would not come forward to speak to me, upon which two persons (C—— and J——) advanced towards me as their leaders to whom I represented the impropriety of their conduct, and advised them to surrender and that I would mention them in as favourable terms as possible to the Governor. C—— replied they would have death or liberty. Quartermaster Laycock with the detachment just then appearing in sight, I clapped my pistol to J——'s head, whilst the trooper did the same to C——'s, and drove them with their swords in their hands to the Quartermaster and the detachment, whom I ordered to advance and charge the main body of the rebels then formed in a line. The detachment immediately commenced a well-directed fire, which was but weakly returned, for the rebel line being soon broken they run in all directions. We pursued them a considerable way, and have no doubt but that many of them fell. We have found 12 killed, 6 wounded and have taken 26 prisoners.

Any encomiums I could pass on Quartermaster Laycock and the detachments I had the honour to command would fall far short of what their merit entitles them to, and I trust their steady perseverance (after a fatiguing march of upwards of 45 miles) to restore order and tranquillity will make their services acceptable.

Mr Provost-Martial Smith, the inhabitants, and constables who voluntarily accompanied the detachment, are equally entitled to my thanks, nor can I be neglectful of the very soldier-like conduct of the trooper who accompanied me.   I have, &c.,

Geo. Johnston, B.-Major

N.S. Wales Corps

Return of arms from the rebels:—26 musquets, 1 fowling piece, 4 bayonets on poles, 1 pitch fork, 1 pistol, 8 reaping hooks, 2 swords.

Letter to Lieutenant-Colonel Paterson, *Historical Records of New South Wales* (ed. F.M. Bladen), Vol. 5, Lansdown Slattery & Co., Mona Vale, NSW, 1979.

Governor Macquarie

Lachlan Macquarie (1762–1824), the recently arrived Governor, hoped to restore the colony to respectability.

No gaming, drunkenness, swearing or fighting

Government House, Sydney,

Saturday, 6th October, 1810.

It being highly necessary that Peace and good Order should be preserved at the ensuing Races, and that no Gaming, Drunkenness, Swearing, or Fighting, should be permitted, His Excellency the GOVERNOR gives this Public Notice, that no Booths, Stalls, or Shops, will be allowed to be erected on or near any Part of the Race Ground during the Race Week, and that any Person selling, or attempting to sell any Wine, Liquor, or Beer, on or near the Race Ground, during the Race Week, will be deprived of their Licences (if they have had any), and prosecuted besides for a Breach of these Orders.

His EXCELLENCY therefore strictly forbids and prohibits all species of Gaming, Drunkenness, Swearing, Quarrelling, Fighting, or Boxing taking place on or near the Race Ground.—Any Person transgressing these Orders, or who is detected creating any Noise or Disturbance, will be immediately apprehended and confined in Gaol; and the Constables will have strict Orders to this Effect.

Sydney Gazette, 8 October 1810.

Thomas Shepherd

Born in Scotland, Thomas Shepherd (1776–1836) trained as a landscape gardener at home before coming to Sydney in 1827, when he was given a land grant in Chippendale to establish a fruit garden and nursery. The estate he describes is that of Alexander Macleay, the Colonial Secretary. Its manor, Elizabeth Bay House, survives.

A delightful situation

… The estate of Elizabeth Bay is situated within the town boundary of Sydney, in a delightful situation, and bound on its north side by the river and harbour of Port Jackson. On one side is a circular bay half a mile in extent, in a commanding style, between rocky promontories of lofty elevation, branching off to the right and left. Between these promontories the ground sweeps round, by a grand and gradual descent into a low and fertile flat of about ten acres, which has been cleared from the natural woods. The outline of this flat ground is also circular, terminating in an abrupt slope, beautifully furnished with rocks, trees and bushes, forming a splendid amphitheatre. A range of luxuriant woods and precipitous rocks follows the boundary of the water on the north side, till it reaches the boundary line of the estate, forming a straight line by the side of a new road, about a mile in length, to a corner of an angle where the main entrance gate is placed. A similar range of beautiful woods and rocks extends from the other promontory for half a mile, by the side of the water of a large bay …

The high lands and slopes of this property are composed of rocks, richly ornamented with beautiful indigenous trees and shrubs. About ten acres have been cleared for pasture, which space has been laid off in two paddocks into two enclosures. The deficiency of pasture is a fault common with every other estate in Sydney and prevents them from being laid off in the useful and ornamental style on a scale of magnitude. Sensible that his land is not calculated for pasture, Mr McLeay has very judiciously applied but a small space of it for that purpose, and has preserved the native trees and shrubs to extend his Landscape Gardening. From the first commencement he never suffered a tree of any kind to be destroyed, until he saw distinctly the necessity of doing so. He thus retained the advantge of embellishment from his native trees, and harmonised them with the foreign trees now growing ... About twenty men have been engaged in these general improvements which have been going on, in a moderate and judicious manner, for several years, and it will require a few more years to complete the work; but when completed the place will probably not be surpassed by any garden in New South Wales.

Thomas Shepherd (1826) in Bernard Smith, *Documents on Art and Taste in Australia*, Oxford University Press, Melbourne, 1975.

James Tucker

The writings of 'Ralph Rashleigh' are usually attributed to James Tucker (c. 1808–88), who was transported for writing a threatening letter and arrived in the colony in 1827. However, this attribution has been disputed.

A straggling range of cottages

The band of Romulus, it is most certain,
· Were ruffian stabbers and vile cutpurse knaves;
Yet did this outcast scum of earth
Lay the foundations of the Eternal City.

Before daybreak next morning the light of Port Jackson was visible from the deck of the *Magnet*, and shortly afterwards that trusty vessel entered the Heads—two bold bluff precipices, between which lies the entrance to that spacious harbour, supposed to be one of the finest on the surface of the globe. A pilot had come on board to direct the course of the ship to her anchorage; and during the run of nearly seven miles from the entrance of the Port to the site of the town of Sydney Rashleigh had ample opportunities for scanning the essential features of the land in which he was destined to find his future home.

The shores of Port Jackson *then* possessed few charms, either natural or acquired; sandy bays opening to great distances inland, bordered apparently by stunted trees; rocky headlands between each inlet, crowned with similar foliage; and far away, on other hand, a background displaying dense forests of sombre green. There were *then* none of those elegant mansions or beautiful villas, with their verdant and ever blooming gardens, which *now* so plentifully meet the eye of the new colonist, affording abundant proof of the wonted energy of the Anglo-Saxon race, who speedily rescue the most untamed soils from the barbarism of nature and bid the busy sounds of industry and art awaken silent echoes of every primeval forest in which they are placed.

Not a single patch of cultivated soil appeared in those days to refresh the sight of the wearied voyagers with evidences that here the foot of civilised man had ever trod prior to their arrival. One of the passengers, who had visited New South Wales before, called the attention of his companions on the poop to an isle called Garden Island, and Ralph looked towards the spot, expecting now, at least, to detect some proof of the reclaiming hand of man. But alas, the so-called *Garden* Island presented nothing to his view but a doubly sterile mass of rugged grey rocks rising from the bosom of one of the numerous bays, and crowned with the same unvarying livery of russet green; but as they rounded the next projecting point they came in view of a small embattled building on a height, which was said to be one of the forts at the entrance of Sydney Cove. Immediately afterwards they saw a straggling range of cottages, mostly of a very small size, which stretched along an eminence, and which were declared by their informant to be a portion of the town of Sydney known as 'The Rocks'.

The *Magnet* was shortly brought to anchor opposite neck of land on which stood a slaughter-house, and our voyagers could survey the greater part of the town from a very favourable position. The dwellings appeared to be chiefly of one story; in fact, most of them deserved no better name than huts. The streets were narrow and straggling; nor did there seem to be more than half a dozen good or convenient private buildings in the town. There was no cultivated land to be seen from their station, and but a very few miserable cottages, peeping here and there out of the trees, stood upon the north shore of the harbour, in various parts of which there were then about six other large vessels at anchor, besides a good number of small cutters and boats which were passing to and fro continually.

James Tucker (1827), *Ralph Rashleigh*, Angus & Robertson,
Sydney, 1975.

Sydney Gazette

The religious residents of Sydney consistently complained of the contempt shown for religion. However, in this case the Baptists showed that they could defend themselves.

The Church militant

BAPTISM.—On Sunday afternoon, three males and a female underwent the ceremony of baptism in Farm Cove, which was performed by the Rev. Mr McKaig. A person undressed himself, and went into the water, and attempted, by catching hold of Mr McKaig's leg, to pull him into the water, but he was prevented from carrying his purpose into execution, and the persons assembling becoming indignant at the conduct of the intruder, pelted him with stones, by which he received a cut over one of his eyes.

Sydney Gazette, 3 September 1832.

Sydney Gazette

Those who wrote for the *Sydney Gazette* achieved a sparse elegance of style. This report does not waste a word.

Fifteen years in the regiment

EXECUTION.—On Friday morning, Thomas Brennan, a soldier of Captain Wright's company in His Majesty's 39th regt. of foot, was shot to death at Dawes' Battery, pursuant to sentence of a Court Martial, for attempting to murder the sergeant of his company, at Emu Plains. The previous day various detachments of troops were marched into Sydney to be present at the awful ceremony. At day light on Friday, the troops in garrison were under arms, and were marched from the barracks to Dawes' Battery, the prisoner following his coffin, which was carried by four soldiers. Having arrived at the spot, the sentence of the Court Martial was read, and the prisoner being pinioned, was left to his devotions with the Reverend Mr Therry. Eight men, with loaded muskets, were drawn from the ranks, and placed within twelve paces of the prisoner. Every thing being prepared, the Reverend Gentleman retired, the fatal signal was given, the pieces were discharged, and Brennan fell a lifeless corpse without a struggle. The troops then marched round this body and from the ground, and the body of the deceased was interred where it fell. He had been fifteen years in the regiment.

Sydney Gazette, 9 April 1833.

Charles Darwin

Charles Darwin (1809–82) came to Sydney on HMS *Beagle* in January 1836 and stayed for eighteen days, managing to fit in a trip to the Blue Mountains.

A fine town

January 12th, 1836.—Early in the morning a light air carried us towards the entrance of Port Jackson. Instead of beholding a verdant country, interspersed with fine houses, a straight line of yellowish cliff brought to our minds the coast of Patagonia. A solitary lighthouse, built of white stone, alone told us we were near a great and populous city. Having entered the harbour, it appears fine and spacious, with cliff-formed shores of horizontally stratified sandstone. The nearly level country is covered with thin scrubby trees, bespeaking the curse of sterility. Proceeding further inland, the country improves: beautiful villas and nice cottages are here and there scattered along the beach. In the distance stone houses, two and three storeys high, and windmills standing on the edge of a bank, pointed out to us as the site of the capital of Australia.

At last we anchored within Sydney Cove. We found the little basin occupied by many large ships and surrounded by warehouses. In the evening I walked through the town, and returned full of admiration at the whole scene. It is a most magnificent testimony to the power of the British nation. Here, in a less promising country, scores of years have done many times more than an equal number of centuries have effected in South America. My first feeling was to congratulate myself that I was born an Englishman. Upon seeing more of the town afterwards, perhaps my admiration fell a little; but yet it is a fine town. The streets are regular, broad, clean, and kept in excellent order; the houses are of a good size and well furnished. It may be faithfully compared to the large suburbs which stretch out from London and a few other great towns in England; but not even near London or Birmingham is there an appearance of such rapid growth. The number of large houses and other buildings just finished was truly surprising; nevertheless, everyone complained of the high rents and difficulty in procuring a house. Coming from South America, where in the towns every man of property is known, no one thing surprised me more than not being able to ascertain at once to whom this or that carriage belonged ...

Before arriving here the three things which interested me most were—the state of society amongst the higher classes, the condition of the convicts, and the degree of attraction sufficient to induce persons to emigrate. Of course after so short a visit, one's opinion is worth scarcely anything; but it is as difficult not to form some opinion, as it is to form a correct judgment. On the whole, from what I heard, more than from what I saw, I was disappointed in the state of society. The whole community is raucously divided into parties on almost every subject. Among those who, from their station in life, ought to be the best, many live in such open profligacy that respectable people cannot associate with them. There is much jealousy between the children of the rich emancipist and the free settlers, the former being pleased to consider honest men as interlopers. The whole population, poor and rich, are bent on acquiring wealth; amongst the higher orders, wool and sheep-grazing form the constant subjects of conversation. There are many serious drawbacks to the comfort of a family, the chief of which, perhaps, is being surrounded by convict servants. How thoroughly odious to every feeling, to be waited on by a man who the day before, perhaps, was flogged, from your representation, for some trifling misdemeanour. The female servants are of course much worse: hence the children learn the vilest expressions, and it is fortunate, if not equally violent ideas.

Charles Darwin, *The Voyage of the Beagle*, J.M. Dent, London, 1959.

Bede Polding

John Bede Polding (1794–1877), a Benedictine priest, came to Sydney in 1835 as Bishop of New Holland. Eight years later he became the first Catholic Archbishop of Sydney.

The very refuse of other callings

Many delinquencies take place in Sydney, in great measure owing to the horrible darkness of the streets. So truly is this the cause, that it is well known not one half of the thefts committed are perpetrated during the moonlit part of the month; add to this the wretched materials of which the Police is composed—the very refuse of other callings, when a man can obtain no other employment, he goes into the Police. In the country depredations are sometimes committed by half-starved cruelly treated men on their tyrannical masters. In England, were a third of such treatment received, ten times worse consequences would ensue. Talk of reform and less leniency [towards?] the Convict population—the Code of Convict law is Draconian. Let us have a better race of masters and the reformation of this country will be speedily accomplished.

> Letter, 28 January 1838, from *The Letters of John Bede Polding OSB*, Vol. 1, 1819–43, Sisters of the Good Samaritan, Glebe, NSW, 1994.

Louisa Anne Meredith

Louisa Anne Meredith (1812–95) was born in England, came with her father to New South Wales in 1821, and went back to England to marry in 1839. She returned to Sydney later that year, when she recorded her impressions. In 1840 she moved to Tasmania, where she lived for the rest of her life writing poetry, fiction, and sketches.

Wool, wool, wool

Fleas are another nuisance they swarm in every room in tens of thousands, and blacken the breakfast table or dinner as soon as the viands appear, tumbling into the cream, tea, wine and gravy with a most disgusting familiarity. But worse than these are the mosquitos nearly as numerous, and infinitely more detestable to those luckless bodies they form an attachment to, as they do to most newcomers, a kind of initiatory compliment which I would gladly dispense with, for most intolerable is the torment they cause in the violent irritation of their mountainous bites.

The ladies, to quote the remark of a witty friend, 'pay more attention to the adornment of their heads *without* than *within*.' That there are many most happy exceptions to this rule, I gladly acknowledge, but in the majority of instances a comparison between the intellect and the conversation of

Englishwomen, and those of an equal grade here, would be highly unfavourable to the latter. An apathetic indifference seems the besetting fault, and utter absence of interest or inquiry beyond the merest gossip—the cut of a new sleeve, or the guests at a late party. 'Do you play?' and 'Do you draw?' are invariable queries to a new lady-arrival. 'Do you *dance*?' is thought superfluous for everybody dances; but not a question is heard relative to English literature or art; far less a remark on any political event, of however an important nature—not a syllable that betrays *thought* unless some very inquiring belle ask, 'if you have seen the Queen and whether she is *pretty*?' But all are dressed in the latest fashion and in the best materials, though not always with that tasteful attention to the accordance of contrast of colour which an elegant Englishwoman would observe ...

Most gentlemen have their whole souls so felted up in wools, fleeces, flocks and stock, that I have often sat through a weary dinner and evening of incessant talking without hearing a single syllable on any other subject ... the eternity of wool, wool, wool, wearied my very soul.

> Louisa Anne Meredith, *Notes and Sketches of New South Wales*, John
> Murray, London 1844.

Joseph Simmons

Joseph Simmons (1810–93), who arrived in the colony in 1830, combined three callings: acting, theatrical management, and auctioneering. The theatrical flourishes of this advertisement omit the unpleasant fact that an aspect of the view from Woolwich was the convict prison on Cockatoo Island, only a few hundred yards swimming distance away.

The finest views of any spot

In directing public attention to the Intended Sale of the above-named Township [of Woolwich], the Auctioneer is almost tempted to deviate from the set rule he at first intended to follow with regard to the length of his advertisements, as far as concerns a description of this magnificent and truly valuable Property, to attempt even an outline of its many advantages would occupy an unlimited space, suffice it to say, the inducements now held out to all classes of the community by the Sale of the Woolwich Allotments are great indeed! Scarcely two miles from the heart and bustle of Sydney, so delightfully situated that as to command the finest views of any known spot in the Colony, first in panoramic form on one side, the Sydney Harbour, with numerous ships, boats, and vessels of all kinds, reclining upon its broad waters, or sailing over the ruffled surface on the other side; the pretty appearance of the Lane Cove River in another direction, the eye is relieved by rich cultivated Lands, and the enlivening scenery of the surrounding Country ...

To merchants, retired officers, tradesmen in easy circumstances, invalids, market gardeners, speculators &c, &c, this is the opportunity. 'Health is a blessing greater than riches,' and all who locate themselves in the new town of Woolwich will have the benefit of enjoying 'health in the breeze.' The whole of the allotments possess ample frontages to the Government Road, leading to Kissing Point, Parramatta, &c, as also to the Sydney Harbour and the Lane Cove River; they vary considerably in size, and are thereby rendered suitable for either the magnificent villa or the humble cottage.

The Auctioneer would seriously advise all who seek to invest their capital in a lucrative way to consider the opportunity now offered—it is well known that the Steam Ferry Boat, intended to ply between Dawes' Battery and the North Shore, will be launched in a few days; the engines are hourly expected from England; on their arrival the boat will immediately commence plying, thereby securing for the inhabitants of the North Shore a speedy and safe passage to and from Sydney several times a day ...

Joseph Simmons in Sydney Gazette, 23 February 1841.

John Hood

John Hood came to Sydney in 1841, after a voyage on an emigrant ship, with one son to visit another, a squatter. Hood was of sufficient status to leave his card at Government House.

Gin palaces and pot-houses

One thing that pains and surprises a stranger, is the vast number of grog-shops, and the conspicuous and public places and thoroughfares selected for those wells of poison. I am told there are at present in Sydney two hundred and fifteen of these dens of iniquity; which gives one public-house, where spirits are sold and drunk over the counter, for every one hundred and forty souls, including women and children! In a community constituted as Sydney is, of mixed materials, it might have been anticipated that some restriction would exist on this point; but so much the contrary has it ever been, that from the first establishment of the colony, such houses have been the foundation of some of the largest fortunes; and the earlier history of its transaction states, 'that his Majesty's Servants made rum a legal tender, and the liberty to sell it was a privilege eagerly grasped at by gentlemen holding at the time commissions in his Majesty's army. I do not mean to assert that such things exist now. But certain it is, that the injury done to the masses by this facility of obtaining spirits, is a disgrace to the country ...

One great drawback to the comfort and cleanliness of the town, is the want of common-sewers, to carry off the water and other impurities. It is true the chief part of the town stands upon a height, and that there is a declivity to the sea at either side. But some of the principal streets are perfectly level; and it is wonderful to me that the senses of the inhabitants are not more offended than they are, and that disease is not more prevalent. The dryness of the atmosphere may in some degree counteract this evil; but the town's people will never do justice to themselves or their beautiful capital until this is remedied, nor until their streets are macadamized and lighted with gas.

Notwithstanding what I have too truly stated, with regard to the number of public-houses in all their varied description, from the bright and seducing gin-palace to the lowest pot-house, still it is not less the fact, that I never was in any town in my life when the streets were quieter at night, or where there was less danger of street annoyance.

I expected to have found Sydney a very noisy, dissolute place, especially after dark; and that vice would 'run down her streets like a river.' But, on the contrary, it is most orderly, and scarcely any drunkenness or licentiousness is to be seen; and there seems to as much respect shown to the Sabbath, in the the public parts of the town at least, as even in Edinburgh, which is acknowledged to be, in this respect, the most exemplary city in the world ...

The first sight of the town and people does not impress a European with the idea of being in a country so distant from his home;—the language, the manners and dress of the inhabitants being for the most part similar to his own. But there are many peculiarities that gradually display themselves, chiefly attributable to the climate. There is a sallowness of countenance in the male, and a delicacy of feature and skin in the female, that I have not seen elsewhere: while you are every now and then instinctively placing your hand upon your pockets, as some suspicious-looking fellow passes you. Nor is this to be wondered at; when it is remembered, that every seventh man you meet in the the street has 'left his country for his country's good'; or is the offspring of those who have done so ...

Many of the private houses in the vicinity of the town are delighful little retreats, placed amid beautiful gardens and scenery, wood and water. Many are magnificent in their architecture and dimensions. When you inquire the names, however, of some of them, you are amused at hearing, in reply, a nickname generally indicative of the calling or origin of its possessor or builder. 'Frying-pan Hall,' for instance, a very handsome chateau in the neighbourhood belonged to a person who, after serving his term of bondage of seven years, followed the useful calling of an ironsmith! It is not safe to be too curious in Australia, as to either fortune or family; we must take the good the gods provide us, and the civilities sometimes vouchsafed the stranger, without much inquiry as to the pedigree of the host, or the mode in which his wealth was acquired. Personal history is at a discount; and good memories and inquisitive minds are peculiarly disliked.

John Hood, *Australia and the East*, John Murray, London, 1843.

Ludwig Leichhardt

Ludwig Leichhardt (1813–48?), a young German naturalist and explorer, arrived in the colony in 1842.

You can buy any article

The activity of the town is astonishing, and a spirit of feverish speculation prevails. The harbour is crowded with ships and there are daily arrivals and departures from and to England, China, New Zealand, Van Diemen's Land, Port Phillip and different places on the coast. There are steamboats going to Hunter's River, Moreton Bay and Port Phillip. You can buy any article of luxury or convenience in Sydney ... And to whom do we owe such astonishing changes in so short a time? In 1788 Arthur Phillip brought 850 convicts here, founded the colony, and began, with convict labour, to make the country productive. From then on, they continued to send convicts here, where they were employed either on public works or were assigned as servants to the free settlers. Convicts whose sentences had expired were set free and themselves became settlers. Even those granted conditional pardon could acquire property and become financially independent. The richest men in the colony were convicts, or the descendants of convicts. But more and more free settlers have gradually been coming here, and there are now about 100,000 of them on the land in Australia. Nearly all these immigrants came here to make money and nothing else. They are willing to devote years of their life to the purpose, in the hope of being able to return Home to enjoy life quietly until they die. Few come here to stay. But many change their minds when they are able to discern the attractions of this rich country, and to find its disadvantages less irksome. Families of this kind, who are taking an interest in this colony, and have come to look upon it as their own country, constitute, in fact, its only real wealth. And it is through them that a powerful state will gradually arise, a state which may possibly consign old Europe to oblivion. Naturally, however, you can't expect existing social conditions in Sydney to be satisfactory, considering the incompatible elements of which society here is composed. No matter how liberal you are, if you're in the company of ex-convicts you'll never banish the thought that you are in fact dealing with people who were once capable of committing serious crimes. True, they have paid the penalty and have returned, white-washed, to society—but has it redeemed them? Do they really merit our confidence? Such considerations, which are by no means groundless, explain why many free emigrants have come to regard themselves as [people of] a distinct and superior class. The effect of their opinion of themselves has been to unite the emancipated convicts. In consequence, we now find two parties, two kinds of society confronting each other. There is hostility between them which often impedes the progress of the colony … I have to admit, moreover, that I'm fascinated when I watch what is happening here. A state is coming into being which may, perhaps in less than a century, break loose from England as did the United States of America, and establish an independent nation or federation.

The Letters of F.W. Ludwig Leichhardt (ed. M. Aurousseau), Vol. 2,
Hakluyt Society/Cambridge University Press, London, 1968.

Sydney Gazette

Governor Macquarie's pious hopes in 1810 that racing in the colony would not be accompanied by gambling were not fulfilled. This passage describes the first meeting of the Australian Jockey Club, which had been founded only a few months earlier, at Homebush.

A glorious turn-out

'A horse! a horse! my kingdom for a horse.' This had been the cry throughout Sydney for several days preceding the races. Horse-flesh was not to be got for love, and hardly for money,—for, those who had but one horse kept it for themselves, and those, who had more than one, had them bespoken for the last week, or ten days. Never have we witnessed a more glorious assemblage, or a more glorious turn-out in the colony, that we had on Tuesday last, at Homebush. About eight o'clock in the morning the heavy baggage of the day (of course we mean the lumbering and springless drays, and dismounted water carts, of which there were a vast number) started. At nine, the spring carts, or, as they are more commonly called, 'shay' carts, and numberless vehicles in that line rolled 'doucelie' along the road. At ten came the gigs, and the hired party of hacks jogging slowly, yet steadily, on their way, whilst ever and anon, horsemen in pairs and threes might be observed threading their way amongst the wheels. At half past ten the 'slashers' were on the road; four in hand, fast trotting horses in gigs, tandems, top boots, crack whips and handsome women all mingling together in the whirling dust in the most admired confusion. Through this scene of dust and beauty did we wend our way in the most stoical composure, but, ever and anon, as our gallant little black, bore us in some measure from the reach of the dust, or as we gained the summit of some range, the beautiful scenery of the country, rendered still more delightful by the shining of old Sol, called us to an enjoyment, a moment of which is worth a world of your dull plodding office days. But, wheugh! the dust from that carriage has veiled the fairy scene by a cloud of dust, and we must fain pursue our road though not without casting dire looks of vengeance at the unsentimental Jehu, who in all the pride of a bottle-green coat, and white nethers, in vain tries to make his roadsters emulate the pace of our own noble animal. After divers hair-breadth escapes, from the Phaeton like propensities of certain ambitious youths, we arrived safe on the course. About twelve o'clock, and as we cleared the rise of the hill, what a joyful and enlivening sight there met our eyes—booths, decked out in all their holiday panoply of flags, their inside filled with eatables and drinkables of every description, were ranged along the run in, opposite the grand Strand, while the numbers who were laughing, talking, singing, shouting or crying, made up a scene in which it was impossible to be sad. The many beauteous smiling faces that everywhere met the eye, would have made even a misanthrope happy. For ourselves, the sight of others receiving pleasure from innocent amusement, is always one of joy, and no matter how sad we might be arriving at a scene such as that we witnessed on Tuesday, yet, in a very short time our face reflected the smiles of those around us. Under these circumstances, then, we spent a happy day, and the beauty of the weather added in some degree to our enjoyment. No less than ten booths, besides the grand stand, were erected on the course, and the numbers that thronged them throughout the day, must have caused an extra smile to the smiling hosts. Fodder and water were provided in plenty at the back of the booths, at a moderate price, considering the day. We do not think we ever saw so many four-in-hands at any race, as we observed on Tuesday. Every thing went off well. The company were delighted with the sport, and the police kept the ground remarkably quiet and orderly. Some of the light-fingered gentry were on the spot, but could do nothing of any consequence, as they were too well looked after. An excellent ordinary was provided by Messrs. Walker and Clarkson, at the grand Strand, at five shillings a head. A band of music was also stationed here, which, between the races played some of the most popular airs. Among the distingushed personages present, we observed,—the family of Sir Maurice O'Connell, E.D. Thompson, Esq., Colonial Secretary, Major Nunn, Captains O'Connell and Innes; several Naval and Military Officers, besides many of our respectable citizens, who, from the admirable manner in which the sports were conducted, seemed highly gratified and amused with the animating scene.

Sydney Gazette, 31 March 1842.

F.G. Brewer

The manager of the *Sydney Morning Herald*, F.G. Brewer, wrote a revealing private memorandum on the first election for the Legislative Council in 1843.

The rowdy denizens of Blackwattle Swamp

The nomination took place on Tuesday, June 13th, at the hustings in Macquarie Place, in front of the old Star Hotel, the balcony of which was used for spectators. Each candidate had his own colours—those of Wentworth and Bland were blue, of O'Connell green—and each was escorted to the hustings by a procession. One came down Bridge Street, another by way of Spring Street, a third by Gresham Street, and the fourth by O'Connell Street. Wentworth and Bland's procession reached Macquarie Place at the same moment as Captain O'Connell's, and a fierce struggle took place for the possession of the hustings. The O'Connellites succeeded in filling the space occupied by the returning officer and his staff, whereupon the Wentworth and Bland contingent stormed the platform and many who attempted to scale it were hurled to the ground. Dr Bland, in endeavouring to get on the hustings, was thrown down with violence and received such severe injury that he was carried to his residence in an unconscious state. Mr Wentworth, Captain O'Connell and Mr Hustler having succeeded in securing positions on the partially demolished hustings, with some of their proposers and seconders, Mr Robert Cooper and his immediate supporters had to content themselves with an omnibus—the only one in Sydney in those days. The row was continued all through the proceedings, which were gone through almost in dumb show. Anything like orderly speaking was out of the question, but Cooper harangued the mob from his 'bus and put forth his claims to election to his immediate surrounders, the rowdy denizens of Blackwattle Swamp, who fell upon all who expressed dissent in so vigorous a manner that Cooper was able to talk away for some time without interruption. The day intervening between the nomination and the day of election was devoted to the delivery of addresses in Hyde Park by Cooper, whose procession thereto was headed by two of his supporters carrying pikes, on each of which half a loaf of bread was stuck. Platforms had been erected for the speakers. The streets on the eve of the election were crowded with excited mobs, the Irish contingent being very demonstrative. The Native Party, who were unanimous for Wentworth and Bland, arranged their tactics for the coming contest, but were not prepared for the outbreak of the following day. The polling commenced at nine o'clock on June 15th, and for the first two hours things progressed in a fairly orderly manner. About twelve o'clock a mob of some 500 persons, wearing Captain O'Connell's colours, went through Prince's Street to the polling booth in Gipps Ward on Flagstaff Hill, tore down the colours of Wentworth and Bland, levelled their booth with the ground, and made a furious attack on their supporters, who fled in all directions. The polling booth was surrounded, and the ingress of voters for any other candidates but O'Connell for a time prevented. One of the persons attacked was a Mr John Jones, the owner of some whaling ships in port, who ran down to his wharf in Windmill Street, and, collecting a number of the sailors, armed them with whale lances and returned with them to the ground. The consequences, had they met the opposing forces, would have been serious indeed: but luckily the mob had gone to another place, and the whalers were received by a detachment of the mounted police, who chased them back to their ships and disarmed them. The riot, while the mob was on the Flagstaff Hill, was so great that the returning officer considered it necessary to adjourn the poll until the following morning. The same mob then proceeded to other polling places, and on their way passed the residence and auction rooms of Mr Samuel Lyons, who was a strong supporter of Wentworth and Bland. Here it stopped and an attack was made on the place; large stones were hurled through the plate-glass windows of the auction rooms and smaller ones were used on the windows of the first and second floors, until scarcely a pane remained unbroken. From here the mob proceeded to Hyde Park, and, seeing Captain Innes, one of the police magistrates, on horseback, they chased him. Being unable to escape by the usual gate, he put his horse to the fence at the northern side and successfully cleared it ...

The friends of the popular candidates, including a number of native youths known as the 'Cabbage Trees,' from wearing hats of that name, were there, and when the mob came back from the chase a short battle took place with fists, resulting in the rioters being driven from the park. They, however, tore up the palings in front of some houses in Elizabeth Street, returned, and, thus armed, again attacked their assailants until the arrival of a body of mounted police restored something like order. The mob made for the southern part of the city and committed other outrages there. In the evening a band of some thirty or forty men, with as many boys, bearing O'Connell's colours, paraded some of the streets, violently assaulted a peaceable passer-by and broke a number of windows. So ended the first election day in Sydney.

Quoted in John Fairfax & Sons, *A Century of Journalism: The Sydney Morning Herald and Its Record of Australian Life 1831–1931*, John Fairfax & Sons, Sydney, 1931.

John Nugent

This stray document turned up in the State Archives a few years ago. Evidently a running diary kept by police inspector John Nugent, whose territory was bounded by the Rocks and Druitt, Park and Macquarie Streets, it is a unique document on Sydney's underworld. Nugent lists 107 'disorderly houses' (i.e. brothels) in his division. The sparse records show Nugent as an Irish Protestant and that he was dismissed in 1845, reason not given.

A place of resort for low strumpets
Norfolk Islanders. Cont.

Riley Joe—one of the most consummate thieves in Sydney—I had him in custody for some days. He was so proud of his deep villainy that he fairly asked my Chief Constable after certain service that he had tendered Police, if Mr Mitchell did not consider him 'one of the most accomplished rascals in all Sydney,' and gloried, I think, in the flattering candid affirmative. He works as a blind at his trade of a shoemaker near the Gas Works ...

... he has given much information but is a dangerous villain—I told him once 'he was the greatest rascal that I had ever met'. 'Well, Sir, I believe not a man can beat me, but if I was not what I am I would not be fit for your purpose.'

In (?) September I hear he is going to New Zealand—he endeavoured to get employed by me, but I object to the employment of such agents because he would plan robberies in order to earn his wages & induce Crime[,] however I would sooner prevent it ...

... Bullies and Thieves (continued)

... 1843. Kent. George. Pitt St took Mrs Brown's House—has two girls and his Wife and his sister. Keeps a cookshop—quiet. McAuliff (Margaret) one of the girls is a sad drunkard. Triff, Harriet, the other girl, is more quiet. Aug. 44 now lives in O'Connel St.

Gamble George. Pitt St keeps an oyster shop. Lives with woman named Mary Harkinson as his Wife—but 4 other girls of the house walk the streets at all hours.

Mc Cann—Castlereagh Street. Drinks but works—his house is a place of resort for low strumpets.

Lewis (Eliza) in Bligh Street. Next to Leeham's—moved—said Smith (Fanny) to be visited by My Inspector tho' he writes of them thus. 'These two are very quiet, and [h]as no interview with any one but gentlemen.' ...

... Bill the Shoemaker. Keeps a brothel of children of 12 to 14 years of age in Globe Street, opposite the grocers' wharf. Wears a large hat ...

... Bloomfield is lately free from Port Macquarie—he dresses and apes the clerical, in his Coat, neckcloth and step ... This gentleman was favoured by a passage here [for] stealing a gentleman's gold spectacles. He was canvassing him as a subscriber to some work (theological of course) [and] the spectacles lay upon the table. Mr Bloomfield dropped his hankerchief over them and mopped them up in it and & have come here ...

... I have lost sight of this personage 1843 ...

[a newspaper cutting, journal unidentified, is pasted in, evidently a year later]

... sent out some years ago *for his country's good*, being then a minister of religion in England, and has till recently been employed as a special, at Port Macquarie. Having arrived in Sydney he attaches himself to a young female whom he puts off as his daughter, and thus sponges on the public in every shape and form. We know of several publicans who have been taken in by this scamp in the last fortnight to a considerable amount. He is a tall jolly looking personage, with a most unfailing stock of assurance, to which he trusts his first introduction of himself to his *patron's* notice upon making a favourable impression; he assumes this familiar style, and what he principally delights in, is having everything round him in [a] homey way; he calls for [a] bundle of cigars and smokes them, and when they have evaporated he turns up his nose and calls it child's play, but dotes on the pipe you have between your lips, because it is so homely; he flirts disdainfully with the tender limbs of a young duck. While he smiles fondly at the ascenety [?] of roast sirloin at the other end of the table, his leisure intervals he fills with glasses of hot brandy and water, but glows into rapture at the pure simplicity of [a] pint of porter; it is so homely; he vents his full flow of benevolent feelings on his supposed daughter and lavishes on 'his dear Ellen' every kindness and affection which paternal affection can suggest. We saw this fellow after having been turned out of a house where he had run a bill of seven pounds, step into a poor woman's shop and having refreshed himself and *sa fille* with ginger beer and cakes to the amount of some shillings, retire with a promise to call again tomorrow *and pay* ...

Norfolk Islanders cont.

Hunt Simon. 4 years from Moreton Bay. Kent St. A Dealer. Once fined £10 for harbouring Bush Rangers. A gambler ...

10 July was taken up on Parramatta race course. Gambles for one month (?). His wife is a prisoner sold there at 2/- a bottle—a cask of porter is on tap ... and the gamblers pay one shilling in the pound for the *good* of the House [in Erskine Street].

His principal customers are flash thieves—among them is

John Bruney. He never works

Nathan and his brother

Paddy fat. N. Islander & a fence an old man

Joseph Taylor—a thief and whore's bully

Farnell, has a Barber's shop in King St.

White, John, a Shingler, gambler, no thief

Barnes, a tin shop man in Market St.: gone to Maitland

Bravo, John

Stanley George—sent up country May 44.

This man [Hunt] is becoming communicative. He knows who committed the Robbery at Mrs Terry's and observed that the jemmy was broken. He says that only 2 (*not 4*) watches were taken—he knows the two brothers Harris—watchmaker & jewellers fences

—His wife was fancy woman of George Stanley

...

Wainwright Will. Is a Leger de main, hocus pocus Man lives Jan 25.45— in Kent St. a few doors above Harris, the Publican's, he is connected with different gangs. Wears a white blouse and ring—black hair ...

... Murphy Will. A school-master. NI expiree—has been taking indecent liberties with his female pupils.

Kept a school on the Rocks in Cumberland Street and has bolted—Oct. 1844.

29 June 1845. My Friend the 'School Master abroad' *turns up* A lte [letter]
is found at Ed Walsh NI Islander—the burglar taken in Rayner's Stores last
night this lte is from W. Murphy stating that he is keeping a School at the
Irish Clarence town Williams River
—Serj. McCook getting up the Evidence forthwith—
Dr McKellar mentioned the fact at first to me—he attended Carr's the
Grocer's child. Mrs Rochester's little girl and orphan, witnessed the Man
commit the crime
1846 May 21. In Sydney. Sent to jail for 3 months, for not registering himself. The Mother Mrs Carr of Clarence Street refuses to prosecute.

> Inspector John Nugent, 'Registry of Flash Men', *Register of Sydney*
> *Police Establishments* 1838–51, Police Inspector General's Office,
> NSW State Archives.

Select Committee on the Aborigines

Mahroot was unusual in being able to support himself as a professional
fisherman at La Perouse.

All over small pox like

PRESENT:—
Richard Windeyer, Esq., in the Chair.
William Bradley, Esq.
Rev. Dr Lang
Francis Lord, Esq.
Charles Nicholson, Esq., MD
J.P. Robinson, Esq.

Monday, 8 September, 1845.

Mahroot, *alias* the Boatswain, called and examined:—
1.   Where were you born?   At Cook's River.
2.   Do you know how long ago?   I cannot tell, not rightly.
3.   What Governor was here when you were born?   The Governor
     before Macquarie, I believe. I have been told I am about forty-nine.
4.   Both your parents were aboriginal natives—black fellows?   Yes.
5.   Do you understand what you have come here for?   Yes
6.   To tell us about yourself and your friends, and what can be done to
     do you good—do you understand that?   I do.
7.   What extent of the country belonged to your tribe—to your family—
     how much land did you walk over?   Only as far as from here to
     Botany Bay and around the sea coast, away from the heads at Port
     Jackson, to the heads at Botany and all inland.

8. How far inland? Not very far inland, where I am now ...

14. When you first recollect, how many black fellows were there in the tribe, who spoke your language, men, women and children? Four hundred I think in my recollection ...

25. *By Mr Robinson:* Were the whole four hundred black fellows in your tribe about Botany? In Botany.

26. *By the Chairman:* Were there many children then? There was.

27. How many children did each woman use to have? I can't rightly say.

28. How many brothers and sister did you have? I had three sisters by another father and the same mother.

29. How many brothers did you have? None; I have got relations.

30. Used other women to have three and four children likewise? Yes, three or four or two.

31. Never more? Some of them more.

32. What did they live upon? Generally on the sea coast side fish, and fern root.

33. And your tribe did not go far from the sea coast? No, always on the sea coast in the bay.

34. When did the number of your tribe begin to diminish? (A pause) When did you find black fellows die off; when did they come to be few? They used to fight about the town, knock about like the deuce in liquor.

35. It was by getting drunk you think? To the degree they took to liquor, at last they went away very fast; it was the only thing that destroyed them.

36. Do you mean that the old men died, or that the children died? (*No answer.*)

37. Used the children to get liquor? I have seen that.

38. Much? I can't say great much.

39. Used the mother and father give it them or white fellow? I have seen mother and father give it them.

40. Did the women have less children after this, after they took to having liquor? Very few after.

41. Was not that because they used to go with a great many white men? That is very true indeed.

42. And the white men used to give them liquor to go with them? Yes.

43. Do you think that was the reason why they had very few children afterwards? Nothing else but that.

44. How many black fellows are there now living, men, women and children where you used to know four hundred? I should say fifty, but not belong to Botany mind you Sir, different people raised up here in former times come.

45. How many are there do you think alive, who were born there, who belong to the old tribe, who speak your language, not the Liverpool language? Only four, three women and I am the only man ...

83. [*By the Chairman:*] You know the devil is very wicked and lives in a place where people will be punished, is Boy very bad or very good? He was very good.
84. *By Dr Lang:* What did he do to the black fellows?   They say he will take black fellows away to where he lives.
85. Do they say he gives them anything?   No, they don't say that.
86. Is there any other person over them besides Boy?   Only Boy.
87. Is there nobody that does harm to black fellows, that steals their children?   No.
88. *By Dr Nicholson:* What does Boy do, you say he takes black fellows away?   That is what they say.
89. Do you think they all go to Boy or that some go to the devil? Some say they will go to be a fish, some turn out to be a whale, that is … what they say.
90. *By Mr Lord:* What is the meaning of Boy in your language?   The devil.
91. What do black fellows mean by devil devil?   Devil devil is its all over small pox like.
92. *By the Chairman:* What is black fellow's word for dead, when life is gone away, supposing black fellow die or sheep die, what does black fellow say?   Boy.

> Minutes of Evidence taken before the Select Committee [of the New South Wales Legislative Council] on the Aborigines, 1845.

Sydney Morning Herald

Robert Lowe (1811–92), a barrister, who addressed this demonstration, was a member of the Legislative Council, elected with the support of Sydney tradesmen and small businessmen. In 1850 he returned to England, where he became a member of the House of Commons and a Cabinet minister, and was later ennobled as Viscount Sherbrooke.

That floating hell

The public demonstration so long intended in the colony upon the arrival of the first convict ship took place yesterday at the Circular Wharf. It is well known that the *Hashemy* had been unexpectedly delayed in her voyage; but though looked for from day to day, the intense interest of the people of Sydney in the event did not abate, and during Saturday and Sunday very considerable excitement prevailed throughout the city. Monday morning was about as unpropitious in point of weather as a day could be for an open air meeting. There was nothing of either comfort or hope about it. Nevertheless at about 11 o'clock, most of the leading merchants and shop-keepers closed their establishments, and large numbers of people began to wend their way to the Circular Quay. The only accommodation there was an omnibus, from the top of which the speakers addressed the meeting, consisting of betwen four and five thousand persons, and who in spite of the continued rain persisted in grave earnestness in fulfilment of their important duty ...

Mr Lowe, who at this moment arrived upon the ground, came forward to second the adoption of the Protest and was received with enthusiastic applause. It was with great pleasure that he undertook the task of seconding the adoption of the protest of the people of the colony of New South Wales, against the outrage which had been so insultingly and offensively perpetrated upon them by the resumption of transportation. The time for discussion on the principle of the convict question was past. They were not met to exclaim against the proposals of the English Government. The threat of degradation had been fulfilled. The stately presence of their city, the beautiful waters of their harbour, were this day again polluted with the presence of that floating hell—a convict ship. (Immense cheers.) They had lived again to behold the cargo of crime borne across the waves to them. In their port they beheld a ship freighted, not with the comforts of life, not with luxuries of civilised nations, not with the commodities of commerce, in exchange for our produce: but with the moral degradation of a community—the picked and selected criminals of Great Britain. These were the people that Great Britain sent here—educated in her crowded streets amongst her starving masses, New South Wales must be the university at which these scholars of vice and iniquity must finish their course of instruction. New South Wales must alone supply the college where these doctors in crime can take their last degree. (Cheers.) Here it was where the rubbish—the moral filth of Great Britain—must be shot; but the colonists at least had done their duty, and he congratulated them on it ...

Let them exercise the right that every English subject had—to assert his freedom. (Cheers.) He could see from that meeting the time was not far distant when they would assert their freedom not by words alone. As in America, oppression was the parent of independence, so it would be in this colony. The tea which the Americans flung into the water rather than pay tax upon it, was not the cause of revolt of the American States; it was the unrighteousness of the tax—it was the degradation of submission to an unrighteous demand. And so sure as the seed will grow into the plant, and the plant to the tree, in all times, and in all nations, so will injustice and tyranny ripen into rebellion, and rebellion into independence. (Immense cheering.)

The protest was put and passed unanimously ...

The meeting dispersed without any noise or tumult, and the conduct of the people throughout was grave, decorous and becoming.

'The great protest meeting', *Sydney Morning Herald*, 12 June 1849.

Charlotte Godley

Charlotte Godley, an English gentlewoman who had lived in New Zealand for some years, passed through Sydney in 1853. She disapproved not only of the bugs but also of the effect of the 'terrible gold fever' on the servants.

All Sydney swarms with bugs

I believe all Sydney swarms with bugs. Mrs Stewart told me they had great trouble in keeping them out of Government House, although a new house; so we were not surprised at anything but the rapacity of our fellow-lodgers whom we had involuntarily disturbed in their strongholds. In our bed, the first morning, we captured more than twenty, and I averaged two every night that I was there, in my own, or Baby's, bed. The Indian matting on the floor was full of the more lively sort of tormentors, and then the mosquitoes completed the picture, and left us very little peace after the candles were lighted. My husband wore gloves, and a pocket handkerchief over his head, even then could hardly sit still to write or read; and though he slept in them, it was of little or no use. I was at last so sleepy from continual short nights, that I could scarcely keep awake if I sat down anywhere for half an hour ...

[Cabs] are not always easy to get, after dark, though we had a stand close by; and so came our little delay. What we did pay was just half that charge [a driver had left them standing when they rejected his charge of fifteen shillings], but the real thing would have been five shillings, and only so much as that since this terrible gold fever, which, with one or other of its effects, meets you at every turn in Sydney, now, and makes it a thoroughly uncomfortable place to live in. It has in fact quite altered the state of society and put an end, comparatively, to all gaiety; made the rich in many cases poor, and the poor very rich. Men come back from the diggings, after a little good luck; buy, at fancy prices, a horse, and a brand new saddle, and ride—perhaps in their digger's clothes—up and down George Street (the Bond Street of Sydney) for several hours together. Or they get into a cab, two or three together, and give the driver ten pounds, desiring him to give them ten pounds' worth of driving about; and when his horses are tired, and he stops, saying it is over now, they either give him another ten pounds, or go to someone else, quite contented at the idea of getting rid so easily of such puzzlingly large sums of money. You hear endless stories of their spending for the very sake of spending. One I heard of, but I think it was at Melbourne, who went with his wife into a shop, and asked for a gown, the most expensive one they had; one was produced, of which the price was eighteen pounds; but he said that it was not enough, had they nothing of a higher price? They said no, really nothing, but if he liked, they could charge twenty pounds for that one!! That was actually accepted, and the gown purchased. When tradespeople and cabmen can make such a harvest by these sort of customers, you can imagine that they much prefer them to anything like gentlemen; for instance, our friend who asked fifteen shillings for our drive; and in some of the shops (indeed all I went into excepting one or two), your dignity must take up an extremely low position in your pocket, or it will suffer proportionately. Domestic servants are, however, I believe, the people who make the difference most felt to the dwellers in Sydney. Hardly a man is to be found contented to remain where he is, unless you can get an unsuccessful digger, whose health has suffered, or who has no luck at all; and the women, who always found it easy enough to 'get a husband', are now, as Johnson's American says, quite at famine price, and you hear endless stories of ladies who have been used to large establishments, and giving parties, now obliged to give up all thoughts of appearance, and open the door even, themselves, or make their daughters do it; give up their carriage, etc., and thankfully receive the services of any dirty girl who will come and help ...

When we were there [a Government House ball] we were much struck with the tendency of all the people to abuse the country, the society, and all belonging to them. I have no doubt that the gold and its consequences was the reason for this in part. Every family is made to feel its inconveniences, in one shape or another; high prices for everything they want to buy, no servants to be had, and many of the best and pleasantest families literally driven out of country by it. All agree that the change in Sydney, since the last two years, is very great, and very much for the worse. Almost all the best families there, members of the Council, even the Colonial Secretary, Mr Thompson (among those we knew or heard of), are going home to England, and taking this opportunity of getting out of the country; most of them hoping to return when things have returned into something like better order, when ladies will not obliged to open their own street doors, etc. ...

We had, on our way to the dinner at Sir A. Stephen, been overtaken by a 'brickfielder'—as they call their strong South winds in the summer. They come, I believe, invariably after some hours of great heat, and northerly wind, and raise a most frightful dust. As we got out of the carriage, in Lyons Terrace, we literally could not see across the road, and I have no doubt that my hair, when I appeared in the drawing-room, was a good deal redder, if not brighter, than you have ever seen it. This was the first burst of it, and we found them rushing about the house, in spite of the heat, to shut up every window and corner where wind could get in, and very soon the lightning began ...

Charlotte Godley, Letters from Early New Zealand 1850–53 (ed. John R. Godley), Whitcombe & Tombs, Christchurch, 1951.

Isaac Nathan

Isaac Nathan (1792–1864) was a musician, composer, and music teacher who came to Sydney in 1841. He supplemented his income by a great deal of journalism for almost every journal in the city. His biographer, Graham

Pont, who is familiar with his style, ascribes this account, which seems to be Sydney's first restaurant review, to Nathan.

A temple to French cookery

We this week present our readers with an illustration of this attractive temple [the Café de Paris] dedicated to the genius of French Cookery. Our English readers will doubtless imagine, when they hear of a restaurant being established in New South Wales, that the most *recherché plats* will consist of kangaroo steaks or parrot pie; indeed, in the illustrations furnished by our facetious friend, *Punch*, there is a bill of fare depicted in which these toothsome dishes figure very prominently. Until the opening of this very excellent restaurant, we are quite of opinion that Sydney was immersed in the thickest darkness in culinary matters.

We can sympathise with our contemporary, the *Empire*, as to the 'tough beef and tasteless mutton' to which he had been unhappily condemned. We have a very strong idea that good cookery would contribute quite as much to the individual happiness of this community as a good constitution, and dreadful as the admission may seem, we would individually barter our elective franchise for a wholesome and well cooked dinner every day, feeling convinced that whatever might be the effect on the political constitution, our corporeal constitution will be exceedingly benefited thereby.

Since the efforts of this French artist have become known, a new taste has arisen in Sydney, a 'soul has been created beneath the ribs of death.' We are happy to find that his success has stimulated him to launch out and extend his means of accommodation. The adjoining house has been taken and opened in humble imitation of those world renowned places of resort the Cafés of Paris. The new room is depicted in our engraving and in it will be supplied coffee, chocolate, a variety of American drinks, and *pour passer le temps* there is an excellent billiard table by Thurston, chess, dominoes and draughts, besides a variety of periodicals. We cannot doubt, but that this spirited undertaking will meet with the success that it merits. Those who have a taste for something better than scorched legs of too-recently-killed mutton or sodden beef redolent of brine, may here gratify their palates. The only drawback to the attractive picture it presents to our imagination is, that indignant Benedicts will rush home in huge discontent at the thought of the fraud that has been so long practised on their ignorance and their forbearance. Great will be the alarm of thrifty housewives, when venturing to put a 'cold shoulder' on the table and loud will be the reclamations of insulted cooks (heaven save the mark!) when told that their 'nice hash' is only fit for the kennel. But out of this kettle of fish let us hope that a gastronomic regeneration will arise, and that some learned professor of the art will establish a college for the education of those who might contribute so essentially to our health and at the same time economise our national resources. We cordially recommend this establishment, as the charges are moderate, the attendance good and the variety of dishes such as cannot be obtained elsewhere in Sydney.

Isaac Nathan, 'The café restaurant', Illustrated Sydney News,
11 February 1854.

Frank Fowler

Frank Fowler (1833–63) was a journalist who visited Sydney from 1855 to 1857 for the good of his health.

Sydney carries the palm

Rising from different parts of Port Jackson are verdant islets, singularly beautiful, and which look like bits of faërie-land—fragments of a dream—slumbrous homes for the companions of Ulysses or Mr Tennyson's later 'Lotus-Eaters.' They are edged with pendulous bushes and tropical water-plants,—which cool their brazen leaves and thirsty tendrils in the tide,—and smothered all over with a sward of matted bush-flowers, veined with the basanite stalk of the trailing melon.

Similar to these were my notes of the harbour on arriving at Sydney. Flocks of sailing-boats were hovering about the ship, and jumping into one of them, I soon found myself on the great public quay of the city. There must have been from twenty to thirty first-class vessels lying along the wharf, and scores of carts and drays were hurrying to and fro with cargo. A couple of cars, drawn by ten or twelve drowsy-looking bullocks, were going, at drowsy-bullock pace, along the wharf, each piled high with wool, and with a swarthy, heavy-bearded driver tramping at the side, whip in hand, and curt black pipe in mouth ...

What first took my attention in Sydney, after I had sufficiently recovered from the bites of the mosquitoes to show myself in public, was the air of well-to-do-ness which characterised every thing about me. The carriages passing through the streets were quiet and elegant; the people were well and soberly dressed; the cabs on the ranks looked more like private carriages than public conveyances; even the cabmen swore and swaggered less, and chinked their money more—having, I suppose, more money to chink—than I ever noticed the fraternity chink, swagger, and swear elsewhere. It was London in good spirits,—as if every man had turned up a nugget or two in his back garden. This was when I arrived: when I left, the roseate light had somewhat mel-lowed. The shops struck me with surprise. George Street, the principal thor-oughfare, is three or four miles in length. Every house is a place of business, and the majority of the marts and warehouses would bear comparison with the run of those in our leading arteries of trade ... One part of George-street is as much like Bond-street as it is possible one place can resemble another ... The Café Français, in this street, is much frequented by the young swells and sprigs of the city. They hold here a chess club, a billiard club, and a stewed-kidney club. Little marble tables, files of 'Punch' and the 'Times,' dominoes, sherry-cobblers, strawberry ices, an entertaining hostess, and a big, bloused, lubberly, inoffensive host, are the noticeable points of the café left on my recollection. They serve eight hundred dinners a day at this house, for which they pay a yearly rent of 2400*l*. Even M. Mivart—if there be such a person—might shrug his shoulders at that …

And at this point it may be as well to state, with becoming brevity, my comparative impressions of the two great metropolises of the Australias. Sydney is about seven times the age of Melbourne—which was a mud village but the other day—and is, it would almost seem as a consequence of this seniority, about seven times more comfortable to live in. In support of this, I may mention that Sydney has, by this time, a well-arranged and all but complete system of sewerage; while the Victorian capital, whose geographical position requires it far more, is woefully deficient in this particular. The climate of Sydney, too, cooled by those perennial sea breezes, is more genial than that of Melbourne; the inhabitants are more staid and steady than the bustling, gold-digging, go-a-head Victorians. Sydney, again, lies with her breast against the sea; at Melbourne, three miles of hot shifting sand, through which it is almost impossible to walk, glares, like a burning lake, between the harbour and the city. So far, then, Sydney carries the palm …

I was much delighted during the early part of my residence in Sydney with the colonial young-stock. The Australian boy is a slim, dark-eyed, olive-complexioned young rascal, fond of Cavendish, cricket, and chuckpenny, and systematically insolent to all servant girls, policemen, and new-chums. His hair is shiny with grease, as are the knees of his breeches and the elbows of his jacket. He wears a cabbage-tree hat, with a dissipated wisp of black ribbon dangling behind, and loves to walk meditatively with his hands in his pockets, and, if cigarless, to chew a bit of straw in the extreme corner of his mouth. His face is soft, bloomless, and pasty, and you fancy if you touched his cheek you would leave the stamp of your finger behind. He baptises female emigrants after the names of the ships in which they arrived, such as Susan Red Rover and Matilda Agamemnon. On the same principle he calls policemen 'Israelites,' because the majority of them came out with the 'Exodus.' He is christened, in turn, a gumsucker and a cornstalk. He can fight like an Irishman or a Bashi-Bazouk; otherwise he is orientally indolent, and will swear with a quiet gusto if you push against him in the street, or request him politely to move on. Lazy as he is though, he is out in the world at ten years of age, earning good wages, and is a perfect little man, learned in all the ways and by-ways of life at twelve or thirteen. Dickens and Albert Smith have given high celebrity to the genuine cockney youth, though for shrewdness, effrontery, and mannish affectation, your London gamin pales into utter respectability before the young Australian …

... Durand's-alley, and the greater portion of the district called the 'Rocks,' in Sydney, are, in roguery and raffery, as vile as Whitechapel. Scenes of riot and debauchery—sin in its bizarre and most lurid aspects—are daily and nightly enacted in these localities. Here, in these Alsatias, the last attenuated remnant of convictism may be traced—the most hideous developments of old and new world ruffianism are presented. This is worth recording; because as all such places in Australia owe their origin and, in fact, their population, to convictism, it is not out of place to inform our governing classes at home of the harm they inflict upon a country by making it, even in its infancy, a depôt for the scum and scoundrelism of the old world. Durand's-alley may be sketched as a fair sample of the 'old-hand haunts' of the colony. And yet, at the outset, the word alley scarcely conveys an idea of the place. It is, at least, a Seventeen Dials of alleys, one running into another, and most of the houses in which are single rooms with earthen floorings, and utterly destitute of windows, chimneys, and doors. Serpent-like gutters, choked with filth, trail before the tottering tenements, and a decayed water-butt, filled with greasy-looking rain-catchings—across which indecent slime-bred flies dart and dazzle in the sun—stands and rots at the end of each court. Brazen women, hulking bullies, and grimy children, loll about the doorways, and employ their time, the first in smashing mosquitoes upon each other's bare and brawny shoulders, after the style of the Italian women described by Mr Dickens, the second in setting dogs to fight; and the third in floating bits of stick in the water-butts and gutters.

The fights and disturbances in this place at night are something terrific. Policemen never venture there alone; and any unfortunate stranger who might happen to stray into the district, would, to a certainty, be hocussed and robbed, and—speaking from more than one past instance—brutally murdered. The awful old women who turn out of the alleys at night to beg and rob, are sublime in their repulsiveness. You can read a history of the blackest crime, commenced in the old world and culminated in the new, in the bleared face of every one of them. 'How came you out here?' I asked of one who solicited alms of me as, in company of half-a-dozen friends, I passed through the place on a tour of inspection. 'I was picked up by a scamp when I was a girl: he deserted me: I made away with his child: I was sent out here for life thirty years ago. *And now what are you going to give me?*' The English reader shudders at a tale like this—with that grim element of stolidity thrown into it by the last words—but I could chronicle far more horrible narratives, picked up in Sydney, did not the heart turn sick at them, and decency demand the curtain to be dropped upon even that single recital as speedily as possible ...

Having mentioned, in passing, a hot wind, let me endeavour to convey some notion of what a hot wind really is. It is early morning, and as you look from your window, in the suburbs of Sydney, you see a thin white vapour rising from the far-off bush. The sheep out there in the distance are congregated beneath the trees, while the old cows are standing knee-deep in those clayey creeks of water that trickle from the heaped-up rocks above. You have seen all this before, and know too well what it means. Before breakfast time, there will 'be' a hot wind.

It comes. The white earth cracks as it passes over it, as though it were a globe of crystal struck by some invisible and mighty hand. The air is hot and murky, as the breath from an oven; and you *see* trees wither—the fruit shrivel and drop from the vines—as though the Last Seal were opened, and the breath of the Destroying Angel had gone forth. The cicadas seem to shriek (their shrill note is always shrillest in hot weather), and the birds drop dead from the trees. The dogs in the street lie down and hide their dry protruding tongues in the dust. Higher and higher rises the mercury in the glass, until now, at noon, it stands at 147°! You stop up every keyhole and crevice in your room to keep out the burning Sirocco, and endeavour, perhaps, to read. In a minute stars dance before your eyes, and your temples throb like pulses of hot iron. You allow the book to fall from your hands, and strive to drop to sleep. It is not much relief if you succeed, for you are safe to dream of the *Inferno* or Beckford's Hall of Eblis. There is only one thing you can do that gives relief. Light your pipe, mix your sherry-cobbler, and smoke and drink until the change arrives.

The 'Southerly Buster,' as this change is called, generally comes

'——sounding on,
Like the storm-wind from Labrador,
The wind Euroclydon,'

early in the evening. A cloud of dust—they call it, in Sydney, a 'brick-fielder'—thicker than any London fog, heralds its approach, and moves like a compact wall across the country. In a minute the temperature will sink fifty or sixty degrees, and so keenly does the sudden change affect the system, that hot toddy takes the place of the sherry-cobbler, and your great-coat is buttoned tightly around you until a fire can be lighted. Now, if you look from your window in the direction where you saw that white vapour ascending in the morning, a spectacle terrible in its magnificence will meet your eye. For miles around—as far as the gaze can reach—bush fires are blazing. You see the trail of the flame extending into the interior until it grows faint and thin along the hilltops, as though a wounded deer had moved, bleeding, upon the road. Nearer, however, the sight is grand and awful, and hints of the Final Apocalypse when the stars shall fall like those charred branches that drop with a thundrous crash and scatter a cloud of glowing embers around them.

No matter where you live in Sydney, looking from your window across the harbour into the surrounding bush, you can always see sights like this after a hot wind. The reflection upon the water itself is very fine. The emerald changes into ruby—the water into wine. The white sails of boats become of 'purple' and 'their prows of beaten gold.' Every thing seems bathed in an atmosphere of romance, and, if the impression were not lowered by the idea, the sheets of flame in the distance might be taken for the crimson walls of Aladdin's palace gleaming through the woods.

Sometimes these hot winds last for two or three days, and then the effects are something lamentable. Scarcely a blade of vegetation is left in the ground—the sere leaves fall from the trees as in a blast of autumn. The same week that I landed in Sydney, a hot wind lasted for four days, on the last of which no less than thirty persons dropped dead in the streets. I remember I had a little garden to my house, and the white-starred jessamine was in full flower in front of the lower windows. Before the wind was over nothing remained but a bunch of dry sticks, kept to the wall by the pieces of cloth with which they were fastened.

Frank Fowler, *Southern Lights and Shadows*,
Sampson Low, London, 1859.

Caroline Chisholm

Caroline Chisholm (1808–77) was a philanthropist who in 1841 established an immigrants' hostel for unemployed young women. After returning to England she campaigned actively for more immigration from England. In *Bleak House* Charles Dickens, who supported her causes, also wrote a parody of her as an obsessive campaigner.

Scenes of immorality beyond comprehension

She must call their attention to the Domain. It had a great deal to do with homes. Many parents might not be aware that there was not a more dangerous and frightful place of an evening, than the Domain. Captain McLerie said of the Domain, in the evening, 'the scenes of immorality were beyond comprehension'. She could not read to them what was said about it, but it was their duty to make themselves acquainted with it. Let them not be earwigged. Every man, some time in his life, had an earwig in his shoulder. Now, the Domain was theirs and their children's, and they ought to see to it that it was properly kept for them. It was quite necessary for mothers to know where danger lay, in order to preserve their children. Let them on no account let their children go into the Domain after seven o'clock at night.

While on the subject of Home, she referred to the report on the state of the working classes, drawn up by Mr Parkes. The lecturer then read a passage from the report and continued. Why was the land surrounding the diggings to be left unpopulated? ('Hear, hear,' by Mr Hoskins.) Great evil resulted from the families of the gold miners being left in Sydney. The houses in Sydney appropriated to the working classes were not fit to be called houses. The houses were utterly unfit for homes. In one case seventy human beings were herded together in a house of six rooms. Other instances of a similar kind were cited. The wages men received were such that a man must let part of his house in order to pay the butcher and baker. The opinion of Mr Aaron, surgeon, on the injurious effects of defective house accommodation on the morals of the community was then cited. Looking at it in a commercial view, no effort was made to induce those who make money here, to stay here, they leave the country, not because they do not like it, but because they have no homes. Hundreds of fine men had here been sent to the grave because they had no homes.

What was a home? was it a fine mansion, with a splendid library, and without a wife and children? What she would call a home was not that, neither was that house in Bent-street [the Union Club], where fine dinners and breakfasts might be had, and which was frequented by a number of bachelor squatters, and even married ones—leaving their wives out of the question. If there was one thing more injurious to the happiness of home than another it was a club. She did not consider these homes; a home in her idea was a cottage, with a piece of ground, a few books in this cottage, and children traversing its neat rooms; their light laughter ringing like music on the delighted ears of the parents.

> From *Radical in Bonnet and Shawl: Four Political Lectures by*
> *Caroline Chisholm* (ed. John Moran), Preferential Publications,
> Ashgrove, Qld, 1994.

Isaac Nathan

This is another piece that Graham Pont attributes to Nathan. Already Sydney was being influenced by the development in England of the seaside resort.

This favourite place of resort

As usual, upon all occasions of public holidays, this favourite place of resort numbered its visitors by the thousands. So early as ten o'clock pleasure parties were afoot wending their way in this direction, taking their passages by one of the many boats which the enterprising proprietors of the Manly beach jetty had provided for the occasion. A very excellent agreement seemed to have been made, though quite accidentally, by which the steamers going to Manly started from one portion of Circular Quay, whilst those for Watson's Bay started from another. As this plan appeared to break the crowds which otherwise would have assembled round the point for embarkation, we recommend its adoption to our police authorities in future, as it gives the constables a much better chance of checking the overcrowding of vessels than they could possibly have if four or five vessels [were] lying together. However, owing as we have said to the excellent provision made of the Jetty, so many boats were provided that no inconvenience whatever arose; on the contrary, some trips[,] were performed by some of the boats with a sufficiency of passengers to pay expenses; but the convenience to the public, from the regularity of the trips was not so great that this plan, though it may not have been profitable, is likely to lead to a very large accession of visitors on future holidays.

At the Pier Hotel, the usual holiday sports were in vogue, in the addition to the now established attraction of the maze. An excellent table d'hôte was also held here from one to three o'clock, but owing to some breach of agreement on the part of the band engaged for the occasion, there was no dancing in the long room of the hotel.

The Steyne Hotel thronged with visitors during the day, the private parlours being occupied, with permission, three deep. Here also a first rate table d'hôte was provided, and we may mention here that so good is the provision that is made, so reasonable is the price, so well are these matters appreciated, that now there are much fewer provision baskets brought by visitors to this locality than there formerly were. The proprietor of this hotel had also added the actual attraction which his situation offered by the erection of a commodious tent in which the votaries of la danse might amuse themselves at their will. This, as was the hotel, was crowded through-out the day.

The Fairy Nook had also its share of visitors, many of those preferred the quiet cup of tea to the fast glass of spirits, selecting this post to 'sit down'. At the same time, Birch's arena of manly sports, and the several other booths, tents, and edifices which competed for public favour, were all more or less patronised during the day. In all spots in which music, even of the rudest kind, could be found, there dancing most certainly formed the most favourite amusement.

Isaac Nathan [?], 'Manly Beach', *Empire*, c. 1860.

Charles Dilke

Sir Charles Dilke (1843–1911) visited Sydney in 1867 prior to a career in politics. The next year he joined the House of Commons, but his political career was blighted in 1885 when it was claimed, in a divorce case, that he had slept with both mother and daughter.

No trace of convict blood

... as we steamed up Port Jackson, towards Sydney Cove, in the dead stillness that follows a night of oven-like heat, the sun rose flaming in a lurid sky, and struck down upon brown earth, yellow grass, and the thin shadeless foliage of the Australian bush; while, as we anchored, the ceaseless chirping of the crickets in the grass and trees struck harshly on the ear.

The harbour, commercially the finest in the world, is not without a singular beauty if seen at the best time. By the 'hot-wind sunrise', as I first saw it, the heat and glare destroy the feeling of repose which the endless successions of deep, sheltered coves would otherwise convey; but if it be seen from the shore in the afternoon, when the sea breeze has sprung up, turning the sky from red to blue, all is changed. From a neck of land that leads out to the Government House, you catch a glimpse of an arm on the bay on either side, rippled with the cool wind, intensely blue and dotted with white sails: the brightness of the colours that the sea breeze brings almost atones for the wind's unhealthiness.

In the upper portion of the town, the scene is less picturesque; the houses are of the commonplace English ugliness, worst of all possible forms of architectural imbecility; and are built, too, as though for English fogs, instead of semi-tropical heat and sun. Water is not to be had, and the streets are given up to clouds of dust, while not a single shade-tree breaks the rays of the almost vertical sun.

The afternoon of New Year's day I spent at the 'Midsummer Meeting' of the Sydney Jockey Club, on the racecourse near the city, where I found a vast crowd of holiday-makers assembled on the bare red earth that did duty for 'turf', although there was a hot wind blowing, and the thermometer stood at 103°F in the shade. For my conveyance to the racecourse I trusted to one of the Australian Hansom cabs, made with fixed Venetian blinds on either side, so as to allow a free draught of air.

The ladies in the grandstand were scarcely to be distinguished from Englishwomen in dress or countenance, but the crowd presented several curious types. The fitness of the term 'cornstalks' applied to the Australian-born boys was made evident by a glance at their height and slender build; they have plenty of activity and health but are wanting in power and weight. The girls, too, are slight and thin; delicate without being sickly. Grown men who have emigrated as lads and lived ten or fifteen years in New Zealand, eating much meat, spending their days in the open air, constantly in the saddle, are burly, bearded, strapping fellows, physically the perfection of the English race, but wanting in refinement and grace of mind, and this apparently by constitution; not through the accident of occupation or position. In Australia there is promise of a more intellectual nation: the young Australians ride as well, shoot as well, swim as well, as the New Zealanders; are as little given to book-learning: but there is more shrewd intelligence, more wit and quickness, in the sons of the larger continent. The Australians boast that they possess the Grecian climate, and every young face in the Sydney crowd showed me that their sky is not more like that of Attica than they are like the old Athenians. The eager burning democracy that is springing up in the Australian great towns is as widely different from the republicanism of the older States of the American Union as it is from the good-natured conservatism of New Zealand, and their high capacity for personal enjoyment would of itself suffice to distinguish the Australians from both Americans and British. Large as must be the amount of convict blood in New South

Wales, there was no trace of it in the features of those present upon the racecourse. The inhabitants of colonies which have never received felon immigrants often cry out that Sydney is a convict city, but the prejudice is not borne out by the countenances of the inhabitants, nor by the records of local crime. The black stain has not yet wholly disappeared: the streets of Sydney are still a greater disgrace to civilization than are even those of London; but, putting the lighter immoralities aside, security for life and property is not more perfect in England than in New South Wales. The last of the bushrangers were taken while I was in Sydney.

Charles Dilke, *Greater Britain: A Record of Travel in English Speaking Countries During 1866 and 1867*, Macmillan, London, 1868.

Sydney Mail

Although both the attempt to assassinate Prince Alfred and the lynch mob failed, the affair touched off bitter controversy in Sydney. The would-be assassin was an Irishman, so Sir Henry Parkes, a member of the government, claimed that the Irishman had acted as part of a wider conspiracy of the Fenians, an Irish nationalist group who espoused violence. There was no evidence to support this claim, but the city was divided in a bitter sectarian struggle.

A most determined attempt

It is with the deepest sorrow that we have to announce a most determined attempt to assassinate his Royal Highness the Duke of Edinburgh. When the Prince left the luncheon tent at the Sailors' Home Picnic ... he escorted the Countess of Belmore to the door of the Royal tent, and then turned to converse with his Excellency the Governor, the Chief Justice, and Sir William Manning. They remained talking a few seconds, and then his Royal Highness and Sir William Manning sauntered across the grass towards the clump of trees bordering the beach, and under which the Galatea band was stationed. The subject of conversation was the Sailors' Home, and his Royal Highness, to mark his appreciation of the institution, handed Sir William a cheque as a donation to the institution. Sir William made his acknowledgments for the donation, and then asked his Royal Highness whether he would go round to Cabbage Tree Beach to see the aborigines ... Before his Royal Highness could reply a treacherous assailant, who had just left the crowd of persons congregated under the shade of the trees, stole up behind him and when he had approached within five or six feet pulled out a revolver, took deliberate aim, and fired. The shot took effect about the middle of the back of his Royal Highness, an inch or two to the right of the spine. He fell forward on his hands and knees, exclaiming 'Good God, my back is broken.' Sir William Manning, hearing the discharge, and seeing his

Royal Highness fall, turned and sprang at the would-be assassin, who then jumped back and aimed the murderous weapon at Sir William. Seeing the pistol directed towards him, Sir William stooped to evade the shot, and, losing his balance, fell. Fortunately the charge did not explode, but as Sir William Manning was in the act of rising, the ruffian took aim a third time; just at the moment Mr Vial (of Castlereagh Street), who also happened to be behind, sprang upon the dastardly assassin, pinioned his arms to his side, and thus the aim of the pistol was diverted from the body of Sir William Manning to the ground. The weapon was discharged, however, and the shot entered the foot of Mr George Thorne, senior, who fainted, and was taken away by Mr Hassall, and other friends.

In the meantime a number of people, attracted by the discharge of firearms, and seeing his Royal Highness fall, ran to the spot, and three or four of them, among whom was Mr T. Hales and a young gentleman named McMahon, lifted his Royal Highness to carry him into the tent. It was evident from the demeanour of his Royal Highness that he was suffering great pain, and he asked his bearers to carry him gently. This was complied with as far as possible, and he was borne into his tent. Here he was taken in charge by Dr Watson, of HMS Challenger, who together with Dr Wright (of Sydney), Dr Powell of the Galatea, and assistant-surgeon Waugh of the Challenger, were immediately in attendance. The dress of his Royal Highness was removed and upon an examination of the wound it was found that the bullet had penetrated the back, near the middle, and about two inches from the right side of the lower part of the spine, traversing the course of the ribs, round by the right to the abdomen, where it lodged immediately below the surface. No vital organ fortunately appeared to be injured, the course of the bullet being, to all appearance, quite superficial.

While this painful examination was in progress another scene, which almost defies description, was going on in another part of the ground. No sooner had Mr Vial grasped the arms of the man who had fired the shots, than Mr Benjamin Mortimer (an American gentleman), Mr Whiting (of the firm of Drynan and Whiting), A.L. Jackson, and other gentlemen seized him; and, had it not been for the closing in around them of the police and other persons, they would speedily have placed him beyond the reach of the Law Courts. The people shouted 'lynch him,' 'hang him,' 'string him up,' and so on, and there was a general rush to get at him. The police, headed by Superintendent Orridge, got hold of the assassin, and they had the greatest difficulty in preventing the infuriated people from tearing him limb from limb. In this the police were ably assisted by the chief Justice, Lord Newry, and the men of the Galatea Band. Both Lord Newry and Sir Alfred Stephen exerted themselves to get the prisoner on board the steamer lying at the wharf, while Mr Orridge, with herculean strength, kept back the crowd as much as possible. The task of putting the prisoner on board the ship was not an easy one, and it was fully ten minutes before they could get him on to the wharf. By that time all the clothing from the upper part of his body was torn off, his eyes, face and body were much bruised, and blood was flowing from various wounds; and when he was dragged on to the deck of the Paterson, he appeared to be utterly unconscious. No sooner was he on board than a number of sailors had a rope ready to string him up, and it was only by the interference of Lord Newry that his life was spared. Some of the police were very roughly used, detective Powell getting about the worst of it. In the scuffle he fell over some stones, and had a chance of being trampled to death. The whole of the police on the ground were under the control of Mr Fosbery.

The people, out of whose hands the prisoner had been rescued, immediately gave vent to their disappointment, and, at an indignation meeting summarily convened, determined to bring him back from the steamer, and dispatch him at the scene of his crime. A rush was then made for the steamer, which had just hauled off a few feet from the wharf, and they shouted to the captain to haul in. For a moment this officer appeared to waver, but the Hon. John Hay, who was on the bridge, doubtless divining the intentions of the crowd, peremptorily ordered the captain to haul off. This he did, and the vessel accordingly proceeded on her way to Sydney.

The effect of this dastardly attempt at assassinating the Prince, among the immense number of people persons congregated at Clontarf, may be more easily imagined than described. A large number of ladies fainted, others were seized with hysterics, and the whole multitude was convulsed.

Sydney Mail, 14 March 1868.

Anthony Trollope

Anthony Trollope (1815–82), author and postal administrator, visited Sydney in 1871.

The very best cabs in the world

One Mrs Macquarie, the wife, I believe, of Governor Macquarie, made a road, or planned a road, or at any rate gave her name to a road, which abuts on the public domain, and is all but in the town. A mile and half from the top of Hunter Street carries the pedestrian all around it. Two shillings does as much for him or her who prefers a hansom cab,—and the Sydney hansoms are the very best cabs in the world. At the end of it is Mrs Macquarie's chair,—with a most ill-written inscription,—but with a view that affords compensation even for that. The public gardens, not half a mile from the top of Hunter Street, beat all the public gardens I ever saw,—because they possess one little nook of sea of their own. I do not love public gardens generally, because I am called upon to listen to the names of the shrubs conveyed in three Latin words, and am supposed to interest myself in the locality from which they have been brought. I envy those who have the knowledge which I want; but I put my back up against attempts made to convey it to me, knowing it is too late. But it was impossible not to love the public gardens of Sydney,—because one could sit under the trees and look out upon the sea. There is a walk from the bottom of Macquarie Street,—not Mrs Macquarie's Road, but the old governor's own street,—leading round by the fort, under the governor's house, to the public gardens. The whole distance round may be a mile and half from the top of Hunter Street, which opens on to Macquarie Street. It runs close along the sea, with grassy slopes on which you may lie and see the moon glimmer on the water as it only glimmers on landlocked coves of the ocean. You may lie there prostrate on the grass, with the ripple close at your feet within a quarter-of-an-hour of your club. Your after-dinner cigar will last you there and back if you will walk fairly and smoke slowly. Nobody ever is there at that hour, the young men of Sydney preferring to smoke their cigars in their own arm-chairs. Then there is the little trip by steam ferry over to the north shore, where lives that prince of professors and greatest of Grecians, Doctor Badham, of the university. I should like to be the ferry-man over that ferry to Lavender Bay on condition that the Doctor met with some refreshment on each iourney. Sydney is one of those places which, when a man leaves it knowing that he will never return, he cannot leave without a pang and a tear. Such is its loveliness.

The town itself, as a town, independently of its sea and its suburbs, was, to me, pleasant and interesting. In the first place, though it is the capital of an Australian colony, and therefore not a hundred years old, it has none of those worst signs of novelty which make the cities of the New World unpicturesque and distasteful. It is not parallelogrammatic and rectangular. One may walk about it and lose the direction in which one is going. Streets running side by side occasionally converge—and they bend and go in and out, and wind themselves about and are intricate.

Anthony Trollope, *Australia and New Zealand*, Vol. 1, Dawson's of Pall Mall, 1873.

The Empire

Boxing was to Sydney's colonial society a continuation of sectarian strife by other means.

Orange v. Green

PRIZE FIGHT.—A prize fight took place at George's River yesterday between two natives of the colony, one named Ross (a cabman) and the other Foley. The combatants and their friends and backers started as early as half-past 3 a.m. for the scene of the encounter; and although the police got scent of the occurrence during the morning, it is said that the affair was decided before their arrival. The fight is represented as having been a desperate encounter, lasting over two hours and a half, and resulting in a drawn battle, although victory was claimed in favour of Foley, who represented the green, while his opponent wore the orange colours. The brutal affair seems to have excited a good deal of interest in certain quarters, as the combatants, although natives, were regarded as representing the two antagonistic sections into which Irish nationality is unfortunately divided. It is much to be regretted that some of those in a higher station who have done, and are still doing, their worst to stir up and intensify the diabolical feeling of party strife in this community, could not be got to hammer each other a little, in proof of the goodness of their cause, as these stupid young men Ross and Foley have done. Both of the pugilists are said to be severely injured, Ross having his wrist sprained or dislocated, and his adversary suffering from severe bruises about the breast and sides.

Empire, 29 March 1871.

Havelock Ellis

Havelock Ellis (1859–1939) stayed in Australia from 1875 to 1879. Influenced by his mother, the priggish young Englishman was a connoisseur of preaching, but in later life he abandoned Christianity and became a pioneer sexual psychologist while remaining a prig.

No good preaching

... Australia has not produced a single poet of the least genius; nor a painter, nor a musician, true there are some men of science but Australia can hardly be said to have produced them. Indeed from what I can see there appears very little intellectual ability of surpassing note in any department. There is most decidedly no orator; the Legislative Assembly is a body of businessmen, merchants, shop-keepers and the like, met together to transact business, and they do it as a board of Guardians would at home ... Neither is there any good preaching. The other day I went to hear a Congregational Minister said to be the best preacher in Sydney. I expected to hear a discourse something after Baldwin Brown's style, but what I did hear was in many respects good; it was eloquent; it was worth listening to, perhaps; it might even be said that it was a cultivated discussion; but there were no marks of powerful thought about it; or of intellectual independence; it was, in fact, hardly what might be expected from the best preacher in the metropolis of New South Wales. The other day I walked through the Museum, a very fair building; but of course very small to our notions of a Museum, derived from the British or South Kensington; but it has a fine collection of the natural history of the country; several curiosities ...

Havelock Ellis, *Diaries*, 1875, Mitchell Library.

The Innocents

The Innocents in Sydney emerged in the second half of 1878 and lasted until early the following year. It was an example of a Victorian genre, occurring in London, which purported to expose immorality but was semi-pornographic. The paper listed more than a dozen sales points in Sydney and country towns. Fifty years later in between-wars Sydney, the publisher would have ended up in jail, but Victorian Sydney shrugged its shoulders.

Unseemly pleasure

Where are the nurseries for all these prostitutes that disgracefully fill our streets, and shamelessly often, and pitifully always, flaunt their abandoned shapes in the glare of the Café? Where, fathers and mothers, have your daughters first learnt to treat slightingly your advice, to stay out late, and to cause you painful apprehension for the safety of their characters? Where, brothers, have you seen your sisters when the first danger of their rectitude struck you with keen despair for them? Where, mistresses, have your servants been most demoralised, and where have they caught the first taste for unseemly pleasure, late hours, dissipation and debauchery, and ultimate lasciviousness which has led them on to ruin? Where but in the dancing-rooms, the 'shilling hops' and half-crown hells, but into which, however, your daughters, your simple-minded sisters, and your domestic servants are enticed by being admitted gratis!

How many a father has been made wretched by suddenly discovering his daughter a frequenter of these enticing nurseries, which are so numerous in this city, who shall tell? How many a mother, seeing her child tainted by the associations and indecent dancing, has lived to regret that she ever gave her daughter birth, after she had brought such dishonour upon her family? Parents, do you want to train your daughters up for *wives*, or prostitutes? Mistresses, do you want servants about you, mingling hourly with your innocent children, who are pure and seemly in their conduct and life, or would you have them sullied by the immoral influences of these dancing hotbeds of danger to the young and susceptible?

Workgirls, many of them of very respectable parents, gather about these places in greatest numbers. They are out necessarily more than servants or girls who assist in domestic duties at home, and they usually claim more license than these, especially as their work sometimes keeps them employed till a late hour. It is easier for them to elude the vigilance of their friends; and the attractions of the dancing-floor, after the sedentary occupation of the day, is made by the cunning proprietors so attractive to them by that 'ladies free', that hundreds fall into the cunningly contrived meshes of the net without questioning the snare. Go to any one of these places whenever you may, and you will find groups of girls descending gradually from that purity of thought which is the brightest gem that can honour girlhood, and drifting away from such unsullied aspirations as fill the minds of those who are content to look forward to wifely honours as their best aspiration in life—drifting away towards the quicksands of passion and desire. The suggestive waltz, too, is the dance most in fashion.

... And let us as we pass the Museum to Bourke-street, wonder at the flitting shapes which hover about our path and peer into our sympathetic eyes with looks full of wicked meaning. These are technically termed 'square corner' girls. William-street has its restless nymphs, too, and at Our Boys' Hotel (which I shall describe in a future number) they air their fancies and show their striped stockings in a most ladylike manner, and keep their stomachs moist with threepenny ginger-wines or kerosene [sic]. Coming to Bourke-street, we turn to the left toward Woolloomooloo-street, and on the right-hand side, at the corner of a lane, we may linger in the shadows of half-a-dozen waving trees in a front garden, which impart quite a tropical beauty to the cottage which nestles away back. And nestling within the walls of that cosy retreat are a merry troupe of girls. Not quite so young as Topsy, yet each might well exclaim with that interesting young lady, 'Oh, golly, I'se so wicked!' There are two rooms in front, and a passage opens from the side which, crossing the house, separates the front from the back rooms, and keeps the girls and their friends from bumping up against each others' partition. This is Belvidere Cottage, and Lizzie Watson (who is as well known to the *habitués* of King-street as Baalam's ass was to the multitude after he had spoken) is the Lady Principal. Although inhabited by nearly a dozen ladies, it is more of an academy for young gentlemen. And however bashful and stiff in their manner some young gentlemen may be on first entering the fatal door, they are never so stiff when they leave.

But to stay all this preliminary, just give the office that 'the Innocent' is within. Ring in the fairies to the best parlour; touch their handkerchiefs with *eau de cologne* lest they smell of cigar ends and stale wine; make a few grimaces at them to bring the dimples back to their love-tired cheeks, and let's plunge down upon the sofa among their rumpled petticoats, streaming hair, and flowing words of love. Never mind your foot upon my knee, dear—so. Your head looks lovely enough against my shirt front, I know—but what abominable train oil have you been mopping up with your hair, miss. Come, fie, Miss Cherry lips, you're not at a prize baptism, to be disclosing your shape beneath one flimsy garment in that way—how dare you, you vulgar girl. Yes, the drinks—a toast—'Here's to the girl,' breaks in Miss Blank, 'who makes more by her "love" than her needle;' then all the girls began wrapping their skirts about them, and chaffed each other about wrapping up the 'whole of their body.' The stout Lizzie Watson, whose weight is currently said to have been the immediate cause of death to a dozen cab-horses, when riding to and fro with the squatters she has captured, tries to keep the girls in as much order as the rapidity of the shouts will allow, but her own exhiliration [*sic*] over her immense profits raises the spirits of the girls, and with their spirits unavoidably their petticoats, so that I thought they were about to perform the Japanese dance of forfeits, which has the effect at last of reducing every girl's covering to their luxuriant heads of black hair …

> *The Innocents in Sydney*. 'Written by The Innocent/The Prodigal/The Town Crier.' Sydney, 1878.

Australian Engineering and Building News

Plus ça change. This report testifies to the perennial nature of plans to end harbour pollution. It also answers the often-asked question of how Sydney acquired a sewage outlet next to Bondi Beach.

Relieving the harbour from pollution

Sir Henry Parkes, like Lord Beaconsfield, is alive to the importance of sanitary measures, and has passed a vote through the Legislative Assembly providing the money required for the efficient drainage of the city of Sydney.

The necessity for this work, for relieving the harbour from pollution, needs no explanation to a Sydney resident; yet, no doubt, many will be surprised to learn that the slops, cooking water, &c., from over eight thousand houses, and the excrementious matter from seven thousand water-closets, are conveyed into the harbour at different points; and they will agree with Mr Clark, 'that the state of the harbour at the outlets of the various sewers admits of no second opinion as to the necessity for some immediate remedy for a daily growing evil,' and to which the returns of the Register General bear evidence as to the death-rate, but not as regards the illness and suffering arising from the causes which produce those deaths. 'In England it is usually estimated that for every death there are twenty-eight cases of preventable sickness,' entailing a pecuniary loss on those who have to work for their living, 'which, when estimated in money, is an amount calculated to startle the strongest.'

In planning the drainage, Mr Moriaty and Mr Bennett, whose scheme Mr Clark practically adopted, by no means started with their hands unfettered, there being about thirty-three and a half miles of brick, stone, and pipe sewers already executed, which have been laid without any reference to the ultimate discharge of the sewage at a given point; yet it was absolutely necessary that the existing sewers should be utilised in any new arrangement, to set aside so large an amount of work, executed at so much cost, being out of the question.

From the report of Mr Clark we find the drainage of the northern area is confined to the interception and disposal of the sewerage which at present falls into the harbour, and into Shea's Creek. It is proposed to construct a sewer, the upper end of which is in the Parramatta Road, near the University reserve, at a level of thirty-two feet five inches above high water line; from thence it runs to a point near the Benevolent Asylum, on to Belmore Gardens, along Forbes Street and Wemys Street to the junction of College and Liverpool Streets; though Liverpoool Street to West Street, and to Lacrozia Valley, crossing the Glenmore Road, Cascade Street, and Point Piper Road. The tunnel is then continued through the hill to the low land at a point on the Edgecliff Road, near Trelawney Street; thence it proceeds in a straight line under the ridge occupied by the Belle View Road, and crossing the low sandy area at the head of Rose Bay, enters the rocky hill which forms the coast line, and eventually falls into the ocean at Ben Buckler, three and a half miles from the mouth of the harbour, a distance sufficient to prevent the possibility of any nuisance arising thereto. At the outlet of the intercepting sewer at Ben Buckler, it has been requisite to devise a plan to over-come the difficulty of the sea, breaking into the tunnel, and in this matter the experience of Mr Moriaty has been of great value. Waves of enormous size and power break upon the face of the rock where the outlet must be made. To overcome the difficulty of entering seas into a horizontal tunnel, it is proposed to form an expanding basin, thirty feet or more in diameter—with a self-acting valve at the mouth of the sewer—at a distance of two hundred feet from the face of the rock, communicating with a gallery one hundred and sixty feet long by fifteen feet wide, at right angles to the direction of the sewer. From this gallery four tunnels convey the sewage into the sea. A further preventative will be obtained by driving blind tunnels into the rock opposite the outlets, by which the entering sea water can be received and it exit facilitated.

'The drainage of Sydney', *Australian Engineering and Building News*, vol. 1, no. 2, 1 August 1879.

Sydney Mail

The word *larrikin* was still unusual enough to be given inverted commas, but soon it was to become a catchcry, especially for the better off, encapsulating everything that was wrong with Sydney.

Ungentlemanly conduct

[The] match was continued today and, we regret to say, was marked by the most disgraceful scene we ever remember to have witnessed on any cricket ground in the metropolis. Such a display of unbridled rowdyism, perpetuated as it was in the presence of His Excellency the Governor, Lady Robinson, and party, and a large number of the prominent citizens of Sydney, and

directed against the English players who are at present our guests, will probably remain as a blot upon the colony for some years to come. The unfortunate occurrence originated in the decision of the English umpire, who, in the
second innings of the New South Wales team decided, on appeal, that Murdoch was run out. The moment the decision was given, the disturbance
commenced, and it is a significant fact the hooting and groaning proceeded
first of all from about a dozen persons in the pavilion, some of whom, at all
events, were known to be pecuniarily interested in the result of the match.
One well-known betting man himself acted as the fugleman, and the crowd
outside, encouraged by this bad example, worked themselves into a state of
violent excitement and presently broke through all bounds of decency and
fair play. All round the enclosure hundreds of people demanded the with-
drawal of Coulthard [the umpire], and before the vacancy created by Murdoch's retirement was filled, a large number of 'larrikins' sitting at the bottom
of the terrace, and within the boundary fence, made a rush for the centre of
the ground and were quickly followed by hundreds of roughs who took
possession of the wickets. The English team soon found themselves in the
middle of a surging, gesticulating, and shouting mob, and one rowdy struck
Lord Harris across the body with a whip or stick. Mr Hornby at once seized
the cowardly ruffian and attempted to bring him into the pavilion. As a general *mêlée* was now imminent a number of gentlemen from the pavilion and
grandstand (including the trustees of the ground and members of the Cricket
Association) hurried to the assistance of the English team, who might otherwise have been seriously maltreated, but as the mob were evidently bent on
rescuing Mr Hornby's prisoner a scene of confusion ensued and blows were
received and returned. The small body of police who were present were too
late to get to the centre of the ground when the rush occurred, and subsequently found it difficult to make their way through the crowd. However, by
dint of determination, and no little physical exertion, the English team were
escorted into the pavilion and Lord Harris's assailant was locked up in one of
the committee rooms, being released afterwards on giving his name and
address. Several of the English team received a few scratches, and Mr
Hornby's clothing was somewhat torn, but beyond this, as far as our reporter
could ascertain, no serious injury was inflicted, and the umpire, about whose
safety some doubts were entertained, came off scratchless, owing mainly to
Mr Hornby's prompt assistance. As there were two or three thousand people
on the cricket area and in front of the pavilion, the bell rang for clearing the
ground, but it was some time before the excitement subsided and an opportunity was afforded to resume the play. Thomson and A. Bannerman and the
English Eleven went out into the field, but as soon as the crowd saw that
Coulthard had not been withdrawn, strong expressions of disapproval were
heard, and the ground was again rushed. Expostulation by Mr Driver and
other gentlemen appeared to have no effect, and another adjournment to the
pavilion took place. Lord Harris and Mr Gregory subsequently discussed the
question of having another umpire, but the majority of the English eleven

decided, naturally enough, to stand by their umpire, and the ground having in the meantime been once more cleared, the players proceeded to the wicket for the second time, but as the more disorderly portion of the spectators were determined not to allow the match to go on with Coulthard, about 300 men and larrikins repeated the performance of taking possession of the ground, and remained there until nearly 6 o'clock, when all hope of resuming play was abandoned. There were about 10,000 spectators present during the afternoon, and it is only fair to say that of this number there were not more than 2000, at the outside, who took an active part in the disorder. A large majority of the public were evidently deeply humiliated by the occurrence (especially after the cordial reception of the Australian team at home), and much indignation was expressed that the scene should have originated by the ungentlemanly conduct of a few persons in the pavilion.

'The English eleven v. the eleven of New South Wales. Second day— Saturday, February 8', *Sydney Mail*, 15 February 1879.

Sydney Mail

This newspaper report describes the first of three Sydney Cups the great racehorse Carbine was to win.

Carbine coming like a locomotive

Betting: 2 to 1 v. Abercorn, 8 to 1 v. Keith and Melos, 9 to 1 v. Carbine, 10 to 1 each v. Plutarch and Papua (late New Guinea), 12 to 1 each v. Honeydew and Lochiel, 20 to 1 each v. Yabba and Recall, 25 to 1 v. Amina.

After a trifling delay, Mr Watson lowered his flag to a splendid start, and the flight of racehorses left the post in a line, the colours of Yabba and Amina showing in the van. Amina was the first to face the hill, when Lady Lyon flashed past her, and the former disappeared from the front for ever. Even thus early it was it was evident that the pace was going to be something to wonder at, and, making every post a winning one, Lady Lyon shot past the scraping sheds six lengths clear from Amina, who had a length advantage of Plutarch and Lochiel, whose immediate attendant was Keith. Settling down to her work with earnestness, the leading light weight showed the way round the bend, ten lengths from Amina, Lochiel, and Recall, who were in a heap, and closely waited on by Pearlshell, who headed a clustered lot, the last of which were Melos and Carbine. No material alteration took place for the next three furlongs, and Lady Lyon, on a mission to help something, showed the way past the stand by about fifteen lengths, Plutarch, with Amina against the rails, and Lochiel on the left, next, a length and a half in front of Pearlshell, Recall and Keith, who had Abercorn on his quarter, with Honeydew and Yabba almost on terms, and succeeded by Papua, Carbine and Melos, who was pulling hard. Before reaching where the rocks used to be Lady Lyon began to falter and when passing Oxenham's house Amina,

Plutarch and Lochiel, still locked together, were within four lengths of her, and after them came Keith and Pearlshell, while the colours of Abercorn could be seen, standing out in relief from the others, and Yabba had joined Papua, Carbine and Melos in the rear. As they opened out in the back stretch the pace became really desperate and Lochiel, Plutarch and Amina closing on the fast-tiring Lady Lyon cut her down in a few strides. The trio faced the ascent for the second time together, but when halfway up the hill the severity of the pace told on Amina, and, amidst a wild burst of excitement, Lochiel carried his yellow jacket to the front, with the beaten Lady Lyon, the fast-tiring Plutarch and Amina within half a length; but all in trouble. The great New Zealander topped the hill, and then shaking them off led everything by a clear length past the sheds. Great as the pace had been it grew stronger here, and as Abercorn was seen to emerge from the ruck a silence fell upon the crowd as it became evident that a terrible battle was about to be fought. Here Honeydew suddenly left the apparently beaten field, and, racing up to Lochiel, the pair swept around the bend fairly extended, with Abercorn next on the outside, and with still a little in hand Lochiel shortened his beautifully even stride as they made the home corner, and after one final and brave effort for the honour of Maoriland reeled in his stride and gave place to Honeydew, who, with Abercorn at his girths, was going as strong as a lion. But, before they were fairly half-way round the bend, Melos and Carbine commenced to battle their way towards the first flight. O'Brien had just began to call on Carbine when one of the beaten field collided with the colt, and he fell back last; but recovering himself only as a lion-hearted racehorse could, he settled down to the bitter and apparently hopeless task of catching the flying column thundering on in front. Honeydew was the first to land in the straight, but being quite unequal to answer the challenge of Abercorn, he suddenly retired from the contest, and as the gallant top-weight dashed to the front it looked as if the son of Chester was going to perform the great task allotted him. But the goal was still more than 200 yards away, and the great racehorse, sobbing under his weight, faltered ever so little, and as he did so Ellis brought the patiently-waiting Melos with a great rush and the pair raced locked level for a dozen strides. Another twenty strides and Carbine on the outside coming like a locomotive drew on terms with Melos and Abercorn, and then like an arrow shot to the front, crossing the other two as he did so. Abercorn was the first of the trio to fail, and the two colts drawing out fought out a never-to-be-forgotten battle in all its bitterness right up to the post, the champion winning in the last stride by a head against a scene of excitement that has seldom been witnessed at Randwick. Abercorn, contesting every inch of ground, was a length and three-quarters away, and beat Keith, who came at the end, by half a length for third place; and then came Papua, Honeydew, Yabba, Lochiel, Pearlshell, Amina, Recall and Plutarch, with Lady Lyon last. Time, 3 minutes 31 seconds.

Sydney Mail, 27 April 1879.

The Express

Holding an international exhibition was to claim a status something like the Olympic Games today. Sydney's exhibition followed on the American centenary exhibition at Philadelphia in 1876.

The garden palace

The Sydney International Exhibition ... was a giant undertaking for a colony whose total population would not fill one fourth of the good city of Paris. It was, further, an undertaking which, for speedy conception, generous national enthusiasm, and swift completion, is perhaps without a parallel in the short annals of International Exhibitions. It must now for ever remain an indisputable historic fact that the first great International Exhibition in the Southern Hemisphere was held where it ought to have been held—in the premier city of the southern seas, the capital of the mother colony of the Australias. There was a magic in the Garden Palace that won all hearts. It became an abode of peace—a place of beauty where all in the city and 'their friends' loved to linger and taste innocent instructive enjoyment. It was a promenade where among the delicous fountains and flagrant flowers and objects of Oriental brilliance, the sons and daughter of our dusty homes might pass to a dreamland of eastern Arcadian splendour. It was a hive of industry where the busiest city men might find abundant profitable employment. To the scientist, to the artist, and to the sight-seer, it was a home, and when the eye grew weary with seeing the multiplied treasures of art and industry, the glorious building itself gave to the lover of genuine picturesque scenery a treat of healthful enjoyment which no other palace in the universe ever did or could. Not in Vienna, not in London, not in Philadelphia, not in Paris, could a view be found comparable to that which might be had in a few minutes from any one of the towers of the Garden Palace. A miniature Eden stretched out beneath, and beyond lay the undulating forest of city houses and public buildings, laved by the weirdly intricate waters of the incomparable harbour, or rather hundred harbours formed by Port Jackson ... The blue mountains bounded the vision in another direction, and in another the deep sea lashed against the cliffs where the mariner from afar is henceforward to be protected by the beneficent rays of our new electric lighthouse—a monument of our scientific generosity during the progress of our world fair. We have reason then on many accounts to be deeply grateful to the men who, despite many obstacles, inaugurated such a work and saved the credit of the colony. The architects who planned the noble structure, the contractor who erected it [and] the men who in season and out of season worked for it, are deserving of all praise ...

'The garden palace', *Express*, 24 April 1880.

Bulletin

The owner of the picnic grounds sued the *Bulletin* and gained one farthing damages, but the journal had to pay £1500 in costs, and when it was late in paying two members of staff, J. Haynes and J.F. Archibald, were briefly imprisoned until the money was raised.

Taking pleasure madly

The larrikins who demonstratively display their evil propensities and outrageous proclivities in full public view do not as a rule belong to the well-to-do classes. They are the idle, the uncared for, the wilful, and the depraved. The peculiar prominence which they attain is clearly attributable to the comparative ease with which they, as compared to the old world, can acquire the means for indulgence and idleness. Under the mild skies of Australia little is needed in the way of home-shelter. Here too, while a shilling goes further towards maintenance than in most parts of the world, it is infinitely more easy to earn or to procure. The youth who chooses to indulge in riotous living does not come to absolute want in the inevitable fashion which obtains in the old country. An occasional spell of work puts him in funds. He can even trust luck for odd jobs and 'rises' obtained honestly or otherwise. Even the business of loafing is not here subject to the over-competition which reduces its profits to a minimum in more populous countries. The ideal and the lazy do not here necessarily disappear under the wheels of the social machine. Where the remedy is to be found is not yet apparent. Primary education does not promise to meet the case, for the larrikin, as a rule, has been to school—some alas! are actually at school. The recent holidays have served to bring this blight upon Young Australia prominently into view. The season, once so sacred, has served as Carnival time for larrikindom. Those excursions, upon which it has been the custom of the daily Press to dilate, as furnishing gratifying evidence of the prosperity which prevails, have served also to expose the numbers and quality of shameful residue. The scene presented by the motley crowd at Clontarf on Boxing Day is one never to be forgotten by an eyewitness. Englishmen have been accused of taking their pleasure sadly. The larrikin takes his and her pleasure madly. At Clontarf it was not an excursion—it was an orgy. Large ocean steamers discharged cargo after cargo of young Australians. Young men, young women, ladies, girls and still more sad children thronged the ground crowded the dancing pavilion (save the mark!) and jostled at the drinking bars. As their blood warmed by dancing, and their passions became inflamed by liquor, the scene within and around the hovels which serve for dancing and drinking became indescribable. Horace has no descriptions more revolting. The dancing was that of satyrs and bacchantes, but of satyrs and bacchantes in soiled tweed suits and squalid finery or rumpled gowns that had at first been stiffly white. Depravity of physique thrust itself upon notice. Young Australia here was represented by faces prematurely old—countenances cunning, debased, dully sensual, surmounting figures undergrown, meagre and angular. There were no manly youths. A six-foot constable towered like a giant amid the seething crowd—a sturdy water-police officer, of middle size, appeared a formidable heavyweight among them. And the girls! There was beauty of feature here and there, blurred by traces of intemperance and ravages of excess. But, worse still, amidst the flushed, panting bevy of young girls clinging in romping abandon to promiscuous partners, were some unworn childish faces with the devil's mark not yet stamped on their foreheads—but obviously preparing to have the seal set upon them before another day. Drink and excitement, inherited impulse, and above all, example and evil associations were doing their work and breaking down the last barriers of modesty. As the orgy grew, and drink, desire, and jealousy inflamed the participants, young girls, comely and shapely enough to make homes pleasant and parents proud, flew wild-beast fashion at one another, boxed like men and and scratched and bit like cats. Female children, not yet in their teens, romped around with gestures and antics they would have shocked a camp of black-gins. The males barely restrained themselves to a semblance of decency—the females resented no familiarity. The ones were inflamed—the others melted. The devil had broken loose. We looked around for the ministers of God and some policemen. We looked for parents and discovered—bawds. Has no one any duty to discharge to these unhappy youngsters? Are Sunday-school picnics the only proper place for clergymen to perform their ministries? Is the enemy only to be fought where he has no enemy? If Young Australia is to grow up to the full height of his opportunities, parents, employers, parsons—aye, and journalists—must do their duty with more determination and less of the mawkish dodging of plain facts and ugly necessities.

Bulletin, 9 January 1881.

Daniel Bandmann

Bandmann, an American actor, had toured Sydney before. Perhaps his alarmist view of larrikins was due to the fact that he put on edifying plays with a Christian message.

A class of vampires

I am sorry to say that I cannot appreciate the 'colonials' of today: neither their taste in art, nor their sentiments in life ... Of late years a class of vampires has grown up, which is known in the country as 'larikans' [*sic*]. They are perhaps better described in this country [USA] as 'hudlums' and yet that word is only a weak designation of these low creatures ... In short, a race has arisen which knows nothing of the ideals of its forefathers in Art, character, conduct; which has no true, strong manhood; and hence the decline of the drama in its loftiest aspects, the increasing demand for sensational amusements; for, in brief, all performances which please the eye, work upon the senses, but do not move the heart, exalt the character, or inform the mind ...

Its [Sydney's] irregularity [of layout] reminds one of Boston, and many of the more ancient towns of England and the continent. In the city itself there is nothing of great interest except the Public Gardens.

Daniel Bandmann, *An Actor's Tour*, Brentano, New York, 1886.

James Froude

James Froude (1818–94), English historian, visited in 1885.

The most venomous of his whole detested race

Ten miles from Sydney the detached cottages became thicker, villages smartened themselves into suburbs. The city spread inland to meet us, and we had been many minutes running between houses before we arrived at the station. Sydney proper—the old Sydney of the first settlement—stands on a long neck of land at the mouth of the Parramatta River, between two deep creeks which form its harbour—that is, its inner harbour, where its docks and wharfs are. Port Jackson, the harbour proper, from which these are mere inlets, is the largest and grandest in the world. A passage about a mile wide has been cut by the ocean between the wall of sandstone cliffs which stretch along the south-west Australian shores. The two headlands stand out as gigantic piers, and the tide from without, and the freshwater flood from within, have formed an inlet shaped like a starfish, with a great central basin, and long arms and estuaries which pierce the land in all directions, and wind like veins between lofty sandstone banks. The rock is grey or red. Worn by the rains and tides of a thousand human generations, it projects in overhanging shelves, or breaks off into the water and lies there in fallen masses.

The valleys thus formed, and widening and broadening with age, are clothed universally with the primeval forest of eucalyptus, and dark Australian pine—the eucalyptus in it most protean forms, and staining its foliage in the most varied of colours, the red cliffs standing out between the branches, or split and rent where the roots have driven a way into their crevices. In some of these land-locked reaches, except for the sunsine and the pure blue of the water, I could have fancied myself among the yews and arbutuses of Killarney. The harbour is on average, I believe, about nine fathoms deep. The few shoals are marked, and vessels of the largest size lie in any part of it in perfect security. Sydney itself is about seven miles from the open sea. The entire circuit, I was told, if you follow the shore round all the winding inlets from bluff to bluff, is 200 miles. There is little tide, and therefore no unsightly mud-banks are uncovered at low water. It has the aspect and character of a perfect inland lake, save for the sea monsters—the unnumbered sharks which glide to and fro beneath the treacherous surface ...

Dead tired, I slept till morning—safe as I fondly believed, behind mosquito curtains. I awoke bitten over hands and face as a young author is bitten by the critics on his first appearance in print. The mosquito of Sydney is the most venomous of his whole detested race. Where he has fastened his fangs and poured in his poison, there rise lumps and blotches which irritate to madness. The blotch opens into a sore, and I was left with a wound on the back of my right hand which did not heal for months. Happily, again like the critic, he chiefly torments the new-comers; I was inoculated that night and suffered no more afterwards. Perhaps the blood is affected and the venom finds an antidote.

James Froude, *Oceana; or, England and Her Colonies*, Longmans Green, London, 1886.

Sydney Morning Herald

In 1885 one of the larrikin pushes had pack-raped a young woman at Mount Rennie. In the outcry of hysteria against the pushes that the case produced the victim was lost to sight. Four were hanged, a kind of revenge of society on the larrikins, in a fearsomely botched execcution.

Hanging the Mount Rennie rapists

... Since the passing of sentence of death upon the culprits they were zealously attended and instructed by the ministers of their respective denominations. On the night previous to the execution several hours were spent in prayer and exhortation, and at 6 o'clock in the morning Mass was celebrated in one of the cells, and the Roman Catholic prisoners received those consolations of religion reserved for such as are *in extremis*. From an early hour in the morning the Presbyterian chaplain and the Rev. T.J. Curtis attended upon the prisoner Read, who, the latter states, 'bore himself consistently throughout as an innocent man.' Breakfast was served to the condemned men at an early hour, but they only took a little tea. There are at present on a rough computation about 700 prisoners in the gaol, and these were permitted to leave their cells, at about 6 o'clock, when they washed and had breakfast. At 7 o'clock sharp they re-entered their cells and were kept under lock and key until after the execution. They were, on the whole, very well behaved, only one or two cries being heard.

From about 7 o'clock in the morning a crowd commenced to assemble at the great gates of the gaol. It was composed of all classes, but chiefly of young men, some of unmistakable larrakin stamp; and there were also a number of women included in it. On the outskirts of the crowd, which must have numbered two thousand or more, a number of carts and drays were drawn up. The crowd was at its largest at 9 o'clock, but scores loitered about the gaol gate for hours after the execution had been carried out. Those having cards of admission met in the principal court, where an unseemly scramble occurred among the large crowd with regard to signing the visitors' book, a duty required from each present. Communications between the court and the gaol yard is by means of an underground passage, and through this those present filed, the general visitors being sent first, and the members of the medical and other professions, the representatives of the press and officials headed by the Sheriff (Mr C. Cowper) and the governor of the gaol (Mr J.C. Read) following. On ascending the steps leading from the underground passage the visitors found themselves in a well kept garden, and winding their way along a path turned the corner of a stone building, and reached the lawn near the Governor's private residence. Here a halt was called, and the press representatives, separating from the main body, went on to the wing where the gallows had been erected, and took up a position in the first gallery, the one above being occupied by the general spectators, and the members of the medical profession being upon the ground floor, where they had the best opportunity of viewing the bodies. It was just upon the stroke of 9 o'clock, at the time when those entitled to be present were finally gathered within the section of the wing, that the execution took place. It may serve to convey some idea of the spot where the scaffold was erected if it be described as a central space from which long corridors lined with cells radiate. There are three stories of corridors and it was from the corridor on the second floor that the condemned men were passed on to the scaffold. The customary formula by the Sheriff of demanding the bodies of the prisoners was gone through, and they were bought from the cells to have their irons removed and be pinioned. The hangman and his assistant performed the latter operation speedily, and as mercifully as possible, and the procession then moved along the corridor, and, ascending three steps, the prisoners reached the platform of the scaffold. The space opposite to the massive and ungainly structure was in the shape of a crescent, against the wall being two galleries. These were lined with spectators the greater portion of the ground space being also occupied by them, so that a ghastly thought of the theatre was suggested. Altogether, including doctors, reporters, and general visitors, there must have been quite 120 present. In addition to these were officials of various grades, warders and policemen. On first entering the wing there had been a buzz of conversation, and the Sheriff demanded silence, the governor of the gaol reminding those present of the solemn occasion upon which they were present. There was no need for a second admonition for with the entrance of the procession absolute silence fell upon all. After the gaol officials followed the first of the condemned youths—two were of 19 and two of 17 years of age—Martin. He was followed by Boyce and Duffy, and then Read. They were placed upon the trap in the following order: Boyce to the extreme left, then Martin, Duffy, and Read. Boyce was attended by the Rev. Father Coonan, Martin by the Rev. Father Byrne and Duffy by the Rev. Dr Murphy. Each of these prisoners had a crucifix hung round his neck. Read was attended by the Rev. T.J. Curtis—who throughout has been unremitting in his attention to the prisoner—by the acting chaplain, the Rev. J.F. Henderson, and by the Rev. Jas. McNeil. For a few seconds the prisoners stood beneath the beam. Boyce was exceedingly pale and throughout kept his eyes firmly turned upward, Martin was less pale and somewhat more stolid looking, Duffy was flushed and his lips moving incessantly, repeated words of prayer, while Read stood with his eyes closed and face turned skyward.

In the midst of most painful suspense and solemn silence the Rev. Mr Curtis in a broken voice said 'On behalf of Robert Read, I desire to say he has made a long written statement, which he has placed in my hands, to be held sacred until after his execution. In this statement he declares his innocence, and says that he will enter into the presence of God, trusting only in the Lord Jesus Christ his Saviour, with a clear conscience, knowing that he is innocent. In this matter—[Here Read turned his head and spoke to the rev. gentleman.] Robert Read wishes me also to say that so far as his small knowledge of the affair extends, and from all he has gathered from the other condemned men, he believes that those who have been reprieved—save Donnelan—that is to say Hill, Miller, Keegan and Newman are innocent.'

The executioner and his assistant then produced the white caps; Mr Curtis kissed Read, and, burying his face in his hands, stepped aside. The halters were quickly adjusted and in a second the bolt was drawn. A scene too painful to describe followed. It was evident that the weight of the prisoners and the drop had not been properly calculated. One struggled for about six minutes, the others for a less time, and when at 25 minutes to 10 o'clock Drs O'Connor and Brownless felt the bodies, it was quite plain to them that death had not at all been instanteous. Of the four, only one— Duffy—had his spinal column fractured. The others were strangled to death. It was stated by a medical man present, that in the case of Martin, respiration did not cease till the expiration of ten minutes. By a mischance, the rope got partly caught by one of his pinioned arms, and this no doubt to some extent checked the fall. So far as those present could judge, the knots of the nooses did not, in at least two cases, appear to have been drawn sufficiently tight. After hanging for some time, after the medical examination had been made the bodies were lowered and removed to the morgue, where a post-mortem was held, and subsequently the City Coroner (Mr Shiell) presided at an inquest, where formal evidence was given, the statement of Dr O'Connor, medical officer of the gaol, being that in the case of Duffy death had been caused by the dislocation of the the vertebrae of the spinal column, and in the cases of Read, Martin and Boyce, by strangulation.

'The Mount Rennie outrage', *Sydney Morning Herald*, 8 January 1886.

Ada Cambridge

Ada Cambridge (1844–1926) was a clergyman's wife who lived most of her life in rural Victoria. She was a poet and bestselling novelist.

Cultivated minds rubbing together

... There was yet another Saturday party—the party of them all. We started out to it in the sweetest weather to be found on earth, sunny and fresh, the living light of the sky the colour of nemophilias and the sea like liquid diamonds under it—poor similes both for the glory of that spring-like winter morning. On foot from Pott's Point to the Quay, by boat to Mosman's, up the ferny sandstone hills to breezy heights where I stood enraptured to look upon the Sound and the Heads and the Pacific outspread below, and down a crooked woodland path to a sequestered beach, we took our way; and if there had been nothing to get to at the end, the walk alone would have been a joy for ever. But on that lonely bit of shore, backed by the steep hills, fronted by the open gateway to the Heads, stood 'the Camp' ... The proprietors were two members of the Arts Club—men with homes and families in the city—who made this their private resting-place and holiday resort. They had gathered a choice assortment of their fellow-members on this occasion; they were 'giving a party.' But no woman had been allowed to take any hand in the affair; their wives were as much guests as I was; their cook was their old sailor caretaker, whose huge blocks of cold roast and boiled, hot potatoes and plum duff, bread and cake from his own camp oven, required no kickshaws to supplement them. It was a banquet for the gods, with that sauce of sea air to it. The permanent tent, combined sitting- and bed-room, was the drawing-room of groups of us in turn; we crowded on the covered-up truckle beds and the floor (of pine boards, well raised from the sand) for afternoon tea; at lunch we sat on planks under an awning, at long plank tables, like children at a school feast. It was a perfect 'spree,' but at the back of the merry trifling was that deep intellectual enjoyment of cultivated minds rubbing together which is so rare in social gatherings. We strolled in twos and threes along the lovely little beach, and sprawled under the bushes, and talked, talked; a few games had been provided, but there were no blanks to fill with them after lunch had crystallised us. The walk back to the boat was the best of all. The sun was setting as we

climbed out of the glen of the camp, and, looking back from points of van-
tage as we rose, we saw the moon swim up over the North Head—black as
ebony above the pale glitter of the water, while all other visible land was
wrapped in that beautiful rosy haze which so glorified every feature of it.
Then the great South Head Light began its revolutions, pouring over us and
the darkening path at intervals of a minute. I do not know how far that long
ray reaches, but I know that it is brilliant in the eyes of the homing traveller
for hours before his steamer makes the Heads.

Ada Cambridge, Thirty Years in Australia, Methuen, London, 1903.

James Tyrrell

James Tyrrell (1875–1961) was a second-hand bookseller, publisher, and
author.

A great place for boys

Balmain was a great place for boys of the Tom Sawyer persuasion in those
days (1880–87). We lived practically right alongside the water, only thirty
yards or so from the jetty, and linked to the romantic world of piracy and
adventures on the high seas by the ships and sailors constantly coming into
the bay. The ship I remember we always specially watched out for was a
barque picturesquely named the *Grecian Bend*, the crew of which seemed
to make our place their shore quarters.

To this day I can see them as if they had just sailed in; coming talking
and laughing from the jetty to our place. They are headed by the pirate-
looking mate, whom we knew as Blake; with him, Norwegian Big Tom and
Bill Petersen; Gustaf Hedburg, a Russian Finn; and Little Tommy, the cook,
a Cockney. He must have been a great-hearted little chap, the same Little
Tommy, with a vast toleration for small boys. He gave us, so to speak, the
freedom of the cookhouse, when we, pirates in fancy and almost in fact,
boarded the *Grecian Bend*, swarming all over her and up into the rigging.

… Blake, with the right appearance for such a career, eventually went off
to the South Seas, blackbirding, like Bully Hayes. Big Toni left his old sea-
chest with us and sailed away overseas; the chest is still in the family doing
service after more than sixty years, and in its time has played many parts,
some of them not usually catalogued in the Seven Ages of sea-chests;
among other things it has been a glory-box. Gustaf Hedburg, on in the
nineties, put the immense sailor Saving of £200 into William Lane's New
Australia scheme for setting up a Utopian community in South America, and
left with the other enthusiasts aboard the *Royal Tar* bound for Paraguay,
whither, in a later party, also went that fine woman and fine poetess who is
now Dame Mary Gilmore. Today nothing remains of the scheme except the

name, which has been revived in calling the current inrush of migrants from Europe 'New Australians' ...

At that time a ferry already ran from the jetty; a paddle-wheeler, taking passengers from Balmain to Erskine Street and the city. What may be called the great Sydney rush to get somewhere in a hurry is not altogether a latter-day development, for even then there were always some either running to leap for the ferry as it moved off, or ready to jump ashore before it tied up.

The ferry was run by Captain Watson, who lived in a large house on top of the hill up from Reynolds Street. He was a man of ships and the water, even to the extent of having a ship modelled on the side of the big house up on the hill ...

I began these recollections with an exclamation about how times have changed ... [T]he sport then most popular [was] sculling...

Our own hero was, of course, Bill Beach. An old Balmain authority assures me that Beach followed another profession which also has as good as vanished: he was a blacksmith, and a mighty man was he even as smiths went. Moreover, he was a member of the Balmain Rowing Club and always rowed in its colours.

When there was a boat-race between Beach and Hanlan, swarms of people, a mixed procession of many thousands, on horseback or in horse vehicles or on foot, made the pilgrimage through Drummoyne and Five Dock to Abbotsford and the river. A sculling match, in those halcyon days, was not merely a sporting encounter; it was the big event of the moment. The crowds went to it, by land or up the river in boats, from all parts of Sydney, and farther afield. Afterwards the stakes were paid over in Larry Foley's hotel, in George Street, near King Street, with white horse for its sign: a famed sporting rendezvous of the time, and a haunt of, among others, Phil May. Larry Foley himself has his niche in the bruisers' Valhalla, where George Borrow could welcome him as the greatest teacher of boxing Australia has known; but the noble art, like rowing, seems to have faded with fashions.

On the last occasion on which Beach defeated Hanlan on the Parramatta, I made my way with the throng to Abbotsford, and after the race walked with the crowd back to Norton Street, Leichhardt, the nearest place for a tram to Sydney. It was a double-decker steam tram, and, with the custom-ary distribution of sparks among the upper passengers, it managed to take some of the enormous crowd safely downhill past Grace Brothers' small shop (as it was then) at Broadway, but the tram, as it generally did, stalled on the hill past St Benedict's, going towards Regent Street. The custom in that case, which we proceeded to follow, was for the tram to go astern back down the hill till it came to rest with its load of cheering and barracking 'sports' of both sexes. There, as was also the custom, we waited till another tram came along behind and gave us a push to the top of the hill, with loud cheers of triumph as the feat was accomplished.

The old steam tram route used to continue on past Redfern station, which, before Central superseded it, was the hub of the State's railways. Thence it passed into the upper end of Pitt Street, across a Belmore Park that was much more extensive than the pocket-handkerchief thing it has since been whittled down to, and so into Elizabeth Street. Neither George Street nor Pitt Street for most of the way had trams in those horse-favoured days, nor had Castlereagh Street. Indeed, the strongest argument raised against the use of trams at all was that they would frighten the horses or interfere with them as they went about their lawful occasions in carts, drays, wagons, buses, sulkies, cabs, buggies, and carriages. No picture of Sydney streets of that time can be imagined without thinking of the literally thousands of horses moving in them.

On this night of the boat-race I stayed, with the tram to Market Street, and finally, not having the penny for the ferry fare, walked home over the Glebe Island bridge to Balmain, arriving at 1 o'clock (a.m.); a passable day's outing for a ten-year-old.

James Tyrrell, *Old Books, Old Friends, Old Sydney*, Angus & Robertson, Sydney, 1952.

H.M. Moran

H.M. Moran (1885–1945) was a general practitioner and surgeon who published three books of memoirs, thinly disguised as novels.

A Crimean veteran at the street corner
The first school I went to called itself proudly the Darlington Superior Public School. The headmaster was a patriarchal man with a long white beard whose most famous son was Grafton Elliot Smith. The actual teaching was very well done. We were required to pay threepence a week school fees, and each Monday morning in every class the roll was publicly called and the pupils paid up. The boys who did not have the money always looked uncomfortable. There was something humiliating about it all, especially as each guilty-faced youngster had to proffer publicly some excuse for the default. I hated the strangeness and the bustle of the crowded playground. The closets were scribbled over with lewd drawings and obscene words. The conversations were almost always low. Filthy expressions were common. This was a new and ugly world into which I had been launched ...

All round us, at that age, there was much drunkenness. We children were brought up in the strict puritan Catholic atmosphere of many Irish families. Ten Commandments there were, but only one sin really mattered—the sin of the flesh. The priests were always declaiming against it. It was an age when hell-fire still had its uses as a figure of speech. Alcholic over-indulgence was therefore deplored, more as a minor error of conduct. The priests themselves were much given to it—was it not part of the price of their celibacy? But the person who sinned carnally was damned— damned irrevocably. Purity, Purity, was the everlasting cry ...

Poverty was wide-spread. The poor used to come to our little shop invoking aid in the name of my mother who had been so good to them. Itinerant beggars were numerous. The hurdy-gurdy with its little monkey was a common sight. We all gathered round more to see the animal tricks than to listen to the illegitimate father of all mechanical discords. But the clearest figure that stands out is of a Crimean veteran who stamped along on a peg-leg, and at the street corner would stop to sing in a bass voice strange songs of war and foreign lands. These had the melancholy note of a Boris Godonov in the last stages of remorse and moral dissolution. Now, I know he must have sung out of that bitterness of heart which the hero feels who once has been publicly acclaimed. The world for him had passed on, and there he was, holding out a hat for stray pennies ...

The Chinese population in Sydney was then considerable. They congregated together in the very centre of the city and had a monopoly of the trade in fruit and vegetables. A Chinaman would shuffle up to our door with two great wicker baskets swinging from a bamboo stick across his shoulders ... He himself smelt like a vegetable garden. His countrymen carried their garden produce to Paddy's market in great deep-bodied carts with high sides ... At Christmas time the Chinaman would bring a little earthenware jar covered with strange inscriptions and enclosing a dark glutinous ginger which was hot and spicy, and had something about it of the mysterious East.

H.M. Moran, *Beyond the Hill Lies China*, Peter Davies, London, 1945.

Arthur Streeton

Arthur Streeton (1867–1943), an impressionist painter, usually lived in Melbourne. At the time of his visit to Sydney he was still to make a name for himself. The first extract is from a letter to Theodore Fink (1855–1942), a wealthy patron, written in April 1890. The second is from a letter of October 1890 to fellow painter Tom Roberts (1856–1931) whom he addressed as 'Bulldog'.

Steamers whistle and flute

... Thursday morning we enter the heads, slow winding up the harbour, past men-of-war who salute & dip their flags in honor of ourselves & RM 'Massila' & one feels beastly proud

> 'And the chest expands with its madd'ning might—
> God's glorious oxygen.'   Gordon

Then Circular quay with many steamers busy & bright—towering behind em Metropole Customs & Morts, & beautiful Sydney all glowing and oriental—Little steamers puffing hard & skipping over the blue water clouds of smoke, next the steamers whistle & flute in different keys & over all the bright harmony the warm palpitating sky of the Sunny South—

Sydney is an artists' city—glorious—Roberts & I go to Mossman's Bay & pull through the lazy green water, & then lunch under the shade in the open air, eggs, meat, cheese, & 2 big bottles of claret grown in Australia— The little Bay seemed all asleep & so very peaceful—Oh Such a rest—Warm balmy air blue orchids & the purple glory of sarsaparilla—

A land of passion-fruit and poetry—

In the afternoon down to Coogee—where the great green rollers tumble in like huge heavy cylinders of liquid glass, spreading glory everywhere, & playing a great symphony of thunder on the golden shore, where lovers sit in safety & watch and murmer, & kiss in the twilight, before they cross the heavy silver sand towards the tram, when the flowing tide comes in ...

Yours truly
Smike

... The confounded strike is damming things here—I wish they would bring the matter to a head, have a fight and get the thing over

Dam & blast the blessed thing.

I say Bulldog the people of Sydney drink more than our people—

Did you notice when you were here how the girls grow—they are women at 15 or 16 & fit to be married—They are rather broad strong & inclined to be short—

I go & dine at Charringtons at Woollahra very often. They are fine people—

She is a very artistic woman & all Sydney are running after her now. Mrs C. introduced me to a Mrs Terry & said I was one of her very intimate friends Mrs Terry told me I was very fortunate &c This occurred at an At Home on the stage of 'Her Majestys' on Thursday afternoon some lovely women there Bulldog & some fine intellectual looking men—she arranged the stage beautifully with Carpets & Chairs Umbrellas & lounges draperies lights & looked herself splendid—music in full swing in the dress circle—

She is the most professional woman Ive met—Her daughter Nora is coming along finely—I have seen 'Frou Frou' 'Macbeth' Dolls House—She is strongest in the latter I think—

—Don't forget to write to

Yours truly
Wretched Smike

Letters from Smike: The Letters of Arthur Streeton (ed. Ann Galbally and Ann Gray), Oxford University Press, Melbourne, 1989.

Daily Telegraph

The 1890 maritime strike was the first major trial of strength between the nascent trade union movement and the employers. The unions suffered a tactical defeat, but the strike stimulated the formation of the Australian Labor Party.

Troopers charged right and left

Sydney was yesterday a scene of unwonted excitement. The occasion of the outburst was the removal of a considerable consignment of non-union wool from the Darling Harbor railway station to the Circular Quay. The regular trolly and draymen having joined the ranks of the strikers, the employers themselves came forward to take charge of the trollies, and several of the best known men in the colony were to be seen driving in a sort of triumphal procession of non-union wool through the streets of the city. The spectacle may have been one for the gods; but was too much for the wharf-laborer and his confreres. Many of the unionists had been disporting themselves at Darling Harbor on the previous day, and they apparently were aware that the wool was to be removed. So one and all prepared for the function. Every dray moved off with the cargo of wool, each load having a makeweight of special constables. Mounted troopers led the way and regular police rendered service on the flanks. Incensed at the sight of the cavalcade every effort was made to disorganise it. Stones were thrown with indiscriminating vigor, efforts were made to block the wheels of the trollies, whilst some very foolishly disputed the ground with the mounted troopers, several of whom were, however, badly injured before the day was over. Amid groaning and every manifestation of displeasure among the unionists, the wool was conveyed to the Circular Quay for storage in Talbot and Co.'s stores ...

The greatest scene of disorder prevailed at the Circular Quay. Here the crowd had assumed the dimensions of a multitude of fully 10,000 people, all more or less excited. Constables and troopers, however, remained cool and self-possessed, whilst the behaviour of the 'specials,' many of them by no means stalwart, evoked a good deal of admiration. Mr Fosbery stood with about 50 troopers on the eastern side of the Quay. For a time he adopted a Wellingtonian tactic of firm resistance; but this would not answer, and it became necessary to order a dispersal at the point of the baton. The trollies drew up in the vicinity of Talbot and Co.'s stores, where the bales had to be unloaded. Some of the most desperate of the men on strike surged to the fore and seemed determined to throw every obstacle in the way of the operations. Missiles of various kinds were thrown, but the work proceeded fairly well under the direction of Messrs H.W. Wright (of the New Zealand Loan Co.) and Mr Row (of Dalgety and Co.). Stones were again thrown after the first waggon had been cleared. Thereupon, at the request of Inspector Fosbery, Mr Nugent Brown, JP, stepped to the front of the platform at Messrs Flood and Co.'s warehouse and read the Riot Act. This [illegible], unusual in the peaceful life of colonial cities, created a profound impression. Chaos was for the time being superseded by first-rate order. But the frenzy of the mind was not extirpated and the people would not disperse. 'Now, men, clear the quay,' Inspector Fosbery cried, after they had formed into line. And they made a very determined effort to obey the command. The people ran wildly in all directions; in fact, to use a favourite expression of the late Lord Beaconsfield, they fairly scuttled.

In two or three minutes it was all over. Troopers charged right and left under Inspector Latimer, several of them venturing on to the floating jetty. It was remarkable that many persons did not fall into the water. There was soon a large open space in front of the wool stores, the populace having banked up the thoroughfares debouching upon the quay. During the encounter one of the troopers was pulled from his horse and another had his cheekbone laid bare. Many people were cut and bruised and some fell under the horses' feet. Several thousand people were massed at the foot of George-street, and many of them looked very timidly on the scenes which were being enacted. When the disturbance broke out there were number of women about, but they appear to have gained safe sanctuary on the Riot Act being read. The police following the troopers used their batons freely, and there were numerous complaints of injuries received. At the bottom of Phillip-street some 200 or 300 of the disaffected laborers stood jeering and hooting the police. Noticing a wagon standing in the vicinity they tried to bring down the driver. One of them called to his companions for assistance to do so, and upon this Senior Constable Golder seized hold of the fellow. The officer was soon surrounded and every attempt was made to rescue the captive. As Golder was being badly beaten a dozen special constables went to his assistance and in this way the indiscreet rioter was lodged in durance vile. By about midday quietude prevailed. In addition to the troopers under Inspector Latimer there were present 200 foot police under Superintendent Reid and about 200 specials under Inspector Lenthall, the latter being kept as a reserve force. All the drays were safely unloaded after the clearance and in the afternoon the bales were being dumped ready for their ocean voyage.

Daily Telegraph, 20 September 1890.

Sydney papers

Quong Tart (1850–1903) was a tea merchant and philanthropist. The Emperor of China appointed him a mandarin of the fourth degree.

With kind treatment they are tractable

Mr Quong Tart has arranged to provide a repast for the aborigines who are camping at Botany, Moore Park, and North Shore. They will be mustered to the number of about 50 or 60 at the Zoological Gardens, Moore Park, on Wednesday afternoon, 26th instant, at 2 o'clock. Mr Matthews, who is well known as a missionary to the blacks, has been visiting the camp lately, and giving special attention to these neglected people, whose needs are great.

Sydney Morning Herald, 22 November 1890.

To those who have not seen the native blacks at their best an opportunity will be given next Wednesday afternoon at 2 o'clock, at the Zoological Gardens, when a considerable company of them will be guests of Mr Quong Tart. Provision is made for white visitors and tea will be spread in the refreshment rooms. Tickets for admission to the repast are 1s 6d each. Mr Daniel Matthews, missionary to the aborigines has been at the various camps and is now, with others, attempting to improve their condition and provide a school for those boys and girls who are totally ignorant and uncared for.

Daily Telegraph, 22 November 1890.

About 40 aborigines partook of Mr Quong Tart's hospitality at the Zoological Gardens yesterday afternoon. Among the visitors present were the Revs Dr Steel, J. G. Southby, J. Oldham, Messrs John Davies, MLC, John Roseby, Abramowitch, Quong Tart, Lyttle, Hawkins, Lieutenant-Colonel Paul and Mr Daniel Matthews. The blacks were principally from the camps at Botany and Moore Park—old gins, toothless and feeble, young lubras, piccaninnies, 'warriors,' and kings without kingdoms. The whole group thoroughly enjoyed themselves, if one could judge from the hearty applause given the few words of thanks spoken by one of the elder men. The poor, old fellow, whose English was almost perfect, grew quite excited as he praised Mr Tart's generosity, but his brief address had its note of sadness as he bewailed the rapid disappearance of his fellows. Mr Matthews and a few of the visitors spoke on behalf of the foundation of a mission station on the coast, where the few remaining blacks could spend their last days and their children be taught the lessons of civilisation. Close on 1000 aboriginals are located within the coastal district of the colony, and it was thought that if one or two stations could be formed much good might be done. There are now three stations in this colony and three in Victoria. The following resolution was carried:—'That further efforts for the moral and physical wellbeing of the blacks, especially in the neighbourhood of Sydney and the coast districts, is imperatively required, and this meeting commends the mission recently inaugurated with that object, having Mr D. Daniel Matthews as its superintendent, to the hearty and generous consideration and support of the public.' A resolution of thanks to Mr Tart and other friends who had assisted that afternoon was also passed.

Daily Telegraph, 27 November 1890.

The Zoological Gardens on Wednesday afternoon wore an unusually animated appearance, when Mr Quong Tart gave a tea to a number of aborigines from the camps in and around Sydney. About 40 sat on the grass under an impromptu tent, where, upon a long strip of oilcloth, good things were served. A substantial meal was eaten by each black, gin, and piccaninny, all of whom greatly relished it, if appearances were anything to judge by. When the meal was over, Charlie Murray, an aboriginal, evidently above the average class, made a pleasant speech, in which, on behalf of his countrymen and women, he heartily thanked Mr Tart for the very kind and liberal manner in which he had treated them. The latter suitably responded, and said that it was his intention to make the affair an annual one. Cheers were given for Mr Tart and Mr D. Matthews, the latter having taken great interest in matters concerning the aboriginals. Cheers for the Queen were also lustily given. The company then dispersed over the grounds.

News, 27 November 1890.

Quong Tart is quite a household word in Sydney, and, indeed, throughout New South Wales. Who, in Sydney, has not tasted Quong Tart's celebrated tea? And who is not familar with his genial face? At any rate the fact of his broad, generous heart is known to thousands who may not have tasted his delicous tea, or are personally unacquainted with Mr Quong Tart. His generosity always takes a practical turn, and we know of several of his acts of liberality that the outside public never heard of. His last kindly generosity to the Aborigines in the Zoological Gardens is more commendable as coming from him, because we find so few of our own countrymen taking an interest in the orginal owners of 'Sunny New South Wales.' On Wednesday last some forty blackfellows, gins and piccaninnies sat down to a hearty meal provided them by Mr Tart. These were brought together from round Sydney by Mr Matthews, who, for some years past, has been identified with the interests and welfare of our poor blacks. We have frequently met parties of them in the back blocks in the western districts. Whilst they certainly have many vices—probably acquired from the civilised whites—there are several redeeming qualities in them, of which their filial affection and gentleness are not the least. With kind treatment they are tractable, and not so lacking in intelligence as is generally supposed. We feel confident that if the experiences of men like Mr D. Matthews were made more widely known, people would not so readily believe our aborigines to be such arrant fools, and so hopelessly degraded as some would have us believe ...

Exchange, 5 December 1890.

Roydhouse and Taperell

Andy Kelly (1854–1913) served a term in the Legislative Assembly until 1894, then ran a pub until returning to the Assembly in 1901. He was still an MLA when he died.

The new Labour politician

Mr A. J. Kelly, third member for West Sydney, was born in Dublin in 1854, and educated at the national schools in that city. He took to the sea when in his teens, but after a year or so he abandoned the life of a sailor in favour of work on the shore as a wharf labourer. He was participant in a Wharf Labourers' Strike at Liverpool, and soon afterwards was once more afloat. He sailed to America and after arrival entered the United States navy. After serving the term of years for which he had signed, he quitted the navy, and having spent a little time in sightseeing, returned to Liverpool as a sailor, only to leave again, however, almost immediately. In sailing from Liverpool to New York in the *Idaho*, he experienced the perils and discomforts of shipwreck, and lost all he possessed. Back in Liverpool once more, he worked as a dock labourer for four years, and then went to London to try his luck there. He found that he could not better himself, and, therefore, wisely determined to set out for Australia. He landed in Sydney in 1881, and soon found that the New World presented better opportunities than the Old to a willing man. He worked as a wharf labourer, and helped to found the subsequently powerful Wharf Labourers' Union. He was President of the Union for a time, and Treasurer for several years. He also assisted in the formation of the Trolly and Draymen's Union, and was President of it. He was President of the Trades and Labour Council for a term, and in that capacity was prominent in the great Labour demonstration held in Sydney at the time of the London Dockers' Strike. He was also prominent in the Wharf Labourers' Strike of 1882, the great Maritime Strike of 1890, and other industrial difficulties in which the Wharf Labourers' Union was concerned. During his connection with Trades Unionism in Sydney, he has been the recipient of several testimonials for services rendered to different Labour organisations. Mr Kelly does not believe as a representative in dissociating himself from the workers in any way, and upon election he made the now famous hustings pledge that the electors would 'never find Andy Kelly wearing a top hat.'

Thomas R. Roydhouse and H.J. Taperell, *The Labour Party in New South Wales*, Edwards, Dunlop & Co. Ltd, Sydney, 1892.

Henry Lawson

Henry Lawson (1867–1922), poet and short-story writer, was seen to speak for the underdogs of society. Although often described as one of the bush poets, Lawson spent most of his life in Sydney. He died opening a bottle of beer.

Board and residence

One o'clock on Saturday, the unemployed's one o'clock on Saturday! Nothing more can be done this week, so you drag yourself wearily and despairingly 'home', with the cheerful prospect of a penniless Saturday afternoon and evening and the long horrible Australian-city Sunday to drag through. One of the landlady's clutch—and she *is* an old hen—opens the door, exclaims:

'Oh, Mr Careless!' and grins. You wait an anxious minute, to postpone the disappointment which you feel by instinct is coming, and then ask hopelessly whether there are any letters for you.

'No, there's nothing for you, Mr Careless.' Then in answer to the unspoken question, 'The postman's been and there's nothing for you.'

You hang up your hat in the stuffy little passage, and start upstairs, when, 'Oh, Mr Careless, mother wants to know if you've had yer dinner.'

You haven't, but you say you have. You are empty enough inside, but the emptiness is filled up, as it were, with the wrong sort of hungry vacancy—gnawing anxiety. You haven't any stomach for the warm, taste-less mess which has been 'kep' 'ot' for you in a cold stove. You feel just physically tired enough to go to your room, lie down on the bed, and snatch twenty minutes' rest from that terrible unemployed restlessness which, you know, is sure to drag you to your feet to pace the room or tramp the pavement even before your bodily weariness has nearly left you. So you start up the narrow, stuffy little flight of steps called the 'stairs'. Three small doors open from the landing—a square place of about four feet by four. The first door is yours; it is open, and—

Decided odour of bedroom dust and fluff, damped and kneaded with cold soap-suds. Rear view of a girl covered with a damp, draggled, dirt-coloured skirt, which gapes at the waist-band from the 'body', disclosing a

good glimpse of soiled stays (ribs burst), and yawns behind over a decidedly
dirty white petticoat, the slit of which last, as she reaches forward and backs
out convulsively, half opens and then comes together in an unsatisfactory,
startling, tantalizing way, and allows a hint of a red flannel under-something.
The frayed ends of the skirt lie across a hopelessly-burst pair of elastic-sides
which rest on their inner edges—toes out—and jerk about in a seemingly
undecided manner. She is damping and working up the natural layer on the
floor with a piece of old flannel petticoat dipped occasionally in a bucket
which stands by her side, containing a quart of muddy water. She looks
around and exclaims, 'Oh, did you want to come in, Mr Careless?' Then she
says she'll be done in a minute; furthermore she remarks that if you want to
come in you won't be in her road. You don't—you go down to the dining-
room–parlour–sitting-room–nursery, and stretch yourself on the sofa in the
face of the painfully-evident disapproval of the landlady ...

The landlady, Mrs Jones, is a widow, or grass-widow, Welsh, of course, and
clannish; flat face, watery grey eyes, shallow, selfish, ignorant, and a hypo-
crite unconsciously—by instinct.

But the worst of it is that Mrs Jones takes advantage of the situation to
corner you in the passage when you want to get out, or when you come in
tired, and talk. It amounts to about this: She has been fourteen years in this
street, talking to boarders; everybody knows her; everybody knows Mrs
Jones: her poor husband died six years ago (God rest his soul); she finds it
hard to get a living these times; work, work, morning, noon and night (talk,
talk, talk, more likely). 'Do you know Mr Duff of the Labour Bureau?' He
has known her family for years; a very nice gentleman—a very nice gentleman indeed; he often stops at the gate to have a yarn with her on his way
to the office (he must be hard up for a yarn). She doesn't know hardly
nobody in this street; she never gossips; it takes her all her time to get a
living; and she can't be bothered with neighbours; it's always best to keep
to your self and keep neighbours at a distance. Would you believe it, Mr
Charles, she has been two years in this house and hasn't said above a dozen
words to the woman next door; she'd just know her by sight if she saw her;
as for the other woman, she wouldn't know her from a crow. Mr Blank and
Mrs Blank could tell you the same ... She always had gentlemen staying
with her; she never had no cause to complain of one of them except once;
they always treated her fair and honest. Here follows story about the exception: he, I gathered, was a journalist, and she could never depend on him.
He seemed, from her statements, to have been decidedly erratic in his
movements, mode of life and choice of climes. He evidently caused her a
great deal of trouble and anxiety, and I felt a kind of sneaking sympathy for
his memory. One young fellow stayed with her for five years; he was, etc.
She couldn't be hard on any young fellow that gets out of work; of course
if he can't get it he can't pay; and she can't get blood out of a stone; she

couldn't turn him out in the street. 'I've got sons of my own, Mr Careless, I've got sons of my own.' ... She is sure she always does her best to make the boarders comfortable, and if they want anything they've only got to ask for it. The kettle is always on the stove if you want a cup of tea, and if you come home late at night and want a bit of supper you've only got to go to the safe (which of us would dare?). She never locks it, she never did ... And then she begins about her wonderful kids, and it goes on hour after hour. Lord! it's enough to drive a man mad.

We were recommended to this place on the day of our arrival by a young dealer in the furniture line, whose name was Moses—and he looked like it, but we didn't think of that at the time. He had Mrs Jones's card in his window, and he left the shop in charge of his missus and came round with us at once. He assured us that we couldn't do better than stay with her. He said she was a most respectable lady, and all her boarders were decent young fellows—gentlemen; she kept everything scrupulously clean, and kept the best table in town, and she'd do for us (washing included) for eighteen shillings per week; she generally took the first week in advance. We asked him to have a beer—for want of somebody else to ask—and after that he said that Mrs Jones was a kind, motherly body, and understood young fellows; that we'd be even more comfortable than in our own home; that we'd be allowed to do as we liked—she wasn't particular; she wouldn't mind it a bit if we came home late once in a way—she was used to that, in fact; she liked to see young fellows enjoying themselves. We afterwards found out that he got so much on every boarder he captured. We also found out—after paying in advance—that her gentlemen generally sent out their white things to be done; she only did the coloured things, so we had to pay a couple of bob extra a week to have our 'biled' rags and collars sent out and done; after the first week they bore sad evidence of having been done on the premises by one of the frowsy daughters. But we paid all the same. And, good Lord! if she keeps the best table in town we are curious to see the worst. When you go down to breakfast you find on the table in front of your chair a cold plate, with a black something—God knows what it looks like— in the centre of it. It eats like something scraped off the inside of a hide and burnt; and with this you have a cup of warm grey slush called a 'cup of tea'. Dinner: A slice of alleged roast beef or boiled mutton, of no particular colour or taste; three new spuds, of which the largest is about the size of an ordinary hen's egg, the smallest the size of a bantam's, and the middle one in between, and which eat soggy and have no taste to speak of, save that they are a trifle bitter; a dab of unhealthy-looking green something, which might be either cabbage leaves or turnip-tops, and a glass of water. The whole mess is lukewarm, including the water—it would all be better cold. Tea: A thin slice of the aforesaid alleged roast or mutton, and the pick of about six thin slices of stale bread—evidently cut the day before yesterday. This is the way Mrs Jones 'does' for us for eighteen shillings a week. The bread gave out at tea-time this evening, and a mild financial boarder tapped his plate with his knife, and sent the bread plate out to be replenished. It came back with *one* slice on it.

The mild financial boarder, with desperate courage, is telling the landlady he'll have to shift next week—it is too far to go to work, he cannot always get down in time; he is sorry he has to go, he says; he is very comfortable here, but it can't be helped; anyway, as soon as he can get work nearer, he'll come back at once; also (ah, what cowards men are when women are concerned), he says he wishes she could shift and take a house down at the other end of the town. She says (at least here are some fragments of her gabble which we caught and shorthanded): 'Well, I'm very sorry to lose you, Mr Sampson, very sorry indeed; but of course if you must go, you must. Of course you can't be expected to walk that distance every morning, and you mustn't be getting to work late, and losing your place ... Of course we could get breakfast an hour earlier, if ... well, as I said before, I'm sorry to lose you and, indeed ... You won't forget to come and see us ... glad to see you at any time ... Well, anyway, if you ever want to come back, you know, your bed will be always ready for you, and you'll be treated just the same, and made just as comfort-able—you won't forget that' (he says he won't); 'and you won't forget to come to dinner sometimes' (he says he won't); 'and, of course ... You know I always try ... Don't forget to drop in sometimes ... Well, anyway, if you ever do happen to hear of a decent young fellow who wants a good, clean, comfortable home, you'll be sure to send him to me, will you?' (He says he will.) 'Well, of course, Mr Sampson ...' etc., etc., etc, and-so-on, and-so-on, and-so-on, and-so-on. It's enough to give a man rats.

He escapes, and we regard his departure very much as a gang of hopeless convicts might regard the unexpected liberation of one of their number.

This is the sort of life that gives a man a God-Almighty longing to break away and take to the bush.

> *The Stories of Henry Lawson* (ed. Cecil Mann), Angus & Robertson,
> Sydney, 1964.

Banjo Paterson

'Banjo' Paterson (1864–1941) was a poet whose name was coupled with Lawson's as a bush balladist. When he wrote this report of an illegal dog fight, Paterson was still a solicitor, so he had to write under his pseudonym.

Concerning a dog fight

Dog fighting as a sport is not much in vogue nowadays. To begin with, it is illegal. Not that *that* matters much, for Sunday drinking is also illegal, yet flourishes exceedingly. But dog fighting is one of the cruel sports which the united sense of the community has decided to put down with all the force of public opinion. Nevertheless, a certain amount of dog fighting is still carried on around Sydney and very neatly and scientifically carried on, too—principally by gentlemen who follow the occupation of slaughterers, and who live out Botany way and do not care for public opinion.

The grey dawn was just breaking over Botany when we got to the meeting place. It was Sunday morning, and all the respectable, non-dog fighting population of that stinking suburb were sleeping the heavy, Sunday morning sleep. Away to the east the stars were paling at the first faint flush of the coming dawn, and over the sandhills came the boom of the breakers. An intense stillness was over everything, and the white-walled cottages of Botany were shrouded in a faint mist. Some few people, however, were astir. In the dim light, hurried pedestrians might be seen plodding their way over the heavy road towards the sandhills. Now and then a van, laden with about 10 or 11 of 'the talent', and drawn by a horse that cost 15s. at auction, rolled softly along in the same direction. These were dog fighters who had got 'the office', and knew exactly where the chewing match was to take place.

The 'meet' was on a main road, about half a mile from town, and here some 200 people had assembled, and hung up their horses and vehicles to the fence without the slightest concealment. They said the police would not interfere with them, and in truth, they did not seem a nice crowd to interfere with. One dog was on the ground when we arrived. He had come out in a hansom cab with his trainer, and was a white bull terrier, weighing about 40 pounds, 'trained to the hour', with the muscles standing out all over him. He waited in the cab, and licked his trainer's face at intervals, to reassure that individual of his protection and support. The rest of the time he glowered out of the cab and eyed the public scornfully. He knew as well as any human being that there was sport afoot, and he looked about eagerly and wickedly to see what he could get his teeth into. Then a messenger came running up to the cab and demanded to know, with a variety of expletives, whether they meant to sit in the cab till the police came; also, he said that the other dog had arrived and all was ready. The trainer and dog got out of the cab, and we followed through a fence and over a rise, and there, about 200 yards from the main road, was a neatly pitched enclosure like a prize ring—i.e. a 30-foot square enclosure formed with stakes and ropes. About a hundred people were at the ringside, and in the far corner, in the arms of his trainer, was the other dog—a brindle.

It was wonderful to see the two dogs when they caught sight of each other. The white dog came up to the ring straining at his leash, nearly dragging his trainer feet in his efforts to get at the enemy. At intervals he emitted a hoarse roar of challenge and defiance. The brindled dog never uttered a sound. He fixed his eyes on his adversary with a look of intense hunger, of absolute yearning for combat. He never for an instant shifted his unwinking gaze. He seemed like an animal who saw the hopes of years about to be realised. With painful earnestness he watched every detail of the other dog's toilet; and while the white dog was making fierce efforts to get at him, he stood Napoleonic, grand in his courage, waiting for the fray.

All details were carefully attended to, and all rules strictly observed. Most people think a dog fight is a go-as-you-please outbreak of lawlessness, but there are rules and regulations—simple, but effective. Possibly one could even buy a book containing the rules of dog fighting. There were two umpires, a referee, a timekeeper, and two seconds for each dog. The stakes were said to be ten pounds a side. After some talk, the dogs were carried to the centre of the ring by their seconds and put on the ground. Like a flash of lightning they dashed at each other, and the fight began. Nearly everyone has seen dogs fight—'it is their nature to', as Dr Watts puts it. But an ordinary worry between (say) a retriever and a collie, terminating as soon as one or other gets his ear bitten, gives a very faint idea of a real dog fight. These bull terriers are the gladiators of the canine race. Bred and trained to fight, carefully exercised and dieted for weeks beforehand, they come to the fray exulting in their strength and each determined to win. Each is trained to fight for certain holds, a grip of the ear or the back of the neck being of very slight importance. The foot is a favourite hold; the throat is, of course, fashionable—if they can get it. These dogs sparred and wrestled and gripped and threw each other, fighting grimly, and disdaining to utter a sound under the most severe punishment. Their seconds dodged round them unceasingly, giving them encouragement and advice. 'That's the style, Boxer—fight for his foot.' 'Draw your foot back, old man', and so on. Now and again one dog got a grip of the other's foot and chewed savagely, and the spectators danced with excitement. The moment the dogs released hold of each other they were snatched up by their seconds and carried to their corners, and a minute's time was allowed, in which their mouths were washed out and a cloth rubbed over their bodies.

Then came the ceremony of 'coming to scratch'. After the first round, on time being called, the brindled dog was let loose in his own corner of the ring, and he was required by the rules to go across the ring (some 30 ft) of his own free will and attack the other dog. If he failed to do this he would lose the fight. The white dog, meanwhile, was held in his corner waiting the attack. After the next round it was the white dog's turn to make the attack, and so on alternately. It, therefore, became evident that the animals need not fight a moment longer than they chose, as either dog could abandon the fight by failing to go across the ring and attack his enemy. While their condition lasted they used to dash across the ring at full run, but after a while, when the punishment got severe and their 'fitness' began to fail, it became a very exciting question whether or not a dog would 'come to scratch'. The brindled dog's condition was not so good as the other's, and he used to be on his stomach between the rounds to rest himself, and it several times looked as if he would not cross the ring when his turn came. But soon as time was called he would start to his feet and come limping slowly across glaring steadily at the other dog; then as he got nearer, he would quicken his pace and at last make a savage rush, and in a moment they would be locked in combat. So they battled on for 56 minutes till the white dog (who was apparently having all the best of it), on being called on to cross the ring, only went halfway across and stood there growling savagely till a minute had elapsed, and so he lost the fight.

No doubt it was a brutal exhibition. But it was not cruel to the animals in the same sense that pigeon shooting or hare hunting is cruel. The dogs are born fighters, anxious and eager to fight, desiring nothing better. Whatever limited intelligence they have is all directed to this one consuming passion. They could stop when they liked, but anyone looking on could see that they gloried in the combat. Fighting is like breath to them—they must have it. Nature has implanted in all animals a fighting instinct for the weeding out of the physically unfit, and these dogs have an extra share of that fighting instinct. Of course, now that the world is going to be so good, and we are all to be teetotal and only fight in debating societies, and the women are to wear the breeches, these nasty, savage animals are out of date, and we will not be allowed to have anything more quarrelsome than a poodle about the house—though even poodles will fight like demons when they feel like it. And the gamecock and the steeplechase-horse and all animals with sporting or fighting instincts must be done away with. Guinea pigs will, perhaps, be safe to keep, though even *they* have a go-in at one another occasionally. And the man of the future, the New Man, whose fighting instincts are not quite bred out of him, will, perhaps, be found at a grey dawn of a Sunday morning with a crowd of other unregenerates in some backyard frantically cheering on two determined buck guinea pigs to mortal combat.

Banjo Paterson, *Bulletin*, 18 May 1895.

Alfred Deakin

Alfred Deakin (1856–1919) played a leading role in the 1890s conventions that brought about federation of the colonies. He later became Australia's second Prime Minister. His very frank account of the conventions and the personalities involved was not published until 1944, long after his death.

Carefully posed for effect

First and foremost of course in every eye was the commanding figure of Sir Henry Parkes, than whom no actor ever more carefully posed for effect.

His huge figure, slow step, deliberate glance and carefully brushed-out aureole of white hair combined to present the spectator with a picturesque whole which was not detracted from on closer acquaintance. His voice, without being musical and in spite of a slight woolliness of tone and rather affected depth, was pleasant and capable of reaching and controlling a large audience. His studied attitudes expressed either distinguished humility or imperious command. His manner was invariably dignified, his speech slow, and his pronunciation precise, offending only by the occasional omission or misplacing of aspirates. He was fluent but not voluble, his pauses skilfully varied, and in times of excitement he employed a whole gamut of tones ranging from a shrill falsetto to deep resounding chest notes. He had always in his mind's eye his own portrait as that of a great man, and constantly adjusted himself to it. A far-away expression of the eyes, intended to convey his remoteness from the earthly sphere, and often associated with melancholy treble cadences of voice in which he implied a vast and inexpressible weariness, constituted his favourite and at last his almost invariable exterior. Movements, gestures, inflexions, attitudes harmonized, not simply because they were intentionally adopted but because there was in him the substance of the man he dressed himself to appear. The real strength and depth of his capacity were such that it was always a problem with Parkes as with Disraeli where the actor posture-maker and would-be sphinx ended or where the actual man underneath began. He had both by nature and by act the manner of a sage and a statesman.

His abilities were solid though general, as were his reading and his knowledge. Fond of books, a steady reader and a constant writer, his education had been gained in the world and among men. A careful student of all with whom he came in contact, he was amiable, persuasive and friendly by disposition. A life of struggle had found him self-reliant and left him hardened into resolute masterfulness. Apart from his exterior, he was a born leader of men, dwelling by preference of natural choice upon the larger and bolder aspects of things. He had therefore the aptitude of statecraft of a high order, adding to it the tastes of the man of letters, the lover of poetry and the arts, of rare editions and bric-à-brac, of autographs and memorials of the past. His nature, forged on the anvil of necessity, was egotistic though not stern and his career was that of the aspirant who looks to ends and is not too punctilious as to means. He was jealous of equals, bitter with rivals and remorseless with enemies—vain beyond all measure, without strong attachment to colleagues and with strong animal passions—weak in discussion of detail, unfitted for the minor tasks of administration, apt to be stilted in set speeches, and involved in debate, he yet was well qualified for the Premiership by great and genuine oratorical ability. A doughty parliamentary warrior neither giving nor asking quarter, he struck straight home at his adversaries with trenchant power. He was a careful framer of phrases and of insulting epithets which he sought to elaborate so that they would stick and sting. He confessed that he passed many of the weary hours in which he sat unmoved upon the front bench of the Assembly in mentally summing up his associates and opponents, fitting to each some appropriate descriptive epigram which he treasured in his memory for timely use. One lean long swarthy hungry-looking enemy he stigmatized as a 'withered tarantula.' An academic radical from Victoria, possessed by what he regarded as impractical enthusiasms, was more mildly entitled 'professor of democracy.' Dibbs consisted of 'a weedy nature and a sprawling mind.' He had a copious flood of sometimes coarse vituperation which he was pre- pared to pour upon any who crossed his path at critical times, and lighter touches of genuine and happy humour emitted under pleasanter circum- stances. At times his irony was of the grimmest and most merciless. Very many admired and not a few weaker men loved him; he brooked no rivals near his throne but all found his personality attractive and submitted more or less to his domination. It was not a rich, not a versatile personality, but it was massive, durable and imposing, resting upon elementary qualities of human nature elevated by a strong mind. He was cast in the mould of a great man and though he suffered from numerous pettinesses, spites and failings, he was in himself a full-blooded, large-brained, self-educated Titan whose natural field was found in Parliament and whose resources of char- acter and intellect enabled him in his later years to overshadow all his con- temporaries, to exercise an immense influence on his own colony and achieve a great reputation outside it.

It was necessary to see Parkes in his own home, on the platform and in Parliament to appreciate his versatility. In the first he was a literary con- noisseur, dilettante and author, retired from a world in which he held the foremost place at will; on the platform he was the candidate whose trans- parent candour could not conceal his great services but whose humility was ceremonial until he was roused to passion, when he became a turbu- lent tribune of the democracy. His sly humour marvellously helped him in encounters with the mob-wits of his meetings. When challenged at Manly by an elector who professed the utmost faith in his sincerity, but none the less marvelled that he had not during all his three years in office as Premier since he last addressed them fulfilled his express promise to have. the quarantine removed, he replied in his low soft squeaky tones that he had no recollection of having ever made any such promise, but if he had, his heckler should be the happiest man in the room since, having announced entire confidence in his good faith, he must feel himself just three years nearer its fulfilment ...

The most conspicous figure of the Convention [Melbourne 1898], its official author and in matters of moment its leader, was the Premier of New South Wales, G. H. Reid, physically as remarkable as his predecessor,

Parkes, but without his dignity, and even more formidable in discussion because less self-respecting. Even caricature has been unable to travesty his extraordinary appearance, his immense, unwieldy, jelly-like stomach always threatening to break his waistband, his little legs apparently bowed under its weight to the verge of their endurance, his thick neck rising behind his ears rounding to his many-folded chin. His protuberant blue eyes were expressionless until roused or half hidden in cunning, and a blonde complexion and infantile breadth of baldness gave him an air of insolent juvenility. He walked with a staggering roll like that of a sailor, helping himself as he went by resting on the backs of chairs as if he were reminiscent of some far-off arboreal ancestor. To a superficial eye his obesity was either repellant or else amusing. A heavy German moustache concealed a mouth of considerable size from which there emanated a high-pitched voice rising to a shriek or sinking to a fawning, purring, persuasive orotund with a nasal tinge. To a more careful inspection he disclosed a splendid dome-like head, high and broad and indicative of intellectual power, a gleaming eye which betokened a natural gift of humour and an alertness that not even his habit of dropping asleep at all times and places in the most ungraceful attitudes and in the most impolite manner could defeat. He never slept in a public gathering more than a moment or two, being quickly awakened by his own snore. He would sleep during the dealing of cards for a game of whist and during the play too if there was any pause, but he never forgot the state of the game or made a revoke. In the Assembly or in a train he indulged with the same facility both of sleeping and waking if necessary with an appropriate retort upon his tongue. His extreme fatness appeared to induce this state and for that his self-indulgence was chiefly responsible since he denied himself nothing that he fancied, sucking ice or sweetmeats between meals and then eating and drinking according to his fancy. In some respects he was the antithesis of Parkes, who used to quote scornfully a confession of Reid's that he never read a book unless it were a sensation novel. Apparently nothing else could keep him awake. He had no taste for literature, for art, for bric-à-brac, or the study of the past. Newspapers satisfied his tastes; he was fond of society and social amusements, but even at the theatre his preferences were those of the crowd. In other respects he resembled Parkes for he was inordinately vain and resolutely selfish, a consummate tactician even more cunning and if anything excelling him in variety and violence of vituperation. He was almost as impecunious but contrived to keep out of debt, whereas Parkes said of himself and another member that they were alike in that they consistently lived above their means. He was as much an admirer of the fair sex, so that when once on a specially dashing woman appearing in the gallery of the New South Wales Assembly, and Parkes being asked who she was, replied in sardonic style: 'Well I don't know myself. I've asked George Reid and Wise and they don't know, from which

I conclude that she must be a woman of good reputation.' … As a platform orator he was unsurpassed. His voice could reach a great crowd and
his deliberate drawl enabled the densest among them to follow him. At his
best his arguments were well shaped and perspicuously expressed with
admirable directness and in the plainest words, often in slang, but always
so as to be understood. He once remarked to a Victorian whom he closely
watched during the Convention, that his manner of addressing that body
was as if he were 'merely thinking aloud.' 'You don't make platform
speeches that way do you?' said he, 'or you cannot reach the people if
you do.' He made his one long appeal to their sympathy and sensibility
and, provided he got it, cared nothing for his own consistency or dignity
or their comments upon his obvious trickiness and insincerity so long as
his cleverness captured their support … Reid was not merely a humourist
but a great actor assisting his low comedy parts with irresistible gesture
and expression. He cared nothing for the heights of outlook or depths of
insight, discarding all decorum of deliverance, finish of style or grace of
expression, aiming always at the level of the man of the street and reaching it by jest, logic, appeal, rant or ruthless abuse as appeared most effective. He always was effective for he possessed a really marvellous political
instinct, a readiness and adaptability, a quickness of repartee and a rolling
surge of *ad captandum* arguments which were simply irresistible. He
knew the average man better than he knew himself for he was the average man in every respect except his amazing platform powers, political
astuteness, and the intensity of his determination to carve out and keep
the first place for himself in New South Wales and in Australia if possible—but in New South Wales at all events until sure of the other by any
means and at any cost.

Alfred Deakin, *The Federal Story*, Robertson & Mullens,
Melbourne, 1944.

George Griffith

George Griffith (1857–1906) was an English writer who had visited the French
penal colony of New Caledonia to write a book. On the way home he called
at Sydney, where he encountered the last outbreak of bubonic plague.

That whistle again

On one side there was the quarantine station—about as beautiful a land
and seascape as those about to die ever took a last look from at earth and
sea and sky.

On the other hand, the varied beauties of 'Our Harbour,' with Manly
beach to the northward, North Shore and its red-roofed villas sprinkled

among the trees; and, away in the dim distance, the spires and chimneys of Sydney. A couple of hours would have taken us to it, but as we looked at it with longing eyes, thinking of what a cocktail at the bar of the Australia Hotel would taste like, it might just as well have been twenty thousand miles away.

It was during those eight days of mingled dirt and discomfort, cursing, and cribbage that I saw as curious a contrast between life and death as you might search the wide world over for.

On the starboard side, which is the right-hand side looking forward, lay the route of the excursion steamers running between Sydney and Manly Beach.

They came past at all hours of the day, and they came near enough for us to hear strains of stringed and wind instruments, which brought back memories of the dear old Thames with painful distinctness.

On the port side, with almost equal frequency, there came a green-painted, white-awninged launch, flying the Yellow Flag and carrying corpses, 'cases,' and 'contacts' from the depot at Woolloomooloo. As she rounded into the jetty she whistled. Day and night for eight days and nights we heard that whistle—and the meaning of it was usually death. But you get hardened to all things in time, and before our durance vile ended we had got to call her the Cold Meat Boat ...

As we were coming back to the quay to go on board we heard that never-to-be-forgotten whistle again, and the green Death Boat swung round the corner. One of the sanitary police on the wharf put up his hand and waved us back.

In the stern there were about a dozen people sitting. Forward there was a long shapeless bundle lying on a stretcher. It was a case. The others were 'contacts,' friends, lodgers, and relations who had lived in the same house with the case. They had come to be isolated for ten days, so that the microbe of the Black Death might show whether or not it was in their blood.

They were taken out of the boat first. Their own feelings didn't matter, for the Black Spectre takes no account of human affections, and permits no other to do so. They were marched away to the quarters set apart for con-tacts. No farewells were permitted, just a look that might be the last, and that was all.

Then the stretcher with the long bundle on it was lifted and carried on to the wharf. Meanwhile the ambulance backed down to the shore-end, the stretcher was put into it, and it drove away up through the trees to the hos-pital. The next journey of that particular 'case' was to the cemetery four days afterwards ...

There was only one passenger this time, and he travelled in a coffin. A common two-wheeled cart backed down to where the ambulance had been the day before. The coffin was carried to it and put in just like any other sort of packing-case might have been. The driver whipped up his horse, and we watched the cart with its load of coffin, corpse, and quicklime, trotting up the winding road which leads to the burying-ground of North Head.

George Griffith, *In an Unknown Prison Land*, London, 1900.

John Norton

John Norton (1858–1916) was a newspaperman under whose ownership *Truth* developed a national circulation with a combination of muck-raking and scurrilousness. He was a regular bender drinker and often insane.

Marvellous Melba

Madame,

Marvellous Melba, Mellifluous Melba, Supreme Singer, Crowned Cantratrice, and Monarch of Matchless Music though you be, your public and private conduct during your short six months sojourn in Australia makes it compulsory that you should be told the truth. Genius is mostly eccentric; the eccentricities of genius are generally pardoned—up to a certain point. You have great genius, which is only excelled by your eccentricity. The public have heard too little of the first, and a great deal too much of the last. The turpitude of a talented termagant can be forgiven ten times ten, but there is a limit of license which cannot be condoned.

I'm not going to dig up the squalid scandal of your married life, or of your grass-widowhood, nor to resuscitate the sordid story of your alleged intrigue with that French royal rotter, the Duc d'Orleans, nor to revive the details of the celebrated action for *crim. con.* brought against you and him. That matter may well be left to lie covered up in the mantle of mystery, under which it was hidden when the proceedings were quashed ...

What has since come to light concerning your champagne capers on the 'Continent,' in gay 'Paree,' in the 'Rue de Revelry,' and elsewhere: in London, at the Hotel Cecil; in 'Frisco, Sydney and Launceston, and last, but not least, at Menzies' Hotel in Melbourne, lends color to the suspicion that your first and subsequent breaches of faith with the Australian people was as much, if not more, due to champagne as to real pain.

You are pretty plain and free of speech yourself towards others, whom you think you can bully and bounce; permit me, therefore, to exercise the same privilege towards you by expressing the opinion that you indulge in intoxicants a great deal more than is good for you and your divine voice. You are in the heyday of your cultured, ripened powers, at the zenith of your fame; and occupying, of right, the position of proud pre-eminence formerly filled by the peerless Patti. Your powers are ripe; your reputation is made; all the world asks of you is the privilege of paying to hear you, and applauding you. What more could woman wish or desire?

Your voice will not last for ever; it should be cherished like chastity, and not submitted to the risk of ruin that banquets and drinking bouts entail. Divas as divine and delightful as yourself have been dethroned and damned by Drink before today. That you can escape their fate, if you follow in their footsteps, is not in the Providence of God, who gave you your great gift of song, in trust, for the gratification of the highest instincts of your generation.

I'm not posing as a moralist, nor pretending to be a teetotaller, or even a temperance man. I'm neither one nor the other, but I daresay that my morals are quite as good as Melba's, and I am quite certain that as far as 'langwidge' goes, I'm just as modest and moderate as she; while I'm certain I'm more temperate than she, simpy because she could drink with impunity what might make me doubly drunk ...

It is altogether too bad to add to the truculence of the termagant, the vagaries of the virago, and the proclivities of the poculent pocharde those of a miserable miser, who, while revelling in wealth and swigging champagne, balances and buncoes dependants who have kept better faith with her than she has kept with the public who have paid her so liberally, and generously forgiven her so much.

I remain, Madame,

Your admiring admonitor,
John Norton.

John Norton, 'An open letter to Madame Melba', *Truth*,
27 March 1903.

H.M. Moran

By this time Moran, the Irish carter's son from the slums of Chippendale, had become a medical student.

The ancient impersonal dead

They loved the lascivious incidents. The smallest things tickled them. There was that joke about the University rowing man who was called on by his tutor to make a pelvic examination. A good oarsman, he was not so much at home in these waters. Behind a screen a small group of students crowded round the bed of a little Scotswoman. The tradition of Victorian decency still forbade the unnecessary exposure of a patient. The hand, which held an oar firmly in inter-University races, got lost amid the tangle of unnecessary bedclothes and apparel. It was still lost when the flustered student and his sniggering friends heard a little voice from the top of the bed call out: 'A little further forward, Sir, and to the right.' ... The story went round the hospital bawdily embroidered under the title of 'the co-operating little Scotswoman.'

Yet, even amidst these coarse interludes, these medical students were becoming serious-minded. How could they fail to be so, listening with their newly bought binaural stethoscopes (so roundly condemned by the older physicians)—listening and listening—fascinated, to the turmoil of the blood around an incompetent heart valve. And it gave them food for thought, beyond any information in a text-book, when they watched the magic of tissue repair. In the dissecting room the skin, shrivelled and dry like leather, never fought back. Now, with the wrapt attention of a child before its first magic lantern show, they saw in an ulcer the pearly shelving edge grow in, redeeming the raw surface. And day by day, with a sense of partnership in that redemption, they watched the shrinking and drying up of the little ruby lake ...

[The medical students] now went into town on Saturday mornings and 'did the block' for an hour. This meant walking in a prescribed circle which had for its diameter King Street. Along the course they always met men friends and girl friends, stopped for a moment to greet them and then walked on to see others. It was Victorian in its simplicity and in its innocent behaviour.

On Saturday nights it was the custom for the ruder sporting types of young men to flock again into town. In King Street players from all the Clubs congregated in little groups, discussed the events of the day's cricket or rugby, argued and talked and, from time to time, went across to one of the public-houses to linger awhile over a drink. In spite of their limited resources the students frequented the 'private bars,' where all the drinks were sixpence (they were only threepence in the public bars). But there was much more in the ritual of these Saturday nights in town than the taking of a drink. They wandered from Madame Telekey's private bar to the American bar, or over to the more sedate atmosphere of the 'Surrey' and then perhaps to the Tivoli. It was a more or less set round and all the time they were meeting with old friends or making new acquaintances. There was a constant exchange of chaff and banter. Ill-feeling was rare. Some drunkenness inevitably occurred, but it was not a vicious drunkenness, and when the bars closed at 11 p.m. nearly all turned home. The medical students who had had such a night in town always felt fresher for work in the following week. It was considered rather despicable to study on Saturday afternoon or evening. One who did it was a 'swot.' Only the highest distinction in examination results could cancel such a breach of the conventions.

It was all a period of adjustment. None of the young men was as case-hardened as he tried to make believe. Most of them had become habituated to the ancient impersonal dead of the dissecting room. But now they were learning to know actual human beings by their pathological physical states. Challis remained, much longer than his fellows, secretly distressed by the spectacle of a man or woman dying, as if, deep in the unconscious layers of his mind, there still rankled and gnawed the memory of the first uraemic death.

His first attendance at a post mortem examination proved an ordeal. Hidden away, like a guilty secret, on the far side of the hospital grounds, was the shabby little mortuary. It was well out of sight of patients or visitors, but conveniently situated for the unperceived comings and goings of the undertaker's vehicle. Its back jutted on the high fence which encircled the University playing ground. Attached to the wall of this mortuary he read as he got nearer the notice of the impending examination: '*Hodie Sectio 4 p.m.*' The use of Latin words painted on the little black board was, itself, evidence of the dislike of publicity. Only the time was written in with chalk.

Challis, wedged uncomfortably in the little gallery, had, for first impression, a sense of the distressing shabbiness of his surroundings. The walls were grimy, and the whole place looked uncared for. The very basins were chipped and dirty-looking. Instead of white cottonwool they used a coarse brown tow. Even the slate-covered table did not look clean and the metal of the water-taps was dull with oxidation. How different from the bright and spotless scene of the surgeons' operating theatre in the hospital! There, hope was still alive, and by its living kept all else luminous. There, men and women spoke softly in whispers out of reverence. It was the sanctum of a cult: let none blaspheme with loud voices against the art that heals and relieves!

But here were repulsion and denigration. Without respect, and roughly, attendants were depositing the white body of a woman recently dead, on the old-fashioned grimy table. They had obviously lost all consideration for it. The doctor was drawing on great clumsy gauntlets like those the motor men were just beginning to use. He had an air of great disdain and, and when he began his work, his manoeuvres were deliberately crude and rough. He seemed to be handling the parts brutally: the great Scots surgeon at his operation had *caressed* those tissues of her, alive. Now vast, terribly vast, incisions were being made with a large wooden-handled knife. Asepsis did not live here and no one thought of the new surgical expression about 'toilette' of the tissues. And, all the while, the rust-covered tap was running noisily, and noisily running away down open channels on the table, was a fluid incarnardined ...

Challis found himself unable to keep his mind on the comments made by the pathologist carrying out the examination ... He was witnessing the dismemberment of a body which had only recently housed warm affections, secreted tears, quivered pleasantly at a man's approach. Now, all was fused—systole and diastole alike—and all the furies of the flesh had abated. Only a white inert mass remained, blanched of the sensitiveness of those who hope and desire.

When the opportunity came he slipped outside, before the end. It was good to breathe once more the fresh air of a sunny day. A sombrely-clothed undertaker was patiently awaiting his prize with the furtiveness of his class. From the Oval shouts were coming, and at times a high-punted ball could be seen, between the tall trees and above the wooden fence.

H.M. Moran, *Beyond the Hill Lies China*, Peter Davies, London; Dymock's Book Arcade, Sydney, 1945.

Thomas Fiaschi

Thomas Fiaschi (1853–1927), an Italian-born physician, came to Australia to try his luck on the Queensland goldfields. He practised in Macquarie Street from 1897. An able controversialist, he opposed teetotalism. He is commemorated by the statue of a boar outside Sydney Hospital.

Wines ordered by medical men

... To avoid misunderstandings, I tell you frankly that I consider the temperate use of wine a valuable support to healthy man in this thorny path of life, and that the judicious use of it has proved itself to me of incalculable benefit in the treatment of the sick and the convalescent.

In making youth is profession of faith. I do not conceal from you that in recent years a small section of the medical profession has started a crusade against all use of alcholic beverages, and of wine also, both in health and disease. Whether they are right, and those who think like me are wrong, is a question that I am not going to discuss tonight. Enough for you to know, that so far the vast majority of medical men believe in the temperate and judicious use of wines, and that whether you individually believe in them or not, it will often be your duty as Nurses to see that certain wines are taken by your patients according to the physician's prescription. The administration of wine, then, remains in your hands, and I think it will not be time lost for you to acquire some idea of what wine is, and what are the wines generally ordered by medical men in Australia ...

Types of wine.—I must limit myself to describe to you five wines generally known in the world as typical wines, and these are claret, hock, port, sherry, and champagne ...

Medical uses of claret.—Claret acts as a tonic and reconstituent, and is a valid aid to digestion. It is not so much used in the treatment of acute diseases as in those conditions of general debility, impoverishment of the blood, and enfeeblement of the digestive powers, which either precede or follow serious diseases. Hence it is especially recommended for delicate and weak people, for dyspeptics, and for the anaemia of the young; also for convalescents from fevers, from prolonged suppurations, and from surgical operations. Nor should we be deterred from giving it in diabetes or chronic rheumatism, if a stimulant is indicated, as the quantity of glucose present is a mere trace. In this climate claret is specially useful on hot days, when the stomach becomes languid and unable to digest the amount of food required to keep up the nerve strain involved in the struggle of civilised life ...

Dose of claret.—The quantity of claret that should be given in the 24 hours should not exceed one reputed pint bottle, and this really means 13 ounces. In exceptional cases this quantity might be increased to one reputed quart bottle (26 ounces) in the 24 hours. This dose should be proportionately decreased according to age in young people. To derive the full benefit of claret it should be given with meals, and diluted with a little water. Thus used, claret will help to diminish the ingestion of other beverages, such as tea or coffee, by far more injurious to the nervous system and digestive organs than claret can ever be ...

Coming now to the economic value of claret, it is well for you to know that Bordeaux claret is sold in Sydney at between 3s 6d and 6s, and Australian claret from 2s to 3s a quart bottle.

[Dr Fiaschi deals with hock, setting the same dose as for claret, and then with the fortified wines, such as sherry and port, with a dose of 7–8 ounces per day, before going to champagne.]

You must remember the old joke: When should you drink champagne? Whenever you can get it. I shall amend such an extreme statement as follows: When should you give champagne to a patient? Whenever a stimulant is required, and the patient's purse is long enough to afford it. With the exception of gout and diabetes, champagne can be given in all diseases where prostration, weak heart action and mental and nervous depression require a spur to tone and cheer up. It is particularly suitable in certain cases of sickness when other stimulants have been rejected, and, as Dr G. Newton Pitt writes, 'it is most valuable when the appetite has failed in prolonged illness or during convalescence.'

Whilst singing the praises of champagne, I wish to remind you that it is distinctly a beverage for the well-to-do. I consider it a cruelty to put struggling people to the expense of champagne when Australian hock or sherry and soda-water would have answered the same purpose at one-fifth of the cost. Never carry your preferences of prejudices too far, for in this world it is possible to find a substitute for almost everything and everybody.

Dose.—For an adult, a pint bottle; exceptionally up to a quart in the 24 hours.

Price, from 11s to 15s a bottle.

'The Various Wines used in Sickness and Convalescence. Lecture to the Members of the Australasian Trained Nurses' Association, by Dr Thomas Fiaschi, on June 27th, 1906', *Australasian Nurses' Journal*, 15 November 1906.

Louis Stone

Louis Stone (1871–1935) was a novelist and playwright. When *Jonah* was first published it received only one review in Australia.

Saturday night at the corner

One side of the street glittered like a brilliant eruption with the light from a row of shops; the other, lined with houses, was almost deserted, for the people, drawn like moths by the glare, crowded and jostled under the lights.

It was Saturday night, and Waterloo, by immemorial habit, had flung itself on the shops, bent on plunder. For an hour past a stream of people had flowed from the back streets into Botany Road, where the shops stood in shining rows, awaiting the conflict.

The butcher's caught the eye with a flare of color as the light played on the pink and white flesh of sheep, gutted and skewered like victims for sacrifice; the saffron and red quarters of beef, hanging like the limbs of a dismembered Colossus; and the carcasses of pigs, the unclean beast of the Jews, pallid as a corpse. The butchers passed in and out, sweating and greasy, hoarsely crying the prices, as they cut and hacked the meat. The people crowded about, sniffing the odor of dead flesh, hungry and brutal—carnivora seeking their prey.

At the grocer's the light was reflected from the gay labels on tins and packages and bottles, and the air was heavy with the confused odor of tea, coffee and spices.

Cabbages, piled in heaps against the door-posts of the greengrocer's, threw a rank smell of vegetables on the air; the fruit within, built in pyramids for display, filled the nostrils with the fragrant, wholesome scents of the orchard.

The buyers surged against the barricade of counters, shouting their orders, contesting the ground inch by inch as they fought for the value of a penny. And they emerged staggering under the weight of their plunder, laden like ants with food for hungry mouths—the insatiable maw of the people.

The Push was gathered under the verandah at the corner of Cardigan Street, smoking cigarettes and dicussing the weightier matters of life—horses and women. They were all young—from eighteen to twenty-five—for the larrikin never grows old. They leaned against the verandah posts, or squatted below the windows of the shop, which had been to let for months …

Suddenly, up the road, appeared a detachment of the Salvation Army, stepping in time to the muffled beat of a drum. The procession halted at the street corner, stepped out of the way of the traffic, and formed a circle. The Push moved to the kerbstone, and, with a derisive grin, awaited the performance.

The wavering flame of the kerosene torchs, topped with thick smoke, shone yellow against the whiter light of the gas-jets in the shops, The men, in red jerseys and flat caps, held the poles of the torches in rest. When a gust of air blew the thick, black smoke into their eyes, they patiently turned their heads. The sisters, conscious of the public gaze, stood with downcast eyes, their faces framed grotesque poke bonnets.

The Captain, a man of fifty, with the knotty, misshapen hands of a workman, stepped into the centre of the ring, took off his cap, and began to speak.

'Oh friends! we 'ave met 'ere again to-night to inquire after the safety of yer everlastin' souls. Yer pass by, thinkin' only of yer idle pleasures, w'en at any moment yer might be called to judgment by 'Im Who made us all equal in 'Is eyes. Yer pass by without 'earin' the sweet voice of Jesus callin' on yer to be saved this very minit. For 'E is callin' yer to come an' be saved an' find salvation, as 'E called me many years ago. I was then like yerselves, full of wickedness, an' gloryin' in sin. But I 'eard the voice of 'Im Who died on the Cross, an' saw I was rushin' 'eadlong to 'ell. An' 'Is blood washed all my sins away, an' made me whiter than snow. Whiter than snow, friends! whiter than snow! An' 'E'll do the same fer you if yer will only come an' be saved. Oh! can't yer 'ear the voice of Jesus callin' to yer to come an' live with 'Im in 'Is blessed mansions in the sky? Oh! come to-night, an' find salvation.'

His arms were outstretched in a passionate gesture of appeal, his rough voice vibrated with emotion, the common face flamed with the ectasy of the fanatic. When he stopped for breath or wiped the sweat from his face, the Army spurred him on with cries of 'Hallelujah! Amen!' as one pokes a dying fire.

The Lieutenant, who was the comedian of the company, met with a grin of approval as he faced the ring of torches like an actor facing the footlights, posing before the crowd that had gathered, flashing his vulgar conceit in the public eye. And he praised God in a song and dance, fitting his words to the latest craze of the music-hall:

> Oh! won't you come and join us?
> Jesus leads the throng;

snapping his fingers, grimacing, cutting capers that would have delighted the gallery of the theatre.

'Encore!' yelled the Push as he danced himself to a standstill, hot and breathless.

Louis Stone, *Jonah* (first published 1911), Endeavour Press, Sydney, 1935.

Archbishop Kelly

Michael Kelly (1850–1940), born in Ireland, was Catholic Archbishop of Sydney from 1911 to 1940. His views on mixed bathing and alcohol place him firmly in the Irish Jansenist tradition, which was closer to Protestant wowserism than either would have conceded.

On mixed bathing and alcohol

'I think promiscuous surf bathing is offensive in general to propriety, and a particular feature of that offensiveness is the attraction it has for idle onlookers,' said Archbishop Kelly yesterday morning when approached by a 'Sun' representative on the subject of surf bathing, to which His Grace had referred in a recent sermon.

While thus expressing his objection to mixed surf bathing as at present practised along our beaches, his Grace was careful to make it plain that as far as surf bathing itself was concerned it had in him a strong advocate. 'I regard it as an invigorating and healthy pastime,' he said, 'so long as it is conducted with a proper respect for domestic modesty. What I strongly object to is the promiscuous commingling of the sexes, which is the chief feature of surf bathing as at present indulged in.'

'Would you suggest a reform in respect of surf bathing?'

'I think that the municipal authorities should take such steps in the regulation of surf-bathing as would eliminate its present objectionable features,' replied his Grace. 'There is no border-line between vice and virtue. Our worst passions are but the abuse of our good ones. And I believe that the promiscuous intermingling of sexes in surf-bathing makes for the deterioration of our standard of morality.

'If we wish to have happy homes, our women must be respected. Every time they appear under immodest circumstances in public there is a diminution of that respect. It is what I would call subversive of domestic respect. For a woman to be exposed to public view as she is under the circumstances of surf-bathing is utterly destructive of that modesty which is one of the pillars of our nationhood.

Separation of the sexes while bathing

'I would that our municipal authorities had taken more mature counsel in this matter, so that arrangements could have been made for the sexes to bath [*sic*] separately. If I might offer advice to our municipal fathers, I would urge that steps in that direction be taken without delay. As far as the dress is concerned, I have no objection to offer. But I would like to see a modification effected, on the lines of assigning separate locations, not only for dressing, but also for the enjoyment of surf-bathing. That would do away with the present abuse of a healthy and popular form of recreation and exercise.

'Surf-bathing has come to stay has come to stay,' pursued the Archbishop, 'so nothing in the shape of a prohibition would be thought of. But there is abundant room for improvement, and I see no reason why such improvement should not be made. In the eyes of strict modesty, the present promiscuous method of surf-bathing constitutes an offence in that it robs our sisters—who are our domestic treasures—of the respect that is justly due to them.

Unrestrained amusement

'There are those who appear to go in for promiscuous surf-bathing as a pastime, and quite apart from its attractions as a healthy exercise, or other legitimate purposes. This unrestrained amusement in promiscuous surf-bathing is simply vicious. It is vicious in the sense of lubricity.

'I have known of this promiscuous bathing at the Channel ports in the north of France, and there it has become decidedly demoralising. Compare what one sees at these Channel ports of France with the decorum observed at the English seaside resorts on the opposite side! On the English side of the Channel the most circumspect person can go and bathe with modesty. Cross over to the French side, and a self-respecting, modest person could not fail to have his sense of the proprieties shocked by even looking on. There are such immodest exhibitions to be seen in those places as furnish the demoralising section of the French papers with improper cartoons. The conduct of the bathers at these places is such as to make it unfit for any self-respecting person to take part in the amusement.

Encroachments upon Christian modesty

'While appreciating the great benefits of surf-bathing, especially in a dry, hot climate such as ours, I feel it incumbent on me to offer a protest against the encroachment of these modern usages upon Christian modesty and reserve. The crowds of onlookers who go to watch the surf-bathers are not, it is to be feared, all actuated by worthy motives. I know of one incident which occurred at Woolloomooloo, where curious onlookers were told by a policeman to go away. "If you want that kind of thing," he said, "you can go to Manly." That was certainly a keen satire on our present immodest system of surf-bathing. ...

No infringement of personal liberty

'I would carefully guard against any infringement of personal liberty,' pursued the Archbishop, 'and therefore I have no desire to be recorded as an opponent of surf-bathing legitimately conducted. Indeed, I have often been pleased to see the bathers at Manly coming briskly along for their morning dip. It is the abuse of a popular and healthful amusement that I deprecate.

'There are certain things which are slippery,' concluded Dr Kelly, 'and if not guarded they will descend to the level of abuses, and result in public corruption. Unless the homes of the people are maintained on a modest basis, and unless people are attracted by real womanly modesty and not by the indelicacies of the so called up-to-date woman, who moves about like a man and has no proper sense of decency, we are not going to build up a good nation.

'Woe betide Australia if she is going to encourage immodesty in her women.'

A plea for total abstinence

Yes, we need abstinence teetotal, when experience convinces us that we slip from self-control even in moderate indulgence. Women should never accustom themselves to intoxicating drink of any kind, or in any quantity. Young men should not add fuel to their passions, by draughts of fermented beverages, or by small portions of distilled spirits. Denial in this respect will obviate woes without number. It will prevent degradation, and maybe an unprovided death. How long, we ask in humiliation, will our thoroughfares and bye-ways be set thickly with the snares of intemperance? How long will we keep up the social habits which prove a bane to many a brother or sister? The evil is unfortunately rooted in society, but let us individually cut off this dangerous occasion of sin.

> Archbishop Kelly, 'On mixed bathing' (1911), and 'Archbishop Kelly's Pastoral Letter, Lent, 1914', in *Documents in Australian Catholic History*, vol. 2 (ed. Patrick O'Farrell), Geoffrey Chapman, London, 1969.

W.J. Chidley

William James Chidley (1860?–1916), a sex and dress reformer, roamed the streets of Sydney dressed in a tunic and trying to sell pamphlets against penile erections, as the source of aggression in the world. He was much harassed by police, courts, and mental health authorities.

In my lonely cell

Sydney, 26th April 1912 (written at 54 Upper Fort Street, Sydney). Just a few words before sending this life back to Havelock Ellis. I had to leave Melbourne to escape prison—or paying six pounds, which I had not. I have appeared several times in the street with my costume on, and been in Darlinghurst Gaol here for a fortnight for lecturing in the Domain on Sunday. The Bench said, 'He's mad, we'll give him two months to enable the medical men to have a look at him.' In a fortnight I paid my fine and came out. The papers (some of them) severely criticized this decision, but no paper, man, or woman will come forward and champion *me*—or my mission. My 'life' ends here—my fallen, worldly life, I mean. I may utterly fail to convey my message to this generation, but I have made my appearance, written my book, and have *tried to*—and am trying still, in spite of ill-health, mental injury, loneliness, melancholy, and despair. I *suffered* in my lonely cell, thought and suffered a lot—thought of Ada, always—always, with tears, and how different it might have been, 'surely', when I had made my discovery. And I thought of Mother and all she suffered—with tears ...

Sunday, 12th December 1915. I was in gaol again a few days ago and was put in the OBS [observation ward]. I met a man there, Tucker—whose brain and eyes were visibly injured with coition (a *terrible* face and head)—who had killed his wife—chopped her head *slowly* with an axe. He had come out of an asylum, Callan Park, some time before, and will no doubt end his days in one. He told me he had *no recollection* of the occurrence. He regretted her death and *his bereavement* with lachrymose tones one minute, and was laughing and jesting the next. The most cheerful of all the inmates.

Once more *I thought a lot.*

The End

The Confessions of William James Chidley (ed. Sally McInerney), University of Queensland Press, Brisbane, 1977.

H.M. Moran

By this time Moran was practising as a doctor in working-class Balmain, which he thinly disguises under the name of Cockle Creek.

War comes to Balmain

The suburb of Cockle Creek straggles untidily towards Sydney Harbour. It occupies a small quadrant of what was the old Convict Colony. Its main street is long and narrow. Potholes deface the surface. Noisy electric trams jolt along the thoroughfare whose worst ruts an incompetent Municipal Council fill from time to time with unscreened stone fragments known locally as 'blue metal.'

The suburb's more important shops are in the neighbourhood of the Town Hall: a pretentious structure on whose front are hung, like a row of cheap medals on a watch-chain spread across someone's waistcoat, the announcement boards of those societies and lodges which hold their regular meetings within: Druids and Rechabites, The Ancient Order of Hibernians, The Holy Catholic Guild, the Protestant Alliance, and the Loyal Orange Lodge. From time to time, to supplement these disfigurements, bills are posted announcing political meetings or charity concerts. At election time slogans are scribbled with chalk or painted in whitewash on the walls themselves. It is a politically conscious little borough.

Further along the main street are tenement houses and weatherboard cottages, interrupted by an occasional vacant allotment carrying an unheeded notice 'For Sale', drunkenly set on a post. Strange! that in a great growing City such delectable allotments should go a-begging! On the exposed side of every house adjoining vacant areas are advertisements. There are also advertisement posters plastered on paling fences, almost cheek by jowl with a warning that 'Bill posters' will be 'prosecuted.' In times of political ferment even the asphalt footpaths—or those of them sufficiently intact—are scrawled over with public notices. At nearly every important road-crossing is a public-house, sometimes two. They offer no facility for eating, but infinite opportunity for drinking, to men—standing up against a bar and hidden behind swing doors. The few women who enter have to go to the 'Bottle Department' at the side.

The still narrower side-streets run off the main thoroughfare without any plan and in open defiance of any scheme for parallel lines. Sometimes they end blindly; sometimes they turn in a curve and enter the main street again lower down. They symbolise all life in the suburb. Cockle Creek just grew, and growing, out-grew its natural beauty. Its dominant note is one of shabbiness. Only the harbour's water at the foot of Mudie Street sparkles greenly in the sunlight. The Municipal Council cannot touch that ...

For diversion, what was there?—Of intellectual diversions there was none. But sporting pastimes were many. Then there were the hotels, open from 6 a.m. to 11 o'clock at night—continuously, every day except on Sunday. Sometimes the partisanship over the competitions of cricket and football assumed fierce proportions. Gambling was widespread but mostly on a small scale. Only a tiny proportion of those who 'followed the horses' could afford to go to a Randwick meeting or up to Moorfield. Many, however, both men and women, placed their bets with a local starting-price bookmaker who usually had his agency in a tobacconist shop. This was illegal but was winked at by the police except when some members of a religious party indignantly drew official attention to what they called a scandal.

On Saturday afternoon young men could be seen hanging around outside such a tobacconist shop, waiting for the telephone message which would tell of their having won or lost, with their bets of a 'dollar' on the favourite or a 'deaner' on the outsider. The numbers who went down to the nearest Oval or across the city to watch the main match in another suburb were, of course, very much greater. On their own local ground 'barrackers' would sit or lie on the grass and make jeering remarks about the player who missed a catch or mulled a pass. They were a good-natured crowd, but they were not easily pleased, and they were niggard of their applause.

For all those who worked at ship-yards or at the abattoirs, in factories or in offices, Friday night was a great occasion. They had been paid that day and at night they all 'went up the road.' There they gathered together within a narrow sector of the main street, met friends, exchanged gossip and 'had a few drinks.' The younger ones talked of women and sport, the older of sport and politics. The women-folk, young and old, passed along, doing their Friday night shopping or meeting their men friends by appointment. The public-houses meanwhile did a roaring trade, with men jostling one another as they passed at the swing doors. The rare women seen in the hotel were at the bottle entrance. Sometimes a fight took place—nearly always as the result of a political argument. Then a great crowd would gather, with supporters urging the fighters on or seeking to make them desist. In a drunken mêlée at times bottles would be thrown. On such occasions the tram traffic became blocked, and to the incessant clanging and braking of the driver, the crowd would answer with cheerful vituperation ...

When the first world-war came to Cockle Creek the people, appalled, ceased for a little while their trivial rounds then slowly resumed the old ways. Two convictions sustained them: one that it was all so far away, and the other, it couldn't possibly last long—why, all the warring nations would rapidly be bankrupt. 'What business is it of ours, anyhow?' shouted an aggressive worker in an early morning tram. The others in the compartment fingered their newspapers and said nothing in reply. Down on the docks and in the slaughter yard violent arguments took place. It was all a capitalists' war! But even as they argued many of their fellow-workers were over at the recruiting posts giving in their names.

H.M. Moran, *Beyond the Hill Lies China*, Peter Davies, London;
Dymock's Book Arcade, Sydney, 1945.

Keith Murdoch

Keith Murdoch (1885–1952), a newspaperman, was later knighted. Born in Melbourne, he came to have newspaper interests in every Australian capital city except Sydney.

The Sydney spirit would not prevail

The Sun Newspaper,
32 Castlereagh Street,
Sydney.

21/6/15.

Dear Mr Fisher,

Since coming across here I have been very busy every hour of the day or I would have written to you before. The Sun is doing exceedingly well and although our policy frightens the advertisers we get a great return circulation which is bounding upwards near the 100,000 mark.

You would have been surprised here by the flatness with which the coalition proposal fell. It did not interest a single individual and only our out and out conservative newspapers touched it. We have the Employers' Council howling for a national government but everyone knows why they want it and the average man dismisses the scheme with the thought: 'This is a put-up job to hold back the referendum.' Much more interest is taken in the manufacture of munitions but even in this there is general apathy and ironmasters' patriotism is only cloaking their desire for profitable orders. Sydney people go about saying that the war position is very serious and that every effort must be made; but they crowd to theatres as usual and are to be seen every day pluming themselves in the newest military fashions. I do not think the Sydney spirit would prevail in a war against the native tribes of Papua. It is a pity the aborigines were not Prussianised ...

Keith Murdoch, letter to Andrew Fisher, Andrew Fisher Papers,
National Library of Australia.

Lloyd Rees

Lloyd Rees (1895–1988) was a Brisbane-born artist who lived in Sydney for most of his life.

A skyline of coral pink

The first glimpse—a picture in a circular frame. Opal-blue water, a band of golden sand, another of olive-green trees; above them a skyline of coral pink shimmering against the limpid air. This was Manly, seen from the porthole of SS *Canberra* bound for Melbourne in early December 1916.

In that first long look Sydney cast her spell and it has remained with me ever since, in spite of her brashness and disorder, the crimes she has committed against herself, and, above all, the opportunities she has allowed to pass—opportunities that could have made her more worthy of her setting.

It was one of those calm early mornings, when all was veiled under an ethereal mist of blue through which the sun struck on golden foreshores and russet trees, and depicted in creamy light the myriad facets of city buildings and the terraces defining the contours of the hills.

The visit was a short one ...

I left Brisbane for Sydney in May 1917.

For those who know only the Sydney of today, my impressions of the city in 1917 may be of interest.

From the harbour, city towers dominated the skyline—St Mary's Cathedral, the Queen Victoria Building dome, the Town Hall, Post Office, and, near the Quay, the Lands Office tower, still to me one of the most beautiful in Australia. Only four tall buildings gave a hint of things to come: Number Four Bridge Street (later distingushed as a meeting-place for artists); the first section of the Commonwealth Bank, on the corner of Martin Place and Pitt Street; the old *Daily Telegraph* building, now a bank, on the corner of Castlereagh Street and King Street—a handsome building with corner domes; and opposite this, in Castlereagh Street, Culwulla Chambers, then the highest commercial building in Sydney.

I think my first impression on entering the city proper was of its beautiful brown tone and its sense of enclosure. This sense of enclosure remains to this day—one cannot see *through* Sydney as one can through the straight streets of most other Australian cities.

And then, as now, Sydney, divides herself into zones, one towards the railway and the other towards the Quay, the difference between then and the present being that the railway end, now so dead, was once the hub of retail trade, while the booming northern end of today had for the most part a quietude and dignity suggestive of an old-world city.

Most buildings in the area between Martin Place and the Quay were of beautiful Sydney sandstone, and in Italian and French Renaissance styles. Their architectural quality was so high that their almost total destruction is something to be deplored. Fortunately, one fine example of Italian Renaissance style has been preserved—the façade of the old Commercial Bank of Sydney which was removed from Martin Place and re-erected in the grounds of Sydney University opposite the Union steps. For this we have to thank the then Professor of Architecture at the University, Leslie Wilkinson, whose judgement and hard work made this preservation possible. Examples of the French Renaissance style still exist today, notably the Government Offices in Bridge Street.

One section of this area did not, however, share the general dignity and quietude, and that was Circular Quay itself, the centre of a ferry service that makes today's look a pallid thing indeed. It served as a clearing house for all the traffic—pedestrian and vehicular—between Sydney and the northern shores, and great was the bustle at peak hours, and on holidays too when,

before the coming of the family car, the ferries opened magic doors to
golden beaches and to woodlands.

At times the Quay could be very beautiful—especially in the evening
peak hours of winter, when in the dusk the ferries would fan out from
Sydney Cove like slow-moving clusters of golden rockets and spangle their
lights across the velvet waters.

Lloyd Rees, *The Small Treasures of a Lifetime: Some Memories of
Australian Art and Artists*, Angus & Robertson, Sydney, 1988.

Christina Stead

Christina Stead (1902–83), a novelist, spent most her life overseas. She
returned only in 1974. Fisherman's Bay is Watson's Bay.

The great sub-tropical moon

Fisherman's Bay. First days of the first poor man.
An October night's dream.
A stirring sermon has no effect on an ill-fated hero.

The hideous low scarred yellow horny and barren headland lies curled like
a scorpion in a blinding sea and sky. At night, house-lamps and ships'
lanterns burn with a rousing shine, and the headlights of cars swing over
Fisherman's Bay. In the day, the traffic of the village crawls along the skyline, past the lighthouse and signal station, and drops by cleft and volcanic
gully to the old village that has a bare footing on the edge of the bay. It
was, and remains, a military and maritime settlement. When the gunners
are in camp, searchlights sweep over the bay all night, lighting bedrooms
and the china on dressers, discolouring the foliage and making seagulls fly;
in the daytime, when the red signal is flown over the barracks, the plates
and windows rattle with the report of guns at target practice. From the
signal station messages come down of the movements of ships and storms.
Flags flutter and red globes swing on its great mast, which is higher than
the Catholic Church, higher than the Norfolk Island pines, higher than the
lighthouse and than anything else which is between the rocky cornice and
the sandy seafloor. In dark nights, from the base of that enormous spectral
pole which points up any distance into the starry world, one looks down
on the city and northern harbour settlements, on the pilot-lights in the
eastern and western channels, and on the unseen dark sea, where
the lighthouse ray is lost beyond the horizon and where ships appear
through the waves, far out, lighted like a Christmas Tree, small, and disap-
pearing momentarily; and where, after half an hour of increasing radiance,
the yellow rim of the great sub-tropical moon comes up like a lantern from
underneath.

Early in the morning, through the open window, the people hear the clatter of anchors falling into the bay, and the little boys run out to name the liners waiting there for the port doctor, liners from Singapore, Shanghai, Nagasaki, Wellington, Hawaii, San Francisco, Naples, Brindisi, Dunkirk and London, in the face of all these old stone houses, decayed weatherboard cottages, ruinous fences, boathouses and fishermen's shanties. Presently a toot, the port doctor puts out in the *Hygeia*; a whistle, the Customs launch goes alongside; a hoot from the Point, and that is the pilot-ship returning to its anchorage. A bell jangles on the wharf where the relief pilot waits for his dinghy, and the ferry whistles to clear the dinghies, rowing-boats and children's canoes from its path. The fishermen murmur round the beach-path, fishing-nets dry in the sun, a bugle blows in the camp, the inspected ships draw up their anchors and go off up the harbour, superb with sloping masts, or else, in disgrace, flying the yellow flag, to the rightabout, with nose in air, to Quarantine, under North Head and its bleak graveyard. Butchers' and bakers' carts rattle, an original milkman yodels, little girls gabble on the way to school, the wind with hands in pockets whistles a tune, and the day goes gaily and blatantly forward.

There is no place in the estuary, though, so suited for an old tale as this fish-smelling bay, first in the port. Life is poor and unpretentious, life can be quiet. The sun rises just over the cliff, and sailing vessels roll in and out as they have done for a hundred years, and a quarter of a mile away unfurl their full sails to catch the Pacific winds ...

... Michael went always on black, rough feet, whose horny skin was split into deep cracks, bleeding in the crevices, from which the winter's dirt could never be washed. He ran with other little boys in frayed trousers to the beach to collect driftwood and coke for the kitchen, and would return late for breakfast with blue hands; he had chilblains and a running nose all the winter. There were stragglehaired little girls with dirty pinafores and pink skirts. They were all cold; they grasped their sponge-boxes and playtime biscuits, called out the names of teachers in brittle voices and squabbled over hopscotch tors.

The beach provided not only fuel, but also dead fish, swollen fruit, loaves, pumpkins, shoes and socks, broken straw-boaters—all varieties of food and clothing cast up from ships and sewers. Once, when a five-thousand tonner was wrecked near the Gap, a hundred tons of butter floated mildly in to the beach. Pegleg salvaged it and sold it. Cases of condensed milk collided with their frail canoes, manufactured in backyards, of canvas and corrugated iron. They went outside the Heads and brought in a butcher's block, and came back, all their coracles white with flour. They could all swim and were absolutely fearless, despite the frequency of squalls and sharks, paddling all over the harbour in unseaworthy tubs. There were crabs in the rock-pools, little oysters spread all round the bay, and the waters were rich in fish. 'If this were a desert island ...' thought all those verminous little heads joyfully, seeing the bounty of the sea. There was even a great house there, in the last stages of decay, weathered by wind and sea, and standing in a neglected garden with old trees, in which they all could have lived at ease, a pirate brood. The front part of the house, of stone and heavy timber, had been added to the large stone military stables at the back, which had served in the early days. The fences were down, and the house was inhabited fraternally by human, barnyard, and vermin tribes. The goats, ducks, geese, dogs and horses left wandering about the streets of the neighbourhood oftener wound up in the backyard than in the pound, and the children after school found the forbidden front garden, with its tall trees and old bushes, the best spot for playing bushrangers.

Annie Pennergast lived with her family in part of the house. The little girl was thin, with black eyes and hair. She scratched her head and body all the time, and always smelled of ingrained dirt. In the corners of the house bats flew, swallows dropped mud and dung from every beam, and from all the cracks of the great whitewashed stones at the back ran cockroaches. beetles and rats. Cockchafer beetles, cicadas and mosquitoes shouted loudly in summer evenings in the tall trees; large spiders hung in the outhouses, and fearsome-looking, but innocent, crickets and slaters dwelt under the bits of wood and sheets of corrugated iron fallen off the roof into the grass. The house attracted Michael and the other children with the same charm as a stagnant gutter.

The little girl, Annie, took him over the house one Saturday afternoon. Its windows were starred by stones which now lay on the naked flooring inside. Annie preceded Michael up camel's-back staircases and adventitious flights of steps connecting the old house with the later front apartments, through heavy doorways pierced in the stone walls. She showed him windows that looked over the barracks, hill and bay, windows without glass or shutters, some surprisingly placed in small cupboards, others letting the dust, sunlight, seeds of weeds, and the swallows into whitewashed landings. Upstairs they went through rooms with sloping roofs, skylights, whitewashed beams hung with old webs, and dusty floors on which their bare feet made tracks. They looked out through open doorways straight down three stories on to the backyard full of plantains and thistles. She led him into the stables, smelling of dung and damp, and held on to his hand with a soft persistence. A stair began in the comer of the stables, passed old plastered walls and withering landings, and ended at last in a garret. In the garret she said, 'Do you want to kiss me?' with indifferent naivety. He looked out at the light spring sky which a puff of smoke and a swallow crossed, and at the open door leading on to a silent landing and sunny attic. He kissed her carefully on her cheek, and they went on with their metallic clatter about the bay, school and personalities.

Rats came up from the waterfront and lived all over the house, with mice and all kinds of small things, bugs, snails, slugs. On a summer night the cockroaches scurried in and out of holes where the cracked asphalt footpath led into the stables' foundations. Michael pored over them full of languor and content for half an hour and more, kicking his heels and watching the officers going home to the barracks and the couples walking with their heads together; when they went past he sometimes hooted at them. Up the hill went the soldiers clinking their spurs. He stood at the corner one fine summer evening, the year he was ten, watched the eight o'clock ferry trail its golden lights out of the wharf, and studied the little creatures running about in their long-tailed suits. The dusk gathered and the street lamps yellowly came on. The cockroaches streaked out of their holes with a slow rustling, flittered round the lamp and dashed in through open windows at kerosene lamps burning in the old cottages; mosquitoes sang ...

The Municipal Library was in the Haymarket Building where the art-class was held. He went there almost every day with Withers, or other fellows, all voracious readers, most of whom had collected library tickets from friends and owned from ten to twenty tickets, instead of the regulation two. Michael did not read much. They entered the great barn of a building from the Town Hall end and passed all the closed shop-fronts where exotic societies, herbalists, mind-readers, jewellers and bootmakers lived, as it seemed, without clients, friends or visitors.

The Library appeared miles away at the other end. In the centre of the building are two large staircases, and a spiral staircase leading to the rooms occupied by the art-school. Just before they reached this staircase, they passed its bare yellow entrance with a bell inside and a small staircase covered with sacking against the inner wall ...

Baruch lived in a room on the fourth floor back, in a side street in Woolloomooloo Flat, not far from the old public school. His window commanded the Inner Domain, the Art Gallery, the spires of St Mary's Cathedral and the Elizabeth Street skyline. On the right hand, as he looked from his window, were the wharves of the German, Dutch, Norwegian and Cape lines. In the backyard was a wood-and-coal shed covered with creepers, pumpkins, old tires, kites'-tails, buckets and old scrubbing-brushes. There was a clothes-line across the yard, on a clothes-prop, and upon the line the tenants' garments, washed by the woman on the ground-floor, appeared in regular succession throughout the week. There were in the house a bachelor Government clerk and Government medical officer, a school-teacher with his wife and two children, a navvy, a bartender, a junior draughtsman in the Lands Department, and a widow with a young child. The house backing on to theirs was only three stories high. A cheap chop-suey restaurant occupied the ground-floor, its private assembly rooms the first floor, while the rooms above were for sleeping and for letting out. A couple of ladders reached from the windows of these upper floors to the roofs of lean-to sheds and outhouses. This house was usually very quiet, although lights appeared at the windows at all hours of the night. On Saturdays and Sundays the whole neighbourhood swarmed with children, and everybody was out of doors with sleeves rolled up. Tiny living-rooms with Japanese screens, fans and bead curtains, and reeking of bugs and kerosene, with bric-à-brac, vases, wilting flowers and countless rags and papers, sent out their heat and animal odours and old dust at seven in the evening when the hot day had gone down into the violet twilight, a deceitfully shady moment promising cool, but bringing in the torrid night. Everywhere couples lounged about, the waists encircled. the lips together; henna Titians, peroxide blondes, and uncoloured women faded beneath their hair still rich and young; women blowsy and painted, worn and tired, with crow's-feet and unequal powder, fanned their bursting bosoms or their empty sacks of blouses, as they slumped in rickety easy-chairs at their doors.

The doors opened directly into the sleeping and living-rooms and alone admitted air. Little boys argued outside the windows, shrieking and punching.

'My mother is not a whore.'

'She is. Why isn't she?'

'No, Willy's mother isn't; she always has the same blokes, and she has only three.'

'Yes, and I know who they are; a thin little bloke with freckles and ...'

'Shut up or I'll gi' y' a lift under the lug.'

The onlookers whooped during the set-to that followed ... The lamps were lighted. The dwellings on the borders of the hot asphalted pavement were holes in which moved dimly a world of heaving bosoms, gasping mouths, fanning arms. There were visible black-socked feet and bare feet in slippers, bare arms starting upwards from a bush of black hair at the armpit; locks 'straight as candles' hung wet and tangled, hairy men's breasts gaped in the vees of open workshirts. The oil-lamps or gas-jets lighted corsets and stockings carelessly thrown on beds, discoloured with sweat and dirt. The rancid breeze blew in from the wharves with the smell of weeds grown on the piles, beer from the saloons, rotten vegetables from the garbage-tins. There came the clanking of winches at ships' sides, and the fitful songs of men at the waterfront. The last cries of children came from the old streets by the Plunkett Street school or from the other side, where they were dashing up into the rank grass of the Domain to wrestle, smother their giggles, lie on their backs, tell inane tales, sing parodies of songs, and contemplate the high southern constellations through the sensuous summer evening ...

The house was still asleep, so he went up into the 'barracks', that is, into the military reserve. The frank aromatic smells of scrub, garden and sea reminded him of early days, forgotten in the middle years of life; he had a memory of soft dark hair falling half across a pale face, not easily recollected now, for he was so old, not the face of any one, he thought, but the blurred visions of years. When he was a child, at this hour, he would come out into the garden with a trowel to dig where the worm and slug tracks lay silver all over the ground from their night business, while sparrows hopped and jabbered in the oleanders. Or else he would go up into the barracks, pursue weed-grown passages, and look at the seagulls scouring the ribbed sea. Even now the early summer day was idle, simple and companionable, and made him feel a little boy for a few instants; but there was an older thought in its red shadows, and the restlessness of the coming heat stirred already in the small dry plants; the season was on the verge of husky maturity.

The blood-red sun rose through a thick veil which stretched some hundreds of feet above the horizon. The water, shining like oil and burnished metal and bearing oil traces from the ships at Garden Island, ran irregularly round the margin of the beach; the tide was midwaydown—in an hour it would be fit for fishing. No ships were in the harbour, the houses were shadowy, the water was a clouded mirror. Michael began to sweat, even on the hill where a faint breeze still moved. The city lay far off, folded in morning lavender. Presently the first tram ascended the hill by the Gap, there was a clatter in the cook's galley in the pilot-ship, the workmen came aboard the dredger; outside the heads sirens, bellowing like the royal bulls at the Easter Show, called the pilot. A fisherman with two dogs went wading along the beach, and Pegleg climbed down the steps and unlocked the boathouse. The chimneys began to smoke in hotel and kitchen leanto; the reveille, so fine and clear in the hill, woke the camp. All began their morning work. Michael looked at the still smokeless chimney of the Baguenaults and walked through the military reserve where the barbed wire fences are tangled and broken. He circumvented the hill full of ditches, grassy trenches and doors into the hill and came to Lady's Haull, where a fisherman stood on the bluff shouting below. In the bay three fishing-boats were driving in the salmon. Beyond the salmon was a ring of dolphins, the outside the shark which had rounded the salmon up, cleaving the water with dark fin, restlessly patrolled the bay. A warship entering the harbour straits saluted the port; the hills reverberated and the dolphins plunged ...

The fishing was good. Michael got up to go to his cousin's for his lines. He would not be able to fish for several days thereafter because a storm was clearly coming their way from far out on the Pacific. The tide hummed ominously round the coast; the wind blew regularly. He started to split cunjeboy and put the red and yellow meat in an old tin. His fingers were stained red; he washed them in the pool and saw the hungry anemones close on the juice and fragments. Dawdling over the pools feeding the anemones, he became too sleepy to go back for his lines. He retired under a big rock, boiled three or four crabs, and fried a fish given him by one of

the men, and fell asleep in the warm blowy noontide. When he awoke an
hour or two later the tide was surging through the mile-wide straits. It was
getting too rough to fish; he had missed the tide. A coalie putting in from
the south sank behind the waves in a frightening way and reappeared regularly, running in on the rollers.

'The storm will come to-night,' called one of the fishermen, passing him
on the way home.

'A coupla days, I should say, it will last,' said another.

'So long,' called Michael.

Christina Stead, *Seven Poor Men of Sydney* (first published 1934),
Sirius Books, Sydney, 1990.

Suzanne Falkiner

Suzanne Falkiner (1952–) is a writer of fiction and history. *Ethel* is the story
of her grandmother, Ethel Falkiner. The comments on the Prince are from
Mrs Barbara Street, who was interviewed for the book.

The Prince of Wales gets drunk

The first time I ever went out to dinner was that year, at Government
House—and you must remember it was just after the war, and we had led a
very austere life in the years before that. I had never gone anywhere. I
remember I was dressing for dinner and I asked my mother, 'What should I
do about wine?' And she told me, 'Well, look at your hostess. If she drinks
wine you may have some put in your glass.'

That first time at Government House Louis Mountbatten took me in to
dinner. I had been at the races, and an aide-de-camp came over and said,
'Lady Davidson would like you to come to dinner tonight.' I was very
excited. My father went with me in the tram, because everyone was going
and all the cars of people we knew were already full, but at the top of the
hill at Kings Cross he saw a taxi and jumped out of the tram and got it for
me. So I was the last to arrive, and I was paralysed with fright. I can remember the last thing my mother said to me was, 'Don't talk about the weather,
dear.' So that left me with nothing.

But in we went, and I had no difficulty at all—he was quite charming,
made all the conversation, asked me about my family, what we did … it
was just sheer pleasure. The Prince had been given a set of drums, and we
all danced after dinner. I only ever saw Mountbatten at parties, but he
always danced with me, and when he left he gave me a photograph of himself which he signed, as a memento.

It was a wild time, it really was. We were all at Dame Edith Walker's on
the Sunday evening—she had a beautiful house, Uralla [*sic*], in Concord,

with a marble hall and a curving staircase. The Prince got very tight that night. He got halfway up the stairs with some wine and poured it down on the heads of everybody down below. It was a disgraceful thing to do in someone else's house—I can remember how paralysed with horror I was, I've never forgotten it. The trouble was, I think, that he did not have an old enough guardian with him. You see, he had his twenty-sixth birthday out here, and Mountbatten was his offsider, his ADC. They thought at twenty-six he was old enough to behave himself as he should, but he didn't really. He was very naughty indeed.

Barbara Street quoted in Ethel (ed. Suzanne Falkiner),
Macmillan, Sydney, 1996.

Jack Lindsay

Jack Lindsay (1900–90), a writer and Marxist historian, left Sydney in 1926. His writing reflects the Virgin Mary/whore view of women of his father Norman Lindsay's paintings.

Annie, Betsy, and Bondi

In Wilmot Street, not far from the Central Police Courts in Liverpool Street, there was winebar run by an Italian named Amendola. Ray [Lindsay's brother] sums up our memories of this place. 'The bar was in the ground-floor front room, and in a back room just off it there was a dining-room where we used to lunch every Saturday afternoon. A group met regularly there and had formed themselves into a sort of club, portentously called *I Felici Literati*. In the chair was always Sam Rosa, a most repulsive-looking man, completely bald—although I believe that in his younger revolutionary days he had had flaming red hair, with brigand-like moustaches—with evil-grinning, flashing skull-like teeth. At that time he was editor of Sydney *Truth*. Others who used regularly to attend were Hugh Brayden, a charming, intelligent Irishman, then school-master, now retired; A.L. Kelly, then music critic of the *Triad*, an amusing chap with a rather ponderous sense of humour: George Goulding, a likeable fellow, then in the Public Service, fat and greying. There were other regulars who were mainly of a political turn of mind and did not interest me. Among the casual customers were George Finey, then *Smith's Weekly*'s most brilliant cartoonist, Mick Paul and various other journalists. The custom was, after spending most of the afternoon eating, drinking and talking at Amendola's, to adjourn to the Greek Club, then in Park Street, where one pulled oneself together with enormous draughts of rich Turkish coffee; and then, if one had still enough strength, to go to Campbell Street, then as now Sydney's Chinatown, and dine on

Long Soup and the Duck for which Percy [another Lindsay brother] had a rhyming but unprintable epithet.'

Amendola's, Ray says, will always remain in his mind as the place where he first saw 'that fabulous beautiful bitch Annie Brennan. I will never forget how, one Saturday afternoon, she came in drunk and danced among the bottles and glasses on the table. It was an old stunt of hers, but to my goggled still-adolescent eyes it was the most spectacular event I had ever seen. I whispered to Hugh Brayden, "Who is she?" "Annie Brennan," he said. "How beautiful," I sighed. "You should have seen her a couple of years ago," he replied, bored. I was horrified at such blasphemy. But that bitch. How she dominated all that crowd in those days. Leon Gellert was inspired to write *The Isle of San* by the thought of her downfall. Everybody was in love with her, even Gruner, although everybody knew what a slut she was. I always think it was a sad waste that her particular choice piece of feminine bitchery has never been immortalised in paint, so many artists were in love with her. But I do not know of any who would have had the ability to record her unique charms. He would have had to possess the bravura of an Augustus John, the sentimental sensitivity of a Greuze, and the bitch-insight of a Toulouse-Lautrec. But her beauty, vivid as it still is to me, was very subtle. Her small delicate features with the Germanic colouring inherited from her mother, her slow smile, the soft cadence of her voice, her grace of movement were all factors that went to disguise the Queen of All Bitches.

'At that time she had a flat in Victoria Street, on the other side of Kings Cross, not far from the Fire Station. I went back there with her that night after I first met her, and I sat there entranced, just gazing raptly upon her beauty, my bladder near bursting point with cheap wine, but too coy to ask where to go and ease it. I'll never forget my relief when I got outside against the wall of St John's Church. I used often to go to her flat in the mornings and sit there bemused and dumbfounded as I watched her dressing and titivating herself after a night's debauchery in expectation of another to come. But the idea of doing more than gaze never crossed my worshipping mind.' ...

But to return to Amendola's bar. The place was taken over by Betsy, a red-haired woman with a limp, who had been married to a very capable IWW speaker and organiser. The marriage broke up in 1920, and the husband, Rudolph, was said to have joined a circus and become an animal trainer. Betsy did not take over Amendola's licence but rechristened the house Café la Bohème, and it certainly became, as Ray says, a 'meeting place for all the madmen in town. It seems to me somewhat amusing, when one realises how close Betsy's was to the Police Station, that the dumb-headed police took so long in raiding her, with all the uproarious carousing that went on there day and night. The site has been absorbed into a hideous bastard Spanish-American architectural monstrosity of a picture show with entrance in George Street. How clearly I remember Betsy, limping and staggering up and down the stairs with her tubercular hip, her untidy, gingery curls dangling from under the lace of a grimy boudoir-cap, and her screeching, birdlike voice vibrating through the place—a voice that could dominate a room full of obstreperous drunks. Many a time have I seen a cantankerous boozer cower in a corner or slink from the room under its lashing. But she really was a very generous and kindly person, and many are the times when I and others have been grateful to her for a meal when we did not have a penny in our pockets. The quality of her cooking was very variable and her menus erratic.' ...

Betsy was abjectly afraid of thunder. She remarked, 'I get under the bed at once or whatever's handy. It makes my head crack.' But she didn't seem afraid of much else ...

Generally I went on Fridays to the *Bulletin* office to collect my mother's allowance for her. There I often met Henry Lawson, whom the *Bulletin* generously paid something every week for old times' sake. Infinitely mild and amiable, bent and showing signs of his nearing dissolution, he began an interminable conversation which continued next week from where it had last broken off. Unfortunately very little of what he said was intelligible. In his extreme deafness he seemed to have no sense of what was or wasn't audible. He smiled with gentle, warm, brown eyes and talked on, now and then exciting himself and gesticulating. Certainly among other things he described the problems he had in getting a drink, so well looked after was he by the capable-faced woman who soon emerged and kindly took him home. I gathered that he had many hiding-places for a bottle, but none good enough to deceive his benefactor for long. I gathered too that he was expressing some kind of goodwill ...

In the pub near the Press Club, a few minutes off closing time. All around the bar a heaving mass of men elbowing, pushing, trampling on each other's feet, and shouting their orders. Reaching over shoulders, waving pound-notes, dropping irretrievable coins. The one time when even the most pugnacious of Australians had no time to pick a quarrel, intent only on attracting the attention of those floating goddesses, the pink-bosomed pneumatic barmaids with sweat in their curly-haired armpits. The daily rush scene in every Sydney pub. And when the door was at last shut and bolted, the retreating beer-swipers would drop bottles at the tram junctions as they pushed and jumped on to the packed trams, or fell off them.

We retired with our drinks to a window-recess and leaned. No good Australians stand when they can lean. Up came Malcolm, a deadly metaphysical Scot, who had an inturned almost-blind look behind his thick glasses, especially when he remarked, standing square with feet wide apart and one arm behind back, raising and lowering his head sharply, 'Now what is your opinion of Kant's Concept of the Moral Law?'

Bondi was still undeveloped. Only in the last year of my stay did the first modest modern flats begin to rise. Opposite us were rambling sand dunes, which led up to the wild ground along the top of the cliffs, and, by thin tracks, to the Gap with its lighthouse and its barbed-wire efforts to deter suicides ... We bathed on the beach amid great billows, with the shark-watcher on the headland. Often in the early morning we saw several sharks hauled up, but we bathed, now and then startled by a flurry of underwater white that turned out to be only disturbed sand, with no sudden teeth. At times the beach was so hot that it stung, and the sturdy brown girls in their grooves of sand looked as if being cooked in some crystal oven of Venus. At times the summer-breeze came flowing, damp and sticky with seasalt out of the north-east of the Pacific vast, gently at its full in the late afternoon and fading with the rapid sunset.

More violent was the southerly buster. One afternoon I noted the violet-darkening sky rushing up over rooftops to the south. I hurried to close the bathroom window and could not have had more than a half-inch left to bring the window in when the wind struck. The whole pane was shattered in fragments in my face. This wind came on us with an express-crash, with doors banging, tiles flying, and trees bending flat on all sides. The rubbish-tin went clattering half a mile off.

Jack Lindsay, *The Roaring Twenties* (republished as *Life Rarely Tells: An Autobiography in Three Volumes*, Penguin, Melbourne, 1982).

D.H. Lawrence

D.H. Lawrence (1885–1930), English writer, arrived in Sydney with his wife Frieda in May 1922 and left by liner in early July. He spent most of his time on the South Coast writing *Kangaroo*.

The bathing suburb

Mr Somers and his wife got into the cab. The cabby left the doors flung wide open, and piled the three bags there like a tower in front of his two fares. The hat-box was on top, almost touching the brown hairs of the horse's tail, and perching gingerly.

'If you'll keep a hand on that, now, to steady it,' said the cabby.

'All right,' said Somers.

The man climbed to his perch, and the hansom and the extraneous tower began to joggle away into the town. The group of workmen were still lying on the grass. But Somers did not care about them. He was safely jogging with his detested baggage to his destination.

'Aren't they *vile!*' said Harriet, his wife.

'It's God's Own Country, as they always tell you,' said Somers. 'The hansom-man was quite nice.'

'But the taxi-drivers! And the man charged you eight shillings on Saturday for what would be two shillings in London!'

'He rooked me. But there you are, in a free country, it's the man who makes you pay who is free—free to charge you what he likes, and you're forced to pay it. That's what freedom amounts to. They're free to charge, and you are forced to pay.'

In which state of mind they jogged through the city, catching a glimpse from the top of a hill of the famous harbour spreading out with its many arms and legs. Or at least they saw one bay with warships and steamers lying between the houses and the wooded, bank-like shores, and they saw the centre of the harbour, and the opposite squat cliffs—the whole low wooded table-land reddened with suburbs and interrupted by the pale spaces of the many-lobed harbour. The sky had gone grey, and the low table-land into which the harbour intrudes squatted dark-looking and monotonous and sad, as if lost on the face of the earth: the same Australian atmosphere, even here within the area of huge, restless, modern Sydney, whose million inhabitants seem to slip like fishes from one side of the harbour to another.

Murdoch Street was an old sort of suburb, little squat bungalows with corrugated iron roofs, painted red. Each little bungalow was set in its own hand-breadth of ground, surrounded by a little wooden palisade fence. And there went the long street, like a child's drawing, the little square bungalows dot-dot-dot, close together and yet apart, like modern democracy, each one fenced round with a square rail fence. The street was wide, and strips of worn grass took the place of kerb-stones. The stretch of macadam in the middle seemed as forsaken as a desert, as the hansom clock-clocked along it ...

It was Sunday, and a lovely sunny day of Australian winter. Manly is the bathing suburb of Sydney—one of them. You pass quite close to the wide harbour gate, the Heads, on the ferry steamer. Then you land on the wharf, and walk up the street, like a bit of Margate with sea-side shops and restaurants, till you come out on a promenade at the end, and there is the wide Pacific rolling in on the yellow sand: the wide fierce sea, that makes all the built-over land dwindle into nonexistence. At least there was a heavy swell on, so the Pacific belied its name and crushed the earth with its rollers. Perhaps the heavy, earth-despising swell is part of its pacific nature.

Harriet, of course, was enraptured, and declared she could not be happy till she had lived beside the Pacific. They bought food and ate it by the sea. Then Harriet was chilled, so they went to a restaurant for a cup of soup. When they were again in the street Harriet realized that she hadn't got her yellow scarf: her big, silky yellow scarf that was so warm and lovely. She declared she had left it in the eating-house, and they went back at once for it. The girls in the eating-house—the waitresses—said in their cheeky Cockney Australian that they 'hedn't seen it', and that the 'next people who kyme arfter must 'ev tyken it'.

Anyhow, it was gone—and Harriet furious, feeling as if there had been a thief in the night. In this unhappy state of affairs Somers suggested they should sit on the tram-car and go somewhere. They sat on the tram-car and ran for miles along a coast with ragged bush loused over with thousands of small promiscuous bungalows, built of everything from patchwork of kerosene tin up to fine red brick and stucco, like Margate. Not far off the Pacific boomed. But fifty yards inland started these bits of swamp, and endless promiscuity of 'cottages'.

The tram took them five or six miles, to the terminus. This was the end of everywhere, with new 'stores'—that is, flyblown shops with corrugated iron roofs—and with a tram-shelter, and little house-agents' booths plastered with signs—and more 'cottages'; that is, bungalows of corrugated iron or brick—and bits of swamp or 'lagoon' where the sea had got in and couldn't get out. The happy couple had a drink of sticky aerated waters in one of the 'stores', then walked up a wide sand-road dotted on either side with small bungalows, beyond the backs of which lay a whole aura of rusty tin cans chucked over the back fence. They came to the ridge of sand, and again the pure, long-rolling Pacific.

'I love the sea,' said Harriet.

'I wish,' said Lovat, 'it would send a wave about fifty feet high round the whole coast of Australia.' ...

... The ship sailed at ten. The sky was all sun, the boat reared her green paint and red funnel to the sun. Down below in the dark shadow of the wharf stood all those who were to be left behind, saying good-bye, standing down in the shadow under the ship and the wharf, their faces turned up to the passengers who hung over the rail. A whole crowd of people down on the wharf, with white uplifted faces, and one little group of quiet Chinese.

Everybody had bought streamers, rolls of coloured paper ribbon, and now the passengers leaning over the rail of the lower and middle decks tossed the unwinding rolls to their friends below. So this was the last tie, this ribbon of coloured paper. Somers had a yellow and a red one: Victoria held the end of the red streamer, Jaz's wife the end of the yellow. Harriet had blue and green streamers. And from the side of the ship a whole glittering tangle of these colours connecting the departing with the remaining, a criss-cross of brilliant colour that seemed to glitter like a rainbow in the beams of the sun, as it rose higher, shining in between the ship and the wharf shed, touching the faces of the many people below.

The gangway was hoisted—the steamer gave long hoots. Only the crisscrossing web of brilliant streamers went from the hands of the departing to the hands of those who would be left behind. There was a sort of silence: the calling seemed to die out. And already before the cables were cast loose, the gulf seemed to come. Richard held fast to the two streamers, and looked down at the faces of the two women, who held the other ends of his paper threads. He felt a deep pang in his heart, leaving Australia, that strange country that a man might love so hopelessly. He felt another heartstring going to break like the streamers, leaving Australia, leaving his own British connexion. The darkness that comes over the heart at the moment of departure darkens the eyes too, and the last scene is remote, remote, detached inside a darkness.

So now, when the cables were cast loose, and the ship slowly left the side of the wharf and drew gradually towards the easier waters of the harbour, there was a little gulf of water between the ship and the wharf. The streamers lengthened out, they glittered and twinkled across the space almost like music, so many-coloured. And then the engines were going, and the crowd on the wooden quay began to follow slowly, slowly, holding the frail streamers carefully, like the ends of a cloud, following slowly down the quay as the ship melted from shadow to the sun beyond.

One by one the streamers broke and fluttered loose and fell bright and dead on the water. The slow crowd, slow as a funeral, was at the end, the far end of the quay, holding the last streamers. But the ship inexorably drifted out, and every coloured strip was broken: the crowd stood alone at the end of the wharf, the side of the vessel was fluttering with bright, broken ends.

So, it was time to take out handkerchiefs and wave across space. Few people wept. Somers waved and waved his orange silk kerchief in the blue air. Farewell! Farewell! Farewell Victoria and Jaz's wife, farewell Australia, farewell Britain and the great Empire. Farewell! Farewell! The last streamers blowing away, like broken attachments, broken heartstrings. The crowd on the wharf gone tiny in the sun, and melting away as the ship turned.

Richard watched the Observatory go by: then the Circular Quay, with all its ferry-wharves, and a Nippon steamer lying at her berth, and a well-known, big buff and black P. and O. boat at the P. and O. wharf, looking so like India. Then that was gone too, and the Governor's Palace, and the castellated Conservatorium of Music on its hill, where Richard had first seen Jack—the Palace Gardens, and the blue inlet where the Australian 'Fleet' lay comfortably rusting. Then they drifted across harbour, nearer to the wild-seeming slope, like bush, where the Zoo is. And then they began to wait, to hang around.

There ahead was the open gate of the harbour, the low heads with the South lighthouse, and the Pacific beyond, breaking white. On the left was Manly, where Harriet had lost her yellow scarf. And then the tram going to Narrabeen, where they had first seen Jaz. Behind was the great lobed harbour, so blue, and Sydney rather inconspicuous on the south hills, with its one or two skyscrapers. And already, the blue water all round, and a thing of the past.

> D.H. Lawrence, *Kangaroo* (first published 1922), Penguin,
> Melbourne, 1976.

Kenneth Slessor

Kenneth Slessor (1901–71), poet and journalist, wrote *Five Bells*, the classic poem of the harbour, after a friend of his, who was on his way by ferry to a party, fell or jumped into the harbour and drowned.

Five bells

Time that is moved by little fidget wheels
Is not my Time, the flood that does not flow.
Between the double and the single bell
Of a ship's hour, between a round of bells
From the dark warship riding there below,
I have lived many lives, and this one life
Of Joe, long dead, who lives between five bells.

Deep and dissolving verticals of light
Ferry the falls of moonshine down. Five bells
Coldly rung out in a machine's voice. Night and water
Pour to one rip of darkness, the Harbour floats
In air, the Cross hangs upside-down in water.

Why do I think of you, dead man, why thieve
Those profitless lodgings from the flukes of thought
Anchored in Time? You have gone from earth,
Gone even from the meaning of a name;
Yet something's there, yet something forms its lips
And hits and cries against the ports of space,
Beating their sides to make its fury heard.

Are you shouting at me, dead man, squeezing your face
In agonies of speech on speechless panes?
Cry louder, beat the windows, bawl your name!

But I hear nothing, nothing ... only bells,
Five bells, the bumpkin calculus of Time.
Your echoes die, your voice is dowsed by Life,
There's not a mouth can fly the pygmy strait—
Nothing except the memory of some bones
Long shoved away, and sucked away, in mud;
And unimportant things you might have done,
Or once I thought you did; but you forgot,
And all have now forgotten—looks and words
And slops of beer; your coat with buttons off,
Your gaunt chin and pricked eye, and raging tales
Of Irish kings and English perfidy,
And dirtier perfidy of publicans
Groaning to God from Darlinghurst.

Five bells.

Then I saw the road, I heard the thunder
Tumble, and felt the talons of the rain
The night we came to Moorebank in slab-dark,
So dark you bore no body, had no face,
But a sheer voice that rattled out of air
(As now you'd cry if I could break the glass),
A voice that spoke beside me in the bush,
Loud for a breath or bitten off by wind,
Of Milton, melons, and the Rights of Man,
And blowing flutes, and how Tahitian girls
Are brown and angry-tongued, and Sydney Girls
Are white and angry-tongued, or so you'd found.
But all I heard was words that didn't join
So Milton became melons, melons girls,

And fifty mouths, it seemed, were out that night,
And in each tree an Ear was bending down,
Or something had just run, gone behind grass,
When, blank and bone-white, like a maniac's thought,
The naphtha-flash of lightning slit the sky,
Knifing the dark with deathly photographs.
There's not so many with so poor a purse
Or fierce a need, must fare by night like that,
Five miles in darkness on a country track,
But when you do, that's what you think.

Five bells.

In Melbourne, your appetite had gone,
Your angers too; they had been leeched away
By the soft archery of summer rains
And the sponge-paws of wetness, the slow damp
That sucks the leaves of living, snailed the mind,
And showed your bones, that had been sharp with rage,
The sodden ecstasies of rectitude.
I thought of what you'd written in faint ink,
Your journal with the sawn-off lock, that stayed behind
With other things you left, all without use,
All without meaning now, except a sign
That someone had been living who now was dead:
'At Labassa. Room 6 × 8
On top of the tower; because of this, very dark
And cold in winter. Everything has been stowed
Into this room—500 books all shapes
And colours, dealt across the floor
And over sills and on the laps of chairs;
Guns, photoes of many different things
And different curioes that I obtained ...'

In Sydney, by the spent aquarium-flare
Of penny gaslight on pink wallpaper,
We argued about blowing up the world,
But you were living backward, so each night
You crept a moment closer the breast,
And they were living, all of them, those frames
And shapes of flesh that had perplexed your youth,
And most your father, the old man gone blind,
With fingers around a fiddle's neck,

That graveyard mason whose fair monuments
And tablets cut with dreams of piety
Rest of the bosoms of a thousand men
Staked bone by bone, in quiet astonishment
At cargoes they had never thought to bear,
These funeral-cakes of sweet and sculptured stone.

Where have you gone? The tide is over you,
The turn of midnight water's over you,
As Time is over you, and mystery,
And memory, the flood that does not flow.
You have no suburb, like those easier dead
In private berths of dissolution laid—
The tide goes over, the waves ride over you
And let their shadows down like shining hair,
But they are Water; and sea-pinks bend
Like lilies in your teeth, but they are Weed;
And you are only part of an Idea.
I felt the wet push its black thumb-balls in,
The night you died, I felt your eardrums crack,
And the short agony, the longer dream,
The Nothing that was neither long nor short;
But I was bound, and could not go that way,
But I was blind, and could not feel your hand.
If I could find an answer, could only find
Your meaning, or could say why you were here
Who now are gone, what purpose gave you breath
Or seized it back, might I not hear your voice?

I looked out of my window in the dark
At waves with diamond quills and combs of light
That arched their mackerel-backs and smacked the sand
In the moon's drench, that straight enormous glaze,
And ships far off asleep, and Harbour-buoys
Tossing their fireballs wearily each to each,
And tried to hear your voice, but all I heard
Was a boat's whistle, and the scraping squeal
Of seabirds' voices far away, and bells,
Five bells. Five bells coldly ringing out.

Five bells.

Kenneth Slessor, 'Five bells', in *Collected Poems*, Sirius Books, Sydney, 1964.

John Kingsmill

John Kingsmill (1920–) grew up in Bondi between the two world wars.

The gab was a family investment

In the 1920s and '30s, when winter came, everybody wore an overcoat. If you were seen going into town without an overcoat in June, July or August, it was assumed you didn't own one. It didn't matter if the day happened to be freakishly warm in mid-winter, you wore your overcoat or, if absolutely necessary, carried it folded neatly over your arm. Just as long as you had it with you, for the world to see. In common with most men's wear of any quality, the great woollen overcoat came from Britain and was made for Manchester winters. In overcoats of good thick wool thin men looked stout and stout men looked enormous. The effect was heightened, if anything, by the addition of a 'self-belt' placed at precisely that point where the stomach is at its peak. A few dashing fellows, invariably tall and thin, would scorn the belt buckle and tie the ends of the belt in a knot. They were automatically classified as 'Flash Harrys', *flash* being a word that encompassed skites and show-offs as well as any man in a brand-new suit: 'You're looking flash today!'

There were regional and some ethnic differences to be observed in Sydney when it came to the question of the overcoat. On the south side of the harbour, the woollen overcoat was to be seen in considerable variety, from heathery tweed to loud check to sober greys and navy blues, with the odd one in rich brown, nothing too showy, that was understood. It was easy to tell the newly arrived refugees from Hitler's Germany. Their overcoats were far longer than ours. They were always of leather, as were their precious, battered briefcases, gripped tightly under the arm or fiercely by the handle. As these refugees became more numerous and more obvious (because of their leather coats and briefcases and strange, pale faces), there were those chauvinist Australians who saw the coats and briefcases as some sort of provocation, and they would wait for a refugee to be heard speaking in his native tongue and tell him to 'speak bloody English'. The leather coats and briefcases slowly rotted away or were replaced by something more likely to mollify the chauvinists and act as camouflage—a tweed overcoat would do nicely, or, if the refugee had moved to the north side of the harbour, a gabardine.

Every right-minded North Shore man wore his gab. It was of a colour by no means certain. It wasn't quite grey and it wasn't quite brown. It was the colour of a muddy river. The gab was a family investment, like the lawn-mower, the ice chest, the wireless, like carpet in the lounge room. That was its attraction to those thrifty, long-sighted northerners (so different from us southerners, reckless wasters all). It kept a man reasonably warm and it was as impervious to rain as a duck's back, which is more than you could say for tweed. The gab was timeless—it always looked old, from the day it was bought. It would pass from grandfather to son and on to grandson without looking out of fashion, for it had no more to do with fashion than an umbrella does. The idea was to buy the gab a size miles too big for the original owner, in case the family produced (from *her* side) a male who grew uncharacteristically up or out or both. The garment flapped about like an unguyed tent unless reefed in by its self-belt with its multi-stitching and big leather buckle. It may well be supposed that some North Shore people only went on breeding because the family gab would do twenty years more, the way it was going. Waste not, want not …

Sydney streets have always been able to rustle up a capricious high wind out of nothing and any man could find himself suddenly, agonisingly, unhatted. That is, undressed. People instinctively understood his feelings as he chased the rolling, bowling, stopping-and-starting runaway hat. Helpful feet would stamp at it, trying to trap it like a soccerball. Cars would do their level best (given the rules about dogs and cats which have no right to be on the carriageway) not to run over it. Little knots of people with not enough to do would stand and wait to see how it would end. The small drama would play itself out. The thing would be caught, dusted off on its owner's sleeve and put back where it belonged, no longer band-box smart, but on, thank God, *on*! The man was decently whole again.

One of the best things about a man's having a hat on was the chance he had to take it off, to raise his hat to a lady he knew, or even if he didn't know her at all but would like to. A little harmless gallantry like this could lead to all sorts of things beyond the cool bow in reply. Men also raised their hats to each other on meeting and parting in the street, but this seemed to be a mark of the upper class. Men took their hats off in lifts and held them against their chests, like people at a wreath-laying ceremony. It got so cramped in some small lifts in big buildings that signs began to appear (an American idea): 'Gentlemen are requested not to remove their hats, in the interests of comfort'. Some crusty old gentlemen ignored this, seeing in it the seeds of revolution, anarchy, or just plain bad manners. They were right. The rot had set in. The meaning of the hat, its function and reason-for-being was under question. But its end was still too far off even to imagine.

There were, in fact, some subtle variations to be played on the theme of the man's hat. These were decided at the point of sale. The hat salesman would have observed the style of the hat about to be replaced and, unless expressly instructed to make a change, would mould the new hat in precisely that style. It might be no more than a simple dent along the crown. It might be that dent plus two pinched dents in front, like dimples. It might even be the flashy new pork-pie look, copied from the style preferred by country men, achieved by lowering the crown with a whirling motion of an expert finger to make a perfectly flat round top. Whatever the style, it was made more or less permanent by being subjected to a blast of steam from a machine which stood in every hat department. That done, the hat would be presented with a flourish to the customer, who had to decide then and there whether to wear it out of the shop or carry it home in a bag. Pessimists would prefer the bag, 'just my luck' they'd say, if the thing blew off five minutes later or they somehow got a spot on it (especially if it was in the fashionable pearl grey, which showed every speck of dirt).

Spots on a man's hat were, again, a sign for the observant. They first appeared at those two front dimples, where a man would grasp his hat to 'lift' it to a lady, unless he was given to the less-respectful tweaking of the hat brim, not lifting it off at all. In that case, the brim took on, eventually, a slightly darker hue than the rest of the hat. Every man who went in for brilliantined hair found himself, after a year or so, with a slowly rising tide of grease marching up the sides of his felt hat, having beaten the barrier of the leather insert band. To counter this, some hats at a slightly higher price had a greaseproof lining. You couldn't be too careful about this—a grubby, greasy hat was the sure sign of a man without money.

> John Kingsmill, *Australia Street: A Boy's-eye View of the 1920s and 1930s*, Hale & Iremonger, Sydney, 1991.

Margaret Molloy

Yachting had been the preserve of the better off until the foundation of the Sydney Flying Squadron in 1890 to run races for 18-footers, a relatively inexpensive craft developed by Sydney boat builders. Crews were working men, often rugby league footballers keeping fit out of season.

I never lifted me head

[George Grant:] 'I wouldn't know what course we sailed because I was just sitting in the bottom of the boat bailing. I never lifted me head; there'd be the sheet hand, the forward hand, the bloke on the helm, assistant sheet hand and ten others. Five would sit on each side and when they went about, the other five would sit on their laps. They used to tell me that if I didn't get me back wet I'd never get back in a boat. If you went over, you just lay in the sails till you got picked up. We all wore football guernseys and had bare feet—anyway, I was glad their feet were bare because they trod all over me! I was too excited to be hurt or scared, I just loved it. But I wasn't good enough so I never got past bailer boy.'

[Ken Beashel:] 'I was bailer boy for Lennie Heffernan, Horrie Balkwell, Alf Beashel and on a few occasions for Billy Barnett. I was bailer boy on 16s on Saturday afternoons, on 12-foot skiffs on Sunday mornings and on 18-footers on Sunday afternoons. I reckon I turned Sydney Harbour over from the time I was ten till I was thirteen, more than anybody else had ever seen water ...

'I first sailed in Lavender Bay where I learned to swim. At the little old *Aussie* boatshed they kept a couple of 18-footers. The crew would arrive on Saturday mornings and put all their quart bottles of beer down a little hatch in the floor, in the tide, to keep them cool. No drinking was allowed before the race. They would sit around and lace all three sets of sails on the spars. The door was left ajar—if it banged hard, they put 3rd rig on, if it didn't bang at all they used the big sail and if it was just swinging they put on the intermediate rig. If they were in doubt, they put the whole lot in the boat and sailed to Bradleys [Head]. If it was a championship, they would put it all on the beach, and it took four or five blokes to lift the gear, but there was a great atmosphere and a lot of jokes were told while they were rigging up. In those days there were fifteen or sixteen blokes, plus hangers on, plus the blokes who wanted to get a tip if you were going to win, so you might have thirty people around a boat.'

Margaret Molloy, *A Century of Sydney's Flying Sailors*, Sydney Flying
Squadron, Sydney, 1991.

Nancy Phelan

Nancy Phelan (1913–) is a novelist and travel writer. *A Kingdom by the Sea* is an account of her childhood in Sydney. In this extract she tells of a visit to relatives at Hunters Hill.

Something dangerous and slimy

To go there was thrilling, even the journey. You took a ferry from Circular Quay, then changed at Valentia Street to a very small boat for Tarban Creek. The service here was so informal that our cousin Charlie and his friends were allowed to steer and the passengers were often navigated up the stream by boys in Sydney Grammar boaters.

Leaving Valentia Street you entered another world. Pale stone houses, grey slate roofs showed among trees; gardens, lawns sloped down to the Creek. The tranquil afternoon light on that secluded backwater did not belong to the Sydney we knew, to our open-air life at home. There was a different smell in the air, of ancient trees and flowering shrubs, of grey stone sunwarmed walls, old gardens and moss and wistaria, the scent, the mellow richness of slow summer evenings in Cornwall, on the quiet creeks of the Helford river.

The Warren stood on the banks of Tarban Creek and its grounds went down to the water. Secluded umbrageous stone steps descended to a boat-shed and swimming-baths. After our crystalline beach and rock pools these baths were rather frightening, dark and sinister, undisturbed by tides. There was the sense of something dangerous and slimy in the obscure depths; you dived in with panic and got out as fast as possible, yet with far more excitement than on our wholesome beach. The boatshed was shadowy and secretive in a disquietening way; it hinted of forbidden doings and had a damp, rather sour marine smell.

To reach *The Warren* by land you drove over Fig Tree Bridge and down a dead-end called Wandella Avenue. Inside the gates—always open—was a tall pine-tree and nearby, among the jasmine and oleander, an ancient two-seater lavatory, an agreeable setting for conversation. There was a circular lawn, an immense magnolia, Moreton Bay figs and Kitty's camellias; then the house itself, an architectural melange, hung round with creepers.

From the circular lawn you could see the original convict-built house, low and simple, like *Brownlow Hill*, with flagged verandas, slim columns and shutters; but the slate roof had been raised for upstairs bedrooms, with dormers and mullions and balconies never envisaged by the first architect. A porch with tiled floor and scented vines faced the drive; there were long screened verandas, a servants' back-stairs, window-seats, all wrong for the classic simplicity of the old colonial building. They made an exotic jumble to the eye and mind of child; so did the the furnishings—a mixture of elegant antiques, striped wall-papers, portraits of ancestors, new utilitarian objects, bed-room walls with rose-covered trellis, fox masks, stag horns, and a grand-father clock in the hall ...

The Warren has gone, but the pine-tree still stands, old, ragged, upright, like a thin battered colonel. All the landscape has changed, it is hard to find your way. You enter Wandella Avenue from an unfamiliar angle and cannot remember these up-to-date, complacent villas with car-ports and venetians and dabs of iron lace.

By a new double-garage, gate-posts lean in a fragment of stone wall; beyond, rough overgrown lands leads to the water. The gates of *The Warren* were always open, but in welcome. This is mere absence of gates.

I walk in, as though trespassing, searching for landmarks. Behind the ragged pine the faint outline of the circular lawn still endures, with tattered magnolia and Moreton Bays ...

But where is the house? Not a trace remains. Nothing. It is hard to visu-alise where it stood. This is a desert, scarred and abandoned; yet as I go on, compulsively, the path grows familar.

Suddenly, among the weeds, my feet are on the old stone steps down to the boathouse, the sinister baths. It is all fresh again ... the breath-held excitement of plunging into the dark tideless water, the shadowy boathouse. Near the baths, now full of slime, are two aloes, hacked about, on the stone embankment where you dried yourself. I remember them; and the twisted roots of the Moreton Bays, the caves and rocks, now scarred by blasting ...

I look for Kitty's garden, her wistaria, her crumbling old blue-washed wall with the arched doorway and sunflowers and banana leaves, through which she would appear at dawn, with secateurs and cigarette hanging and dark amused eyes. A fresh hard breeze from the west blows down the upper reaches of Tarban Creek and the sky shines with a ruthless blue glitter. It is a harsh beautiful day without poetry. All round, on *The Warren's* subdivided land, new split-level, architect-designed Contemporary Homes have survived, sensible, sanitary, sane. They flourish discreetly, in excellent taste, round this elegy where I stand.

Nancy Phelan, *A Kingdom by the Sea*, Angus & Robertson,
Sydney, 1969.

Sid Barnes

Sid Barnes (1916–73) was an international cricketer, who was not always deferential to discipline.

A rent collector at seven

I was given an important job when I was seven. Ma would make out the rent receipts and off I would go to collect the rent.

I would walk along the edge of the Leichhardt stormwater channel. This channel took rainwater off the street and in bad weather the channel ran at a terrific pace. All mothers warned their children against this channel and, in its time, it claimed many a victim. But, childlike, we ignored all the warnings.

Little tributaries ran off the main channel. They were closed in and used to run under the houses and factories. Picking a fine day, we would proceed with torches and candles along these side-channels and would walk for a mile or so along them, finding spiders, frogs, lizards and the like.

Fat boys were taboo. They were never allowed in as some of the pipes, at their beginning, might not be more than two feet across. We had many a tight squeeze and it was always a thrill to push up a manhole, come out in the street and find where we were, and then walk home.

We used to chalk arrows on the walls in these excursions to guide us back. If one went up a narrow pipe, he would take a ball of string and jerk it if in trouble. Luckily, nobody got into serious trouble. I don't know what we would have done if they had. Then, too, we would find old cricket and tennis balls, dead ducks and fowls in those pipes. They were a world of delight to us little chaps, and my mind vividly returned to those days when I saw Harry Lime in the 'Third Man,' with all their activities in the Berlin sewers.

Ma used to object pretty strenuously to my taking a short cut for the rent across the stormwater channel. I was only a little chap and sometimes I would have a lot of money on the way back. I hope she was most concerned about me, not the rent-money; but I was like Bill Ferguson, the famous scorer and baggageman, he never lost a bag; I never lost any of Ma's quids.

They were hard times—the beginning of the depression. Ma was a generous soul. She had had her money worries and knew that some of her tenants were feeling the pinch. She was no female Shylock. 'Do your best, Sid. Just get what you can', she used to say to me as I set out.

She had married again by this time and my stepfather and two elder brothers had given up the job of rent-collecting. They couldn't do much good but I got results and I stayed on the job.

Sid Barnes, *It Isn't Cricket*, Collins, Sydney, 1953.

Sumner Locke Elliott

Sumner Locke Elliott (1917–91) worked as an actor and writer for radio after he left school. He lived overseas from 1948 after his play *Rusty Bugles* was for a time banned for bad language.

Would the bridge hold?

The Coleses got up at a quarter to four in the morning so that they might be among the first people to cross the Bridge when the ribbon was cut. But they found that thousands had spent the night sleeping and camping out along the approaches so that by the time they arrived in the beginnings of the first light of day the whole population of Sydney seemed to have collected in the shadows of the pylons. Oh well, never mind, Mrs Coles said, at least we're here and, Nance, you'll be able to tell your grandchildren. But I wonder just the same, she said looking up at the immensity of the steel, if it's safe. Safe? Oh, they laughed at her. Well, all this mob crossing at once, would the Bridge hold? Don't be a galoot, Edna, Mr Coles said. Hadn't they lined up a fleet of obsolete train engines end to end for months to test the strain of the arch? Anyway, Mrs Coles said, it's my opinion they ought to have limited how many could come the first day, they should have had a lottery so the whole world and his wife couldn't have got here before *us*.

Never mind, the day was dawning. The first hooters started from the ferry boats below, the sun was coming and as it did there was a concerted breath from the thousands of mouths in the faces looking up. For years they'd seen it from below on the ferries but to be up *on* it, the stone pylons as high as a New York skyscraper and rising from the pylons the immense arch, the longest single-span arch in the world, not just Australia, not just the Southern Hemisphere but the *world*, mind you, Mrs Coles said. At the peak of the arch, one thousand six hundred and fifty feet long, where the girders, wide enough for two cars to pass, met the sky, the Southern Cross and the Union Jack fluttered.

If something could buckle this mighty, beautiful thing so that it would not stand for a thousand years, it could have been the shout from all those throats letting go when the sun caught the first glittering girders against the sky; the noise shook the air (as the first planes swooped overhead in formation) all the way down the harbour to North Head. At last there was something to cheer about in this year of misery, 1932.

Hours later they were still cheering when the loud-speaker announced that the Premier of New South Wales was arriving, the Honourable J. T. Lang was arriving to cut the ribbon. The motorcade roared by. Silver and brass and gleaming leather precipitated the anticlimax of Mr Lang in his walrus moustache, in his diacritical bowler hat. *Him*, in a limousine, Mr Coles said, I'm Labour to the backbone, but Lang, a bloody Bolshie, trying to close the banks only a year ago and bring in Socialism, even the unions don't like the bugger, riding in a limousine, it's a disgrace him having the honour to open the bridge, Mr Coles said and spat.

But the Coleses were too far back to see what happened, could only hear the startled cries, the dramatic interruption to Mr Lang's droning voice, the man shouting, 'I open this bridge in the name of his Majesty the King and all decent people.'

They never saw the cavalryman race forward, the sabre flashing, the ribbon cut, the horse gallop across the Bridge to the crowd's wild cheering. Pushing over the barricades, the entire mob started across the Bridge in the wake of the horseman.

Late in the afternoon, young Nance Coles wrote to her friend Beryl in Wollongong all the way down the South Coast.

> ... anyway, enough of my attempts to describe. Words fail to express the magnificence of it, you and Brian will have to come up and see for yourself. Sufficient to say one of the wonders of the world and we now have it all over those Melbourne snoots whom look down on their noses at us Sydneyites. The most dramatic thing was, at the last moment a Captain of the Light Cavalry rode forward and cut the ribbon with his sword so that Mr Lang got cheated out of it and everyone cheered like Billy-oh. Of course they stuck the ribbon together again but that was like locking the stable door. Tonight I'm going with my second cousin Don (Brandywine) to a posh party in Point Piper to see the fireworks display. Of course I am not too keen on him as you know but I wouldn't pass up a chance to see these Mazzinis' house which is said to be an exquissite home and have a squiz at the fireworks so I'll have to cut this short, Ber as I must dash to iron my pink georgette and silverfrost my evening shoes. Hoo-roo, love.
>
> Nance.

Sumner Locke Elliott, *Water Under the Bridge*,
Picador, Sydney, 1997.

Lennie Lower

Lennie Lower (1903–47) was working for the *Labor Daily* when he wrote his novel *Here's Luck*. Later he went as a columnist to the *Women's Weekly*, from which he was sacked by the proprietor, Frank Packer, for being rude to Noel Coward.

The earnestly genteel

Chatswood is one of those places that are a stone's throw from some other place, and is mainly given over to the earnestly genteel. Here, respectability stalks abroad adorned with starched linen and surrounded by mortgages. The clatter of lawn-mowers can be heard for miles on any sunny Saturday. Sunday evenings, the stillness of death descends on the place, but if one listens very attentively one may hear the scraping of hundreds of chewed pens as they travel the weary road of principal and interest and pay-off-as-rent.

Agatha's mother's home tucked its lawns about its feet and withdrew somewhat from the regular line of houses in the street. It had been paid for. My mother-in-law's chief occupations were writing letters of complaint to the municipal council, and calling upon God to look at our so-called democratic government and blight it. She also laid a few baits for the neighbours' dogs, kept a strict eye on the morals of the whole street, and lopped off any branch, twig or tendril which thrust itself from the next-door garden over the fence and so trespassed on her property. What spare time she had left was used up by various communings with God about the water-rates, and the only really light work she indulged in was when she seated herself behind the window-curtain 'and watched for small boys who might be tempted to rattle sticks along the front fence, Altogether, she was a busy woman. And then, of course, there was the parrot. The parrot was also an opponent of governments, cursed the municipal council, squawked miserably over the water-rates and was withal highly religious. Whether this spiritless subservience to local opinion was due to force of example or merely a desire for a quiet life, I do not know. In this description of my mother-in-law's mode of life I think I have written with a certain amount of tolerant restraint. She is an old lady and the age of chivalry is not dead while a Gudgeon lives. Perhaps a different son-in-law might have described her as a senseless, whining, nagging, leather-faced old whitlow not fit to cohabit with a rhinoceros beetle. But I wouldn't.

Arriving at the house, I paused. The lawn needed mowing. I crossed the road and stood regarding the place. That the grass of the front lawn needed mowing may seem a very little thing and not sufficient to make anyone pause, but I had bitter memories of my infrequent visits to this place in my earlier days. I would enter and be given a cup of tea, then—'Ha! Now we have a man in the house.'

In other words: 'Ha! Here is a work-beast. Let him paint the tool-shed; let him mend the wheelbarrow; bring out the hedge-clippers and the lawn-mower and point out to him the location of the axe and the woodheap.'

That, of course, would be when I was comparatively welcome.

And now?

As I gazed across at the place, a window-curtain quivered. I had been seen. I could not now retreat with dignity so I crossed the road, took a deep breath, and knocked at the door. Wiping my feet industriously on the mat, I waited. I could imagine the scurryings and the whisperings that were going on inside. I knocked again. I had expected this sort of thing, and after waiting a few moments longer I turned and made for the gate as though about to leave. The strategy was successful. The door opened a few inches and the hideous beak of my mother-in-law protruded from the gap.

'Well,' she snapped, 'what do you want?'

I doffed my bowler.

'I've come to see my wife.'

'You've come to see your wife, have you?'

Lennie Lower, *Here's Luck*, Angus & Robertson, Sydney, 1938.

Sumner Locke Elliott

Sumner Locke Elliott (1917–91) wrote *Radio Days*, a collection of stories about Australian radio in the 1930s and 1940s.

The man with 1000 voices

All those diamonds at ten o'clock in the morning.

Two on each third finger, blue and white on one hand and greenish and yellow sunburst on the other. A solid diamond wristwatch with diamond strap and a face so small as to be virtually useless and a heavy diamond brooch with a little chain safety device. The young woman also wore a wedding ring of diamonds flanked by one of sapphires and one of rubies. She was in her late twenties and she was dressed in rich glossy black satin which came fashion-ably then to the middle of her calf, and she wore a wide brimmed black velvet hat with a rhinestone pin in it and a great deal of mascara and lipstick. Her hair was a very bright henna red and it had been artificially formed into hard waves and curled into innumerable little anchovies around her oval face. To a more discerning eye the young woman might have looked like a barmaid who had won the Irish sweepstakes or else had got herself up for the role of a hussy in some thirties movie, but I was thirteen and she appeared to me to be the most glamorous object I had ever laid eyes and she was the nearest I had ever come to being in the presence of fame. She was Nell Stirling the radio star and I was being auditioned by her among seven other pimply-faced boys for the role of the dying young Tsarovitch in *Ivan the Terrible*.

Every Sunday evening at eight, several million Australians from Sydney to Perth clustered around their imitation oak radios (the well-to-do had what was known as a console but there were few well-to-do in 1934) to hear a whiz-bang followed by a drum beat and the announcement: 'THE STARSHELL HAS BURST, BRINGING YOU GEORGE EDWARDS, THE MAN WITH THE THOUSAND VOICES, AND NELL STIRLING', followed by the theme music of the Valkyries. The play was wild melodrama, sometimes sexily rearranged history, the bloodier of the Biblical stories, tampered-with classics; anything in the public domain. What the play *was* made very little difference. What the audience was waiting for and had been making bets on was the unique announcement of the players at the end. In a voice choking with carefully simulated incredulity the announcer would say: 'You have been listening to the George Edwards production of Charles Dickens' *Great Expectations* and the cast was as follows: Miss Havisham was played by Miss Loris Bingham, Pip as a boy was played by Master Spencer Teale and Estella by Miss NELL STIRLING.' Drum roll followed by the announcement (in shaking tones of calculated awe) that the roles of Pip as a man, Magwitch, Mr Jaggers, Mr Pumblechook, Herbert Pocket, Compeyson, Joe Gargery, the Dragoon, the Judge, the Innkeeper and all other parts were 'ALL PLAYED BY MR GEORGE EDWARDS'.

It was in days of flagpole-sitting and marathon dance contests and it was symptomatic of the times that the public would take to George Edwards and his miraculous larynx. The Depression public took to Mr Edwards and his thousand voices with a fervour that verged on the hysterical. Nor was it a nine-day-wonder event, because I first worked with Mr Edwards in 1934 and when I left for the United States in 1948 he was still going strong with as many voices as ever. But in the first year or so of his bursting upon the public I can remember that whole families would not leave the house in the evening excepting on Fridays and Saturdays. Actually Mr Edwards and Miss Stirling (Mrs Edwards in whatever time they had to call their private life) began their broadcasting at eight in the morning with a family dialogue known as 'Darby and Joan' which was nothing but a string of corny jokes purporting to be the breakfast jollity of a 'typical' family all portrayed by Mr Edwards at once and including the crusty old aunt, interposed by Miss Stirling.

Downstairs in the studio building in a dark little cubby-hole of an office with four stenographers pounding away on very decrepit typewriters was another freak. Maurice Francis was the writer of these serials and just as Mr Edwards could reproduce hundreds of voices, Mr Francis was capable of turning out hundreds of situations a week, often twenty fifteen-minute scripts a day. That was facilitated by the fact that he dictated at rapid speed and as one steno finished she raced the script to the typewriter while the next episode was being dictated to another steno, who then rushed it to the typewriter while a third began. Mr Francis was also capable of keeping as many as seven or eight long-running stories in his head without ever getting the characters or events mixed up.

After this mind-breaking day, Mr Francis went upstairs to the studio and supervised production with Miss Stirling and sometimes stepped in to a role to relieve Mr Edwards of perhaps having to play seven voices in one scene. Their evening began at 6 pm with 'David and Dawn', a children's serial, with George and Nell portraying two tiresome tots with hideous Australian accents who had underwater adventures with numerous fish and molluscs all acted out by Mr Edwards. One of my earliest memories of him is his performance of a menacing clam; if a clam could have given utterance it would have sounded the way he did it, clammish. This show was immediately followed (literally only time to pass round scripts, which were seldom if ever rehearsed) by 'The Missing Link' adventures in Africa with the star portraying both a young and an old explorer, and numerous African dialects. The came 'The Swiss Family Robinson' with the duo again, she as Swiss mother and he as the entire rest of the Swiss family plus a friendly ape or two. Next they paused five minutes for a news break and then he swallowed water and plunged into 'The Laughing Cavalier', a mys- teries series which he literally played entirely alone, it having to do with a men's club and having a deliberately all-male cast. Nell worked frantically during this fifteen minutes marking his scripts for the rest of the evening and next day and readying effects and putting on more mascara. By eight o'clock they were ready with 'Inspector Scott of Scotland Yard' in which Mr Edwards, with a vaudeville Scottish accent, had a fine time of committing a new crime every week and arresting himself and in which Nell first devel- oped her famous scream; when she stood back and let it rip she was said to threaten the coaxial cable. At eight-thirty an ashen-faced secretary (all the stenographers worked until nine each evening and Mr Francis was still dictating the next day's shows) appeared with two trays of now lukewarm sent-in-dinner, and by nine they were back at the microphone in 'Birth of a Nation' which was history adapted to suit their kind of melodramatic acting styles and containing continuous bloody acts. Finally at ten o'clock came 'Famous Trials' providing the indefatigible Mr E with the chance both to defend and prosecute himself on the stand and to interject and cross- examine himself as attorneys and accused and overrule himself as the judge; it was probably his virtuoso performance and nobody in the nation went to bed until it was over.

So I was thunderstruck with awe at meeting him and thrilled when I was chosen for the Tsarovitch (he was limited in playing children's roles to one child voice) and astonished at his ordinariness. He was small and portly and in his middle fifties but the real surprise was that he stammered badly (a secret well-kept from the public) and it was unlike any stammer I have ever heard. It occurred in the middle of a word so that 'bottle' came out 'bot-OT-le' and 'telephone' became 'tel-EL-ephone'. When upset he could skip along syllables like a stone across water. Like, 'Let the damn spon-on-sor stick-ik to sell-elling his god-od-od-dam com-od-od-ODities. ' I never heard him stammer on the air, not once in all the twelve years I was in the Edwards' organisation. He would come off the air after a spectacular display of batting back and forth a dozen roles from falsetto to bass and say in a little-boyish way that he nearly made a 'mud-UDDLE in the mid-IDDLE of that bas-ASTARD'.

Only the odd couple of actors who were hired to play what amounted to breath-givers were able to watch him perform and it was an extraordinary experience.

Removing the jacket and tie but never dispensing with his constant cigar, he shuffled through the pages of the script. There was rarely any rehearsal of the shows, so thickly were they piled on each other, so Nell had a unique code of marking which he read like shorthand. In big markings in red and blue pencil they instantly communicated to him the type of voice, blue for young, red for old, blue circle with red dot inside was middle-aged, criss-cross in red was Chinese, large capital blue B was British, red C for cockney, red A for American and so on. I later did the markings for him and was not surprised to find there was a clef-like symbol for 'untrustworthy Chinese'.

To watch him perform, especially for the first time, was an incredible, even eerie, experience. You were not always sure where the voices were coming from; there was something ventriloquial about it and especially the knack he had for overlapping one voice upon another, a manner of interrupting himself. For example a scene from *Oliver Twist* in which he would be playing Fagin, Sykes, the Artful Dodger and Oliver. He would bend slightly to the side of the microphone for Fagin hardly raising his voice from a whine so that, 'Ah, come here my pretty' appeared to be coming from his nose alone and then he would pull back quickly, becoming taller and menacing for a deep, rasping voice that was Bill Sykes and then, springing a little to one side, came the piping voice of the Artful Dodger, and squatting down and rolling his eyes up he produced the child's voice of Oliver. Sometimes he seemed to be like a person in extreme physical pain and discomfort, bending this way and that, dancing little pavanes and waving the dead cigar while the various voices boomed, sang, croaked, snarled, twittered and Nell Stirling (always in the scene somewhere) darted in and out and thrust a word or two here and there to give him a breath while all the time she kept an eye on the stopwatch and if they were in danger of running overtime she would dart to his side of the microphone and point to the last line of the script which they would cut to, regardless of whether it made sense.

Sumner Locke Elliott, *Radio Days*, Imprint, Sydney, 1993.

Donald Horne

Donald Horne (1921–), historian, social commentator, and journalist, has been editor of the *Observer*, the *Bulletin*, and *Quadrant*. He was a child in the 1930s.

A fifty-mile stretch of suburbs

The families in Sydney that seemed important to us were the families that had established the retail stores: the *palazzi* of Sydney were the retail stores themselves, whether the founding families still owned them or not. When we went shopping we were participating in one of the few significant ceremonies of Sydney. Each of the *palazzi* had its own character: David Jones was a House of antique but not remarkable origin that had suddenly become more vigorous than any of the others, an ascendant House; Farmers was somewhat more grand; with its Corinthian pilasters, scrolls and pediments, Anthony Horderns was the oldest and greatest of all Houses, but now in decline; Mark Foys was a tricky and unpredictable House; Hordern Bros a reliable but dull House; Grace Brothers a House that appeared to have over-extended itself; and so forth. Beneath the great Houses the lesser Houses, the big stores that specialised in furniture or men's clothes or whatever, played the part of the gentry among the lords. The smaller retail stores that tended towards cheapness and the chain stores that specialised in it were a radical bourgeoisie threatening established privilege. Many of the heads of families ruling over the retail stores became knights; several of them had patronised the arts; most of them used their money to acquire power in politics; they all of them, between them, were the city's main arbiters of taste, often travelling overseas, looking for some new thing to sell. With the familiarity of the citizens of a city discussing its oligarchs, even schoolboys used to talk about these families, the Hordern family in particular, which, in the English fashion, had sold out of trade and acquired land.

The city was the heart of a fifty-mile stretch of suburbs, with patches of bushland filling them out, but with already a million and a quarter people living in them. What identity did it have for us? There were the *palazzi* of the retail stores to pay tribute to, and the cathedrals of the picture shows to seek inspiration in. There were the two annual pilgrimages across the Harbour—a day at Manly and a day at the zoo. There were acts of witness at the races and cricket matches. There were the festivals of Christmas shopping, the Royal Agricultural Show, and Anzac Day (along with the suburban festivals of Christmas dinner, Mother's Day and Cracker Night, when children let off fireworks to celebrate Empire Day). And there was the Australian Museum, where we could look at stuffed birds, Egyptian mummies, New Guinea head-dresses, Australian opals and dinosaurs' bones, or the Technological Museum, where we could look at an imitation of the Strasbourg clock, or the Art Gallery, where we could see one of the worst collections in the world. These made up the public nature of the city. Sometimes I would go into the city and seek something else: I would walk around the imitation Gothic of the two cathedrals and the hybrid imitations of the two main civic buildings, or peer at the statues in the parks, but this didn't seem the real thing. Sydney was women shoppers jamming narrow pavements between nondescript buildings, some of them carrying large suitcases to pack their bargains in, grimly pursuing their 'day in town'.

Donald Horne, *The Education of Young Donald*, Penguin,
Melbourne, 1988.

Allan Brown

Members of the Brown family worked as stonemasons at Rookwood Necropolis since 1867. In 1988 Allan Brown (1908–) recounted the story of his family and their involvement with the Necropolis.

The stones of Sydney

The early quarries had been established in areas such as Pyrmont, Bondi and Maroubra, all in Sydney. They later extended to Wondabyne on the northern side of the Hawkesbury River Bridge. All sandstone was quarried from this vast area known as the Hawkesbury Basin. Many of the old stone buildings in Sydney, including the Sydney Town hall, Queen Victoria Building, General Post Office, St Mary's and St Andrew's cathedrals, and numerous government buildings, were constructed of stone from Pyrmont and Bondi. The stone from these quarries was of good strength and lasting quality. When a stone was taken from the quarry and cut to size, care had to be taken to ensure that the 'bed' or natural grain of the stone ran the same way as it did in the quarry. If this were not done, the face would split and crumble. In the trade we call this 'fretting'.

In 1927, I worked on some restoration work inside the Queen Victoria Building while I was serving my apprenticeship. I also worked on the interior of St Mary's Cathedral, including the altars, pulpit, and down in the crypt, and the old Tattersall's Club, which has long disappeared. I worked on a scroll over the doorway. It was made from trachyte, a very heavy, hard stone, and I was only learning at the time. We used chisels and pneumatic hammers to carve the scroll ...

To create a monument [for Rookwood], it was necessary to place the stone upon a table built with a box or 'truck' underneath. In the monumental yards, small trucks of about 18 inches to two feet in height were supported on wheels which ran along wooden rails in order to make the transportation of heavy blocks about the yard as easy as possible. Usually there were masons who worked in the yard and others who worked in the cemetery.

Once at the cemetery, the stone would be placed on a hand truck with two wheels which would be pulled and guided by a long pole. From the delivery dray or truck, the stone would be manoeuvred onto the hand truck and taken to the place where the monument was to be erected. Masons who carried out this work in the cemeteries were known as 'fixers'. Trenches were dug and the kerbing set into the ground. With tall headstones, which were common in those days, a base was set on the head or 'socket' end of the kerbing. Into the top of this base a groove or channel would be sunk to a depth of three to four inches. A corresponding tongue or 'tang' would be worked on the bottom of the headstone and fitted neatly into the groove and wet in hot sulphur or cement. Iron dowels were not used in those days, but in later years a copper dowel was used. In many instances today, the stone can be seen to have broken away from the tongue. With dampness, the expansion of the sulphur or cement was greater than that of the stone, forcing the stone out and causing it to break away. That is why so many headstones have fallen at Rookwood Cemetery ...

Early marble stones were imported from Italy and were already shaped and worked. Marble from Carrara, a white stone with very few veins running through it, was more or less reserved for statuary. Sicilian and southern Italian marble has a vein in it and is slightly harder than carrara, which makes it more suitable for monumental work ...

Granite was imported from Scotland and Sweden. It is interesting to note that much of the granite was shipped out as ballast on the ships coming to Australia. This was a cheap and easy way to import stone. Australian granite was not used until the 20th century. The Australian granite at Rookwood came from Sodwalls, in the Lithgow area, Moruya, and Goulburn. The pylons of the Sydney Harbour Bridge are built from Moruya granite. Imperial black granite is quarried in South Australia and red granite in Tasmania.

Allan Brown, 'The stonemason', in *The Sleeping City: The Story of Rookwood Necropolis* (ed. David H. Weston), Society of Australian Genealogists in conjunction with Friends of Rookwood Inc. and Hale & Iremonger, Sydney, 1989.

John Kingsmill

John Kingsmill describes Bondi tram etiquette in the 1930s.

The Bondi tram

There was romance and excitement in every penny tram ride, certainly on the Bondi line. From Waverley Park, the land falls in a great slope towards the sea. Down this slope, Bondi Road, the tram would rush, in a series of stops and starts, bell clanging to let the world know whose tramline, whose street it was. Then, at the foot of that long hill, there had to be a diversion, for the land falls away sharply, so the tramline took a turn and another and another, like a road down a mountainside. There was even a deep cutting in the sandstone rock that roared at the tram as it dashed through.

There was something else, something every Bondi man, woman and child knew and valued—the sea breeze in the afternoon and evening to bid you welcome home at last. On a scorching hot summer's day, when that sea breeze hit the tram, people would catch the eye of those opposite and lift an eyebrow or crimp a little smile of thanks for small mercies. Because it was a Bondi breeze, it was ours. It went with the suburb. And there were days when that gentle breeze, by the time the tram shot out of that sandstone cutting, had turned into a southerly buster, a gale. Hands placed firmly on hats, newspapers folded away skew-whiff, faces set in brave or disapproving grimaces, men knew then why they were the sex chosen to sit 'outside' to take what comes when the weather turns nasty. Behind their closed doors, 'the womenfolk' had the advantage, except for those who had chosen that very day to wear their best to town.

It was at this precise point in the journey that Bondi people knew themselves blessed compared with people whose tramline ended in a drab tramshed, a mere terminus. For us, there was a climax unmatched in Sydney (and, for all we knew, anywhere). Regardless of the weather, good, bad or merely capricious, our tramride ended in a scene that was dramatic, operatic, symphonic. It took a particular dourness to resist looking at it no matter how many hundreds, thousands of times, you'd seen it before—the view across the great bay from the peak of the southern hill, where the tram stopped for a moment before making its final dash downhill past majestic stands of tall Norfolk pine trees through which you could see what the surf was like—flat or ferocious, a different scene every day if you had the eye for fine variations. On days when there were 'white horses', you could see them away out to sea, as far as the horizon, with maybe a coaster making its way, a ragged plume of black smoke torn from its funnel. On days of big storms, the bay was one roiling mass of foam and the vast waves boomed like cannonades. On the gentlest of days, the serenity of it was a balm and a consolation no matter what else had happened to you that day. Our beach. Seen from our tram. All that, for a penny! Or, if you were grown-up, fourpence.

The Bondi trams, indeed, most Sydney trams in the 1930s, were what we called 'toast racks', that is, eight compartments the full width of the tram, with footboards along each side for the tram guard (and as a step to get you aboard) and a glass-enclosed cabin for the driver. The driver's cabin was spartan enough, even though it sported two splendid brass handles and a handsome brass bell, but at least the driver was shielded from the weather behind a windscreen. He was therefore a prince, a king, compared with the life-threatening habitat of his mate, his colleague, the tram guard.

Picture him, lashed by wintry wind and rain, clawing his way along the narrow footboard, his frozen fingers plucking at sodden tickets and giving change in shillings, sixpences and fingernail-size threepenny-bits. It used to unnerve me, even in fine weather when the going was good, to see a tram guard, leaning into the crowded compartment, with his big leather ticket-holder in one hand, using the other hand to collect and distribute money and tickets. What was holding him to the tram but willpower—and fear of terrible injury or imminent death? I used to detest people who airily offered a five pound note or even a one pound note for a fourpenny fare. The man, obliged to accept legal tender, would peer into his great leather change-pouch hanging by a heavy belt around his waist, find the notes and coins for the change (and he would hear about it instantly if he got it wrong: 'I gave you a fiver!') and he would laboriously count it out, coin by coin, into the hand of the unthinking, unfeeling passenger. Where was God if He didn't strike them down for mindless cruelty? I noticed, too, that often enough it wasn't the ladies in furs who put tram guards through such torture so much as someone only one or two social rungs above them.

The toast-rack tram needs to be explained in some detail. You stepped up from the street onto a footboard and up again into a compartment. (When you could no longer do this you knew you were old and finished with 'getting about'.) Men and unaccompanied boys went into the open 'Smoking' compartments, two at each end of the carriage, while the women and children went into the four central compartments ('Non-Smoking'). The women's compartments had small sliding doors to shut out the wind and the rain, always a consideration when you had a good hat to think about. The men's compartments were manfully left exposed to the weather unless there was windswept rain, and then the man on the weather side would pull down the roller blind of stout brown canvas on a heavy metal frame. Rather, he would *try* to pull it down, for these blinds had minds of their own. (Sometimes they would fly up of their own accord, whoosh!)

If a blind didn't want to be pulled down, it resisted all force and simply skewed at an angle and there was no budging it. Thus two men facing each other on the weather side would be wet from head to foot or from waist to foot, depending on the angle of the blind. On a wet day, every boarding male passenger had to cope with the blind, pulled down to its farthest extent and with a boot thrust through the grip-hole to keep it down. Having flung it up and got aboard, he would then have to face the resentful eyes of those already seated and comfortable, their newspapers blown askew. Once settled, however, the newcomer became part of the compartment establishment, entitled to glare at the man at the next stop as he joined the sodden band. Words were unnecessary. Underneath the reproachful looks there was a camaraderie we all felt for each other in foul weather. One thing you never did—you never glared at the conductor when *he* pushed the blind up, for there he stood, clinging to the rail in his rubber raincape and sou'wester, freezing in midwinter or sweltering in late summer humidity. Only the uttermost churl could fail to sympathise with him. There were various small facial grimaces to show your awareness and sympathy, but the gulf that yawned between him on the footboard and us snug and safe inside, with our newspapers and our city offices to go to, was unbridgeable. And he knew it.

If your luck was in, you would get a seat facing the way you were going. Facing backwards all the way was better than standing all the way, but not preferred, so that 'wrong way' people would read their newspapers with one eye on the others to see who would get off and leave a vacant seat facing the right way. At this very instant, two men might make their move. Holding their papers in front of them, scarcely losing their laps, half crouched, but with gymnastic adroitness, they would half-rise and swivel their backsides, to land neatly in the vacant seat with a scarcely concealed smile of satisfaction. The man who moved too slowly would return his backside whence it had come. No-one likes to be a loser and *seen* to be a loser. The race was to the swift. That split second of triumph and defeat would usually be settled by an eloquent glare, a settling of ruffled feathers. The loser was unlikely to risk a second attempt. Practising Christians had their faith tested every time they got on a peak-hour tram.

The tram seats were long, slatted, wooden strips stretching the width of the tram and varnished to a high creamy shine, but varnish or no, the bottoms of the millions kept them buffed to a mirror finish. There was just enough space between these face-to-face seats for knees to protrude and for people to stand between the two rows of knees, with not a fraction of an inch to spare. Thus it was that the toast-rack trams made a unique and precious contribution to Sydney life and to the way we saw each other.

Ten people, total strangers or at best on no more than nodding acquaintance, would sit facing each other, five a side, as though at a long narrow dining table which had been whisked away leaving them cheek-by-jowl and almost knee-to-knee. There was no ignoring each other. If you weren't reading the paper, it was a question of knowing where to look for the half-hour journey to town. The seats were built to take five but if a man or a woman happened to be overweight or had a territorial need for space on each side there would be mimed scenes as in a silent movie and piercing looks exchanged. It was usually just a matter of everybody wriggling a bit to make the fat or the selfish one cooperate. Whereupon a latecomer would wedge himself finally into place, like the last sardine into the tin. He would set his jaw and harden his eyes as if to say: 'I'm in, no thanks to you!' ...

The tram guard shared his footboard with another species altogether, a cheeky, raffish, irrepressible freebooter, the newsboy. The Sydney newsboy was a fearless athlete with the balletic skills of a Nijinsky. He wore clown clothes—a hand-me-down football jumper, dirty sandshoes, drooping football socks not matched to the jumper or each other, with winter accoutrements of cloth cap and ancient waistcoat. He wore a leather bag at the waist for his money and a wide leather strap over his shoulder to hold an enormous bundle of newspapers to his hip. He could not survive a day without knowing by instinct, to the last ounce, how to balance the weight and shape of that bundle as it diminished, the weight and angle of his body being the counterpoise.

He did not so much *work* the trams as give performances on them. The tram would leave the boy's territorial base, the tram-stop where his neatly piled stock of *Herald*s and *Telegraph*s lay (a scatter of coins on top, newspapers and money as sacrosanct as the Grail), and, nimble as a jungle monkey, he would dart forward, leap up and land on the footboard as though the moving tram had acted as a magnet.

The longer a boy (they were all called *boy* regardless of age) worked the trams, the less need there was for him to ask what paper the customer wanted. He knew. Man with grey Stetson hat and grey moustache, *Herald*; lady with knitting and big bosom, the *Tele* (never given its full name). Everything done at top speed—the paper, the payment, the change supplied (boy flashily looking everywhere but into his change bag, knowing by the feel), hands, fingers working like a concert pianist's. A daily show given freely by the little ragged master.

John Kingsmill, *Australia Street: A Boy's-eye View of the 1920s and 1930s*, Hale & Iremonger, Sydney, 1991.

Lydia Gill

Lydia Gill (1913–) lived at Clovelly in the 1930s and worked in the city. She wrote her memoir when she was over 80.

Sargent's

Sargent's shops were Sydney, they were everywhere: wonderful restaurants, famous pies, coffee cake and walnut buns, sponge lady fingers apple charlotte, huge chocolate eclairs, and seasonally tiny little Christmas puddings. These were sold over the counter, but for a quick meal one could have a large pie with tomato sauce, a crisp, crusty bread roll, plenty of butter, a delicious pot of milk coffee or tea, all for 1s. They had the noisiest shops in Sydney. Pies were in their own little tins; then, before serving, the tin was placed in a container. 'Placed?' it was thrown! Even now if someone has a noisy kitchen, we who were there say, 'Sounds like Sargent's!' Over the counter the buttered bread roll would cost twopence, a pie threepence, apple pie and cream three or four pennies. According to the size of pie and our purses, we would say, 'Not too much butter, please' or 'Not too much cream.' ...

Having gone down Market Street to the State, one can't return to George Street without mentioning Sargent's main dining room next door to the State. On the ground floor was a huge tearooms with counters in front for taking away goods, where the assistants kept up the Sargent's tradition of 'throwing' the pie tins into the big containers. One floor up, by elevator too, was the main dining room. One was met by a waiter with a spotless napkin over an immaculate dress suit. He would guide us to a table where with equally spotless white cloths, gleaming sliver, and in peace and quiet, hot foods were served hot, and cold, cold. The menu was bouillon or consommé, lamb and mint sauce and three vegetables, roast beef with Yorkshire pudding, or roast pork with crackling and apple sauce, then sweets, fruit salad and cream, apple pie and cream, baked bread-and-butter custard or steamed pudding. All this with roll and butter and coffee or tea, all for 1s 6d. If we had sherry trifle we had to pay threepence more and it was really sherry. The next floor up was for functions, weddings, etc. Even then Sargent's was only for high days and holidays, when we could run to this dinner. We enjoyed it all the more, and in the suburbs there were still long queues at soup kitchens for the really poor ...

Friday night down at Paddy's [Markets] was a trip to another world. Chips cooking, pie and peas; though I hated the pets' corner: chooks, puppies, kittens and birds. I'd have bought them all if I'd had the money and space, but the beautiful flowers and plants did compensate a little. Once again, I'd chase my fussy little brown boronia, such staghorns and elk horns, bird's nest ferns and stalls packed tight with flowers, colourful chrysanthemums, gladioli and the sweet heady perfume of stocks when in season. Poppies were sixty for sixpence with some free green! The clever thing to do was to buy the bud poppies, then leave them next day in the sun to open. Most times it worked.

The crowd at Paddy's was very mixed: high society, Lascars from the ships looking for cheap clothing, real buyers after bargains in fruit and vegetables, and bacon, home-made sweets, fresh honeycomb, ornaments, factory seconds perhaps slightly chipped, and then dozens of people 'just looking' as we were. Perhaps buying bits of coloured braid or ribbons for trimmings and for our 'geisha silk' frocks. I think every female of dancing age, any age, had yards and yards of brightly coloured geisha silk made into evening frocks. It was sixpence a yard and 36 inches wide.

Lydia Gill, *My Town: Sydney in the 1930s*,
State Library of NSW Press, Sydney, 1993.

Bruce Beaver

Bruce Beaver (1928–), poet, was born in Manly and has lived there all his life.

Manly it was

At Manly one mild and salty night at the southern end of the Ocean Beach's esplanade approximately fifty years ago between four and five years of age dressed in a blue overall suit I watched the carnival monkeys racing in their silver cars around and around a circular track. They were dressed in coloured silken shirts and tiny hats held to their heads by elastic bands that came under the bristly chins. One of them had a metal mirror that it kept looking in. They crouched over the wheels as they whizzed around. Perhaps people bet on them. I ran suddenly behind a deck chair when people began to laugh at my onepiece gaitered suit. The leggings covered the tops of my shoes like spats and elastic bands tethered them to the shoes as the monkeys' hats to their heads. I hid furiously, sickeningly, self-consciously aware of my apparent absurdity. I would not come out from behind the deck chair until a thumb was caught excruciatingly in the back of one and the approaching fragrance of my grandmother's Evening in Paris and my grandfather's Corona convinced me that walking out in my gaiters was preferable—even being laughed at—to being trapped by a thumb. I was given a cigar band to bandage the injury.

Manly it was and monkeys there were in the early thirties, and even Venetian Carnivals when people would parade in fancy dress. So much of it seemed silken, from the monkeys' shirts to the pierrots' costumes but it must have been another cheaper material—crepe de chine or even of frilly paper. As we walked beneath paper lanterns and on the harbour front the junks and galleons and gondolas rocked in the warm salty evening air.

And Manly it was on warmer days at the big beach when the sand modeller shaped oh so carefully, so painstakingly, the tableaux of sand formed figures and objects—What could they be? What would they become? Kingsford Smith and the Southern Cross, Don Bradman, Malcolm Campbell and the Bluebird, or maybe the Death of Nelson with Hardy kissing or maybe listening to the last words (my grandfather could tell)—all in profile in biscuit coloured beach sand until with water from a jam tin the brushed surface smoothed and held the chalky water colours. What blues, reds and yellows placed as carefully on those outlines as if it all were a sandy Sistine Chapel. Then the pennies would fall on the cloth, though some were aimed at the painted sand models that would have to be patiently repaired. But before the day's end all would be ceremoniously destroyed by the artist in steady unreluctant movements.

It was at Manly on the promenade where the canvas tower of Punch and Judy drew the children to the squeaking buzzing voices of the tragedy of Punch with the additional character of a crocodile strayed from Peter Pan, a green backed yellow bellied fellow that gobbled them all up instead of the Devil, dragging them down to the depths inside the canvas booth. But once I stopped the show, for in agitation at the fate of Judy or in diabolical cynicism—Wasn't Father Xmas a fraud—I threw into the booth the metal headpiece and tone arm of a dismembered gramophone. Everything came to a sudden halt. The squeaking rasping tones ceased. For a second or two all was silent, the figures not to be seen on their stage. Then from the side of the tent emerged a very ordinary man rubbing his head and holding the tone arm, enquiring who had thrown the bloody thing. With one voice the watching children accused me and I fled in terror, the man too stunned to pursue.

And it was in Manly on fine Sundays that the preaching men and women invaded the beach and gathered around their blackboard and easel the same gullible Punch drunk watchers, coaxing them to sing in flat and reedy voices simple songs like Brighten the Corner Where You Are while Mac and I made farting noises at them and fled into the frothy shallows or ran between the backward rushing and the forward shooting wave that met not all at once but in a flurrying line of spray like a torpedo's track which we would leap along the bulk of the waves' weight met in the middle of their course and we would leap into the air from the centre of the exploding waves and yell our heads off.

All this was at Manly in the depression years when people could not afford to throw pennies on the sand modeller's mat or go to the movies more than once a week where the families reserved seats in the stalls for Saturday nights and turned to the neighbours behind them and asked what was showing that night although everyone should have known it was the Green Hornet or Speed Gordon. And some even had no money for Saturday night films and had to go to bed early or listen to radio serials.

And the pines grew tall and dark green at Manly and the tideline of the bigger beach was full of matches that could be used as soldiers and sailors. From the top of the seawall we'd leap Mac and I, and Smokey my dog would leap and hit the sand with a thud and a muffled yelp not of pain but of excitement, then tearing around on the wet and dry sand the three of us ran and Mac and I became men and strangers while the eighty-foot pines stopped growing and started to die from age and salty detergent until I walk past their stumps and limbless trunks and look past the worn wall and the biscuity sand at the jade waves and the pine green depths.

Bruce Beaver, 'The village', in *Headlands*, University of Queensland Press, Brisbane, 1986.

Lennie Lower

Lennie Lower again, no respecter of persons or history.

Lower away for the landing

Just fancy! It was way back in 1788 that Captain Phillip and I landed in Botany Bay. How time flies!

As we sailed into the bay we got a whiff from the boiling down works. 'My goodness this country smells!' said Phillip.

'I told you we were landing in the wrong place,' I replied. 'Why couldn't you land in some genteel place like Rose Bay?'

'Who's Governor of this colony?' he replied heatedly. 'All right! All right!' I said. 'Don't do your block in front of the convicts.'

So we landed at Farm Cove. Thus is history made.

It was a pretty wild spot, and the natives were a bit suspicious. 'Blime!' said one convict. 'Tike me back to Dartmoor!' We put him in irons.

'I think we'll build a gaol first,' said Phillip. The first sign of civilisation was the gaol. Then we built the barracks.

After that I said to Phillip: 'What about lunch?' 'Good idea!' he said.

'Lunch ho!' I bawled, and there was a great clashing of leg-irons as the convicts collapsed in their tracks.

'I'm glad you thought to pack some sandwiches before we left England,' I said. 'There doesn't seem to be much to eat in this place.'

'I think of everything,' said Phillip, somewhat boastfully, I thought. 'I've even brought a couple of rabbits and a potted prickly pear which I intend to plant shortly. They ought to do well in this country.'

We were sitting down munching on our sandwiches when Sir Joseph Banks came rushing up with a piece of lantana in one hand and a sprig of Bathurst burr in the other.

'Look what I've found!' he cried delightedly.

'How quaint!' said Phillip. 'We must plant a lot of that, too. Come and have a sandwich, Joe.'

We had just finished the last of our sandwiches when a soldier came up, saluted, and said, 'Sir, one of the convicts has just bitten a piece out of his pick. Did it deliberately.'

'Hang him,' said Phillip.

'Yessir.'

And that was that.

'You're a bit drastic, aren't you?' I asked, when the soldier had gone.

'We can get plenty more convicts, but we're a bit short of picks.'

'I suppose you're right.'

'Of course I'm right!' That was the sort of man he was. Bombastic.

'What's this track they're cutting here?' I asked him.

'That's George Street. I called it after the ship's parrot. Holy Moses!'

'Wasser matter?'

'It's all right. It must be the heat. I thought I saw a big brown thing standing upright on two legs with a long tail and it jumped fifteen feet and disappeared into the bush.'

'You want to lay off that rum,' I told him. We found out later that they were real. Kangaroos—not rum, after all.

All this time, Blaxland was away in the hills with Lawson and Wentworth. We were beginning to get a bit anxious about them. However, they came back after a while and said they had discovered three railway stations. They had had the effrontery to name them after themselves. Phillip immediately named a street after himself. He was very annoyed. He even went so far as to name a whole bay after himself and called it Port Phillip in order to make it sound more important.

He was a man who was inclined to bicker about trifles. One day when he found me fraternising with the aborigines he was quite furious until I told him that I had learned a number of real good names for towns, such as Wagga Wagga, Coonamble and Wantibadgery. That soothed him a bit.

After a few months, when we had the town pretty well fixed up and had imported a few bushrangers to liven things up a bit, darn me if Macarthur didn't arrive with some merino sheep he'd picked up somewhere.

'You fool!' said Phillip, bitterly. 'They'll eat the grass and then how will my rabbits get on?'

'I never thought of that,' said Macarthur, biting his nails.

'A fine team of colonists I've got,' went on Phillip.

'You must admit,' I said, 'that we have made progress. When we first landed here there was nothing else to see but scenery. Now look at it. We've put up two new scaffolds, we've got a street, planted a whole lot of prickly pear ...'

'Yes! Yes! I know all that, but nobody is ever here when they're wanted. There's Bass and Flinders gone off in a boat somewhere, fishing, I suppose. They can get somebody else to be Governor. I'm fed up.'

It was a very nasty scene and has rightly been left out of most history books.

Still, when I look around today and see the result of our labours I say to myself, 'Well we certainly gave the town a good start.'

I'm still able to give the town a bit of a start when I've got the money. The old pioneer spirit lives on.

The Best of Lennie Lower, selected by Cyril Pearl and Wep, Lansdowne, Melbourne, 1963.

Kenneth Slessor

Slessor was also good at comic verse.

Come to Sydney!

'The opening day of Sydney's Sesquicentenary celebrations will be packed with spectacle and atmosphere. There will be an historical pageant through the city ... and a host of professional events. Days and nights of festival will follow, with band-championships, the National Eisteddfod, sports championships and a week of juvenile show and pageantry. Other items include the National Rifle Association's meeting, an angling-competition, a Chinese festival, and a commercial and industrial pageant. This is a programme which does not depend on night-life for its attractiveness.'—J.M. Dunningham, Minister in charge of Sydney Celebrations.

Oh, the scurry and rush of excitement,
    The scenes of hysterical fun,
When Sydney goes gay in a devilish way
On a diet of biscuit-and-bun!
There'll be spelling-bees, also eisteddfods—
    Imagine the hubbub and din!
And hectic debates on colonial dates
    With a lantern-slide lecture chucked in.
There'll be dozens of bands tooting tubas,
    And riflemen banging like mad;
And Scotsmen, by Cripes, playing tunes on the pipes,
    In the Highland Society's plaid.
There'll be thousands of tots around maypoles,
    Wherever you happen to look,
And picnics and jaunts to historical haunts,
    With a series of talks about Cook.
There'll be Japanese crackers and lanterns
    To light up the beautiful dark,
And fishing, by Jove, off the wharf at Lane Cove,
    With a prize for the best-looking shark.
So come to the circus in Sydney—
    The programme's a positive gem—
Where bottles go pop till festivities stop
    At 5.57 p.m.!

Kenneth Slessor, *Collected Poems* (ed. Dennis Haskell and Geoffrey
Dutton), Angus & Robertson, Sydney, 1994.

Meg Stewart

Meg Stewart (1948–) collaborated with her mother, the artist Margaret Coen, to write this memor of bohemian Sydney. Elizabeth Bay House crops up again, derelict, long shorn of its gardens.

Artists and bohemians of Circular Quay

Circular Quay was a world of its own in those days, a world of artists and bohemians. From Martin Place to the Quay was like a rabbit warren, so many artists either rented rooms to paint [or] even lived there. Moving into my own studio in Margaret Street meant that the Quay, its character and its characters, quickly became familar to me.

I might meet Percy Lindsay on the steps of the *Bulletin* newspaper offices; Perc with his rosy complexion, shiny white hair and alert blue eyes was an unmistakable figure dressed in white tropical suit and white solar topee. Percy had a cold shower every day of his life, which perhaps accounted for his particular sparkle.

I might see Bea Miles jumping off a tram, a young, boyishly pretty Bea, also always in white, white frock and white beret. She had a round face and short brown hair …

A shop at the Quay sold every sort of pie: rabbit, pork or beef, apricot. Pies were a staple of our diet. Round the corner in George Street was Plasto's hotel, where the women could safely have a beer in the upstairs lounge. Old Nick's was another cafe in George Street with plates, cups, saucers all printed with a grinning devil and pitchfork. We could have chicken cooked any way we liked—steamed, boiled, roasted—for 2s 6d there.

Maniaci's, the Italian fruit shop, arrived later at the Quay. Before that, there were two Chinese fruit and vegetable shops opposite each other in Pitt Street. Fruit wasn't so varied then. We never saw an avocado or a pawpaw, but the Chinese fruit shops did sell rice whisky on the side. They couldn't have had a licence but nevertheless they dispensed a fierce alchol that burned a fiery track down your inside. Chinese whisky came in full, round-bellied bottles with a brown glaze. Each one was a bit different, a bit crooked-looking, because they were hand-made. There wasn't a studio in town that didn't have a Chinese whisky bottle for still lifes …

Number 4 Dalley Street, where Alison and George had their studio, was also a condemned building (owned by the Electricity Commission) so Alison and George paid cheap rent for a large room, plenty big enough for parties, except that the caretaker made it almost impossible.

The caretaker was a crabby old man who used to shut the outside door at six o'clock and refused to let anyone in. One Saturday a few of us from the Royal Art came round for an evening with Alison and George. We banged and banged on the door, to no avail. The caretaker wouldn't let George open the door. 'Nobody's having a party here tonight,' he snapped.

The studio was on the third floor, the top storey. George had a brain-wave. He put his head out the window and lowered a long string—it must have been a whole ball of string—with cooked frankfurts down to the street. We were having a downgrade party that night; punch parties were upgrade, frankfurts and beer were downgrade. Beer bottles followed on another string and we had our party sitting outside in the gutter …

Janna Bruce knew a group of artists who lived, or rather squatted, in Elizabeth Bay House. Wallace Thornton and Wolfgang Cardimatis were two. Elizabeth Bay House was very rundown. They had no right to be there, but the alcoholic caretaker turned a blind eye and they lived for nothing amidst the ruins of colonial splendour. The upstairs bedrooms had a wonderful view straight out across Sydney Harbour, the only disadvantage being the loose floorboards.

Janna went to a party there. The electricity had been cut off so the guests took their own candles for light. The party was a success, despite the care-taker's being drunk as usual and screaming abuse at them, but not doing anything to stop the party. There was an awful lot of noise but surprisingly the neighbours didn't complain. At midnight they were deciding to disband the party when suddenly every candle burnt down at the same time and they were plunged into blackness. It was terrifying, Janna said, having to pick her own way across the holey floorboards, then make her way down to the ground floor, clinging to the curving staircase.

Meg Stewart, Second Half: Autobiography of My Mother, Penguin,
Melbourne, 1988.

Shirley Hazzard

Shirley Hazzard (1931–), novelist, has lived overseas since 1947, mainly in New York and Capri.

Refinement was a frail construction

A toast-rack tram, discoloured yellow, rocked them on wooden benches glossed with human passage. There were office girls with rolled hair and sailor hats of felt or straw; but there was no Dora, surely. The men sat in their open compartments at each end of the tram, their heavy waistcoats unbuttoned in the heat; flinging tobacco butts on slatted floors and leaning out to spit. In the rain, a canvas blind drew down for them on a rod. In the inside compartment Grace stood between her mother's knees and Caro swayed against an assortment of standing thighs. One and two halves, like the fare; and no Dora.

Dora's own mother had died when she was born, as happened in stories. Dora was twenty-one, but had given up Teachers' College.

Where they got down from the tram there were windows brilliant with coloured gloves and handbags and silk shoes, and shopping arcades lit like rainbows. The women passing along Pitt Street or Castlereagh had cooler faces and wore hats of violets or rosebuds, with little veils. Kegs of ale were nonetheless drawn on drays right past the best shops by pairs or teams of Clydesdales: chestnut necks straining in collars of sweated leather, great hooves under ruffs of streaked horsehair. And the driver collarless, frayed waistcoat open, no jacket, with his leather face and stained mop of horse-hair moustache. Manure underfoot, and a bruised smell of dropped cab-bage trodden by blinkered ponies harnessed to vegetable carts. Along the curb, barrows of Jaffas and Navels, or Tasmanian apples. All this, raffish and rural, at the fashionable conjunction of Market and Castlereagh streets.

At the same corner they would come upon spectres dreaded by Caro and by Grace; and, from the looking and the looking away, by all who passed there. Apparitions of the terrible kind were dispersed throughout the city and might be expected at any shopping centre of the suburbs. For a dead and atrocious certainty they awaited you at this particular and affluent corner, which for that reason seemed not to be a street at all, but a pit or arena.

Some of them stood, including those with only the one leg. The legless would be on the ground, against shop-windows. The blinded would have a sign, to that effect, around the neck—perhaps adding SUVLA or GALLIPOLI. Similarly, on the placard GASSED that hung beside pinned medals, might appear the further information, YPRES or ARRAS. Or the sign might say MESOPOTAMIA, quite simply, as you might write HELL.

They took up separate places, perhaps having a dog with them or a child, or a gaunt women silently holding out the cap. More usually, each alone. Who or what they had singly been, however, was sunk in the delved sameness of the eyes. Nothing more could be done to them, but their unsurpassable worst would be sustained forever and ever. Stillness was on the eyes even of the blind, closed on God knows what last sighting.

What music they made, and how they sang, that ghastly orchestra in lopped and shiny serge, with unstrung fiddles and wheezing concertinas and the rusted mouth-organ grasped in the remaining and inexpert hand; the voices out of tune with everything but pinched extremity. How cruelly they wracked, for Depression pennies, an unwilling audience with their excruciating songs—'The Rose of No Man's Land,' and 'The Roses of Picardy,' and 'The Rose of Tralee,' and ' Oh My, I don't want to die, I want to go home.' The war of the roses, roses, and smile, smile, smile.

> *Ighty-tiddly-ighty.*
> *Carry me back to Blighty,*
> *Blighty is the place for me …*

... Caro and Grace walked home uphill in raging heat. Brick houses were symmetric with red, yellow or purple respectability: low garden walls, wide verandas, recurrent clumps of frangipani and hibiscus, of banksia and bottlebrush; perhaps a summerhouse, perhaps a flagpole. Never a sign of washing or even of people: such evidence must be sought inside, or at the back. Caro was beginning to wonder about the inside and the back, and whether every house concealed a Dora. Whether in every life there was a *Benbow* that heeled over and sank.

You felt that the walls of such houses might topple inwards, that they would crush but not reveal.

Refinement was maintained on the razor's edge of an abyss. To appear without gloves, or in other ways suggest the flesh, to so much as show unguarded love, was to be pitchforked into brutish, bottomless Australia, all the way back to primitive man. Refinement was a frail construction continually dashed by waves of a raw, reminding humanity: the six-o'clock shambles outside the pubs, men struggling in vomit and broken glass; the group of wharfies on their Smoke-O, squatting round a flipped coin near the Quay and calling out in angry lust to women passing. There were raucous families who bought on the lay-by, if at all, and whose children were bruised from blows or misshapen by rickets—this subtler threat contained in terrace houses whose sombre grime was a contagion from the British Isles, a Midlands darkness. Britain had shared its squalor readily enough with far Australia, though withholding the Abbey and the Swan of Avon.

Shirley Hazzard, *Transit of Venus*, Penguin, Melbourne, 1981.

Donald Horne

Donald Horne describes professor of philosophy John Anderson, instigator of the Sydney Free-thought tradition, who exerted a great influence over several generations of Sydney students, writers, and intellectuals.

The university's main rebel
The University carillon had been built as a memorial to graduates who had died in the Great War, and when there was a carillon recital three of the University's most conservative professors usually made a point of standing in the middle of the Quad, as much to safeguard the sanctity of the dead as to listen to the music. They were on the lookout for students who did not stand up for 'God Save the King'; however, it was notorious that they were also watching for the same Professor John Anderson whose article in *Hermes* had informed me that the aesthetic object was to be pursued for its own sake. Anderson would sometimes walk through the Quad when 'God Save the King' was being played and defy the three professors, who had

become his greatest enemies. On the day I first arrived at the University I saw Anderson walking along the cloisters in the Quad: someone pointed him out as the Scottish radical who was the University's main rebel, a renowned atheist, not long ago a Communist, censured in the New South Wales Parliament and by the University Senate. Anderson seemed the most important person at the University. I began to feel a yearning when he walked by; even if I saw him only out of the corner of my eye my skin might stiffen and my hair prickle at the roots. He was in his forties, very tall, stooped, gangling, striding loosely past in a brown suit and a green hat with an upturned brim, usually sombre, with his pipe jutting out from between his teeth. He seemed an embodiment of what was grave and constant in human suffering, but sometimes he would wave an arm at a student, loosely, as if it were a puppet's, and smile, strong teeth bursting out beneath his full black moustache. Recognition. Sunshine. His huge, sad brown eyes seemed to sag right down into his face, pulling the cheeks down with them, lost in wisdom. Sometimes he seemed very tired, both tough and fragile, bearing a great load, but still walking briskly. Then he would laugh, or wave his arm. I was gripped by the need to know him.

Light came into the philosophy lecture theatre, where the Literary Society held its meetings, through leaded glass windows, and on either side of the blackboard there were murals of famous classical and modern philosophers. There was the sense of an inner temple about this room when early in term Pritchett and I sat in it to hear Anderson give his annual address to the Literary Society, of which he was President. When he began speaking in an urgent Glaswegian sing-song the room seemed stilled by significance. Most of the time he spoke strongly, but occasionally his voice hovered and fluttered while he stuttered for words, by this hestitation building up a pressure that then burst through into a confident and sustained high note. The style of his address was intensely serious, but lightened now and again with a wisecrack, or with sarcasm. Most of the small audience took notes of what he said, and in the discussion that followed some of them stood up and elaborated parts of what they had just heard, holding their notes in front of them without referring to them, in the manner of someone at church who sings from memory, but with the hymn book open at the right page. Anderson sat silent, hunched over the rostrum as he wrote on a piece of paper, looking up from time to time, deep-eyed and intent. Then, when the discussion was over, he made a triumphant ending, flowing strongly again, correcting errors and confusions and bestowing agreement like a final blessing. It took only an hour, but we felt that we had just witnessed an important new contribution to the theory of aesthetics.

Donald Horne, *The Education of Young Donald*, Penguin,
Melbourne, 1988.

Elizabeth Harrower

Elizabeth Harrower (1928–), novelist, was born in Sydney. Apart from radio, the second great source of information in the 1940s was the newsreels.

Another heartless band

There was a war on.

On Saturdays at the pictures, newsreels showed the bombed cities of Europe and later still the deserts of the Middle East and the northern jungles, streaming jungles where trees walked and killed. Callow, shallow, safe, ashamed, the Vaizey girls were part of an audience that witnessed the destruction of the light of the world from cushiony red seats in the lilac-scented disinfected dark. They were pressed back on themselves and their few square inches of knowledge and experience. They felt in themselves and each other the inadequacy, hollowness and frustration of one seeking water at a dry spring.

Walking slowly home they talked with an empty excited despondency. Laura more easily wound herself up to judge, pronounce, and theorize, but Clare only ground the soles of her shoes harder into the footpath and, grated, said, 'What's the use? We don't *know*. We don't *know*. I mean—' She only meant it felt something like blasphemous, something like licentious, for their ignorance to speak, improvise opinions, consider its emotions in this situation. 'I mean—we don't know anything.'

Laura stood in a thicket of people where the bare sunburned arms of strangers touched each other, to watch the soldiers marching down Elizabeth Street to the Quay and the waiting ships.

'It's a shame the kids are all at school. They should give the boys a proper send-off on a Saturday when—'

Trumpets came level suddenly, sopping up voices, eyes, attention, flashing, passing. Drums, boots, a mesmerizing march tune that compelled the most blasé-seeming of pedestrians to fall in with the '*left*, *left*, I had a good job but I *left*' of marching boots. Slouch hats, khaki, bayonets glittering, flags performing in the wind.

'North. That's what they say. That's where they need 'em.'

Brown-faced soldiers, and more soldiers. (*Left*, *left*, I had a good job but I *left*.) Another band playing with pitiless gaiety.

'They look pretty tough, eh? Look like fighters, don't they? Good old Aussies—'

Again the crowd cried out, and again cheered, and soon another heart-wrenching band was heard in the distance approaching.

Laura watched, and was not the only one to glance up and away from the *left*, *left*, of sparkling tan boots to the high brick walls of the insensible department stores and office buildings opposite.

Elizabeth Harrower, *The Watchtower*, Macmillan, Melbourne, 1966.

Sumner Locke Elliott

Sumner Locke Elliott's keen ear captures the edgy bad temper of Sydney at the end of the war.

Overpaid, oversexed, and over here

There, joy of joys, across the street was a taxi and she ran to it, but two young American lieutenants reached it at the same moment.

'No, you saw it first,' she said, backing away as they held open the door politely.

'We're going up to the Cross,' one of them said. 'Any use to you?' Kings Cross was exactly where she was going. 'No use, thanks just the same,' she said and, walking away, felt that they were saying something both amusing and ugly about her. Taxi sharing was mandatory and it was a rare luxury to ride alone. Everyone had amusing stories about exasperating fellow passengers: about riding with men who made passes at you, drunks, mad old ladies, vulgar servicemen. But it seemed to her these stories were greatly exaggerated. It was blood-curdling, what had not happened to her.

She waited for the Kings Cross tram in the brownout winter twilight. Cars went by sluggishly with their muffled headlights and overhead the filtered street lamps gave out a weak gingery light, and when the tram came grinding up King Street, it too was lit with the same weak, muddy light by which people strained their eyes to read the thin evening newspaper. Like everyone else, she was inured now to the colourlessness of everything—brown lights, khaki, yellowish newspapers, books printed on cheap paper which turned brown and then quickly to fine dust. The dreariness of brown was everywhere. She could not remember Sydney before the war and, like children who were now beginning to grow up never having seen neon signs, she could not imagine the city starting to glow and twinkle at dusk. She could not visualise what the General Post Office had looked like before they had taken down the clock tower and stored it way somewhere against the possibility of Japanese bombers. She was accustomed to the big stores with unlit show windows and wire where there had been plate glass and all these precautions which, like the air-raid sirens, regularly practising their dismal warnings, had been made for invasion, death, parachutists, the terrifying days of 1942 when these things had seemed possible, when they had drawn the secret, invisible line across the continent to the north and said we will defend from below here, before the Americans came and the threat had gradually rolled back to New Guinea, the Philippines, the Marianas, and had left behind it the drab colour of war and a feeling of anticlimax.

And what is a more ridiculous-looking thing than a camouflaged double-decked bus? Could anyone conceive of the 6.22 bus to Roseville being set on fire by a dive-bomber?

There was something unreal about it all. It might have been a huge hoax on the population, mesmerized into believing a mighty war was being fought. Even when the *Queen Mary* appeared overnight in the harbour like a giant grey squid, one had to deny it was the *Queen Mary* in case the Enemy Was Listening ...

Six o'clock was a bad time, pig-swill time. The bars closed at six o'clock. It meant that the boys had pushed down six or seven big schooners of heavy dark lager in perhaps ten minutes to beat the clock and then hit the cool air of the brown, cheerless street frustrated; nothing to do until the cinemas opened at seven-thirty, nowhere to go except the coffeehouses or the barren, spiritless YMCAs and Red Cross Entertainment Centres. Just after six o'clock the streets were crowded with fiercely thirsty adventurers, brawlers and the lonely ...

When Hilda, Stevie's housekeeper, opened the door, Bea said, 'Oh, I thought you were—' Off for the night, she had almost said, realizing immediately that, of course, she had been tricked.

'They're in the study,' Hilda said and then clapped her hands angrily. 'Bed. Bed,' she called out and Bea looked up to see Miranda's face peering through the banisters with the look of supreme indifference she had inherited from Stevie. Bea waved but Miranda continued to stare. She was able to withstand all exhibitions of human affection with the same equanimity with which she withstood hurt. She had been handed down from her grandmother. 'And here's Bea,' Stevie said, unsurprised, knowing without a doubt Bea would come. The two Americans stood up in their beautifully pressed beige uniforms.

'My sister, Bea St James. Captain Alcott.'

'Orcutt.'

'Orcutt. Corey Orcutt? Oh, American *names*. And you know Gabriel.' The Colonel, the older man, said, 'Hello there, Bea. What will be your poison?'

'Scotch,' Bea said, seeing there was plenty of it. Stevie's house was stocked with genuine Scotch, American cigarettes, Juicy Fruit, Kleenex, Coca-Cola, the GI editions of new novels. She handed out lipsticks and said 'God-awful' a lot. The American voices so constantly around her were infectious and little burrs and flattened vowels had penetrated into her speech.

'Good to see you, lover,' she said.

She was stretched out on the red leather sofa. In her black velvet pants and white silk shirt tied at the waist with a wide scarlet sash, she looked like a young vivandière. She seemed slightly above everything; she was swimming in her success. If she said there would be fish for dinner the Colonel seemed to find it entrancing; so discovered to be dazzling and adorable, she glowed. She had never been so extraordinarily a beauty as she was now and she had acquired a whole new set of mannerisms to go with it. She had always been a sometimes haughty and often scathing girl but she had now softened and was full of little winning ways. The Colonel called her 'baby' and patted her affectionately.

'Go on with the story,' Stevie said. 'He was telling us a story about what's-her-name.'

'I was telling them,' the Colonel said, putting Bea's drink by her, 'about Evalyn Walsh McLean.'

Stevie said, 'But tell, go back a minute and tell how it happened. Tell Bea the name of the man you were with.'

'H. Dean Longswiller.'

'H. Dean Longswiller,' Stevie said. 'Don't you love it?'

'Anyway—' 'If I didn't know you better, I'd say you made it up. H. Dean Longswiller, Bea. Are you ready?'

'Any*way*'— the Colonel patted Stevie gently to cede the floor—'I was with H. Dean at this purrticularly large party in this purrticularly large house in Washington. Washington, DC, that is, and H. Dean had to go to the john—'

'The loo,' Stevie translated.

'The john. Had to go to the john and he was gone a helluva long time. Well, finally he came back downstairs and … you see, this is a tremendous big house in Washington—'

'DC,' Stevie said.

'Let me tell it, baby. So eventually, after a helluva long time, H. Dean came back and this is what he said to me, this is no paraphrase. This is exactly what H. Dean said to me.'

Here the Colonel paused for attention and spread out his large pink hands as he had probably done a thousand times telling the story.

Sumner Locke Elliott, *Edens Lost*, Penguin, Melbourne, 1974.

George Johnston

George Johnston (1912–70) grew up in Melbourne, worked as a war correspondent, and then came to Sydney with his wife, Charmian Clift.

A cocky, callous place

When Cressida came back she said, 'Have you been along to the bathroom yet?' and I said no, I'd been waiting for her to clean up, and asked her why. 'Oh, it's interesting,' she said.

The bathroom—there was only one to each floor of the Princeton Apartments—was at the far end of a corridor angled around a euphemistic light-well from which came weird clankings and groanings and the catarrhal cleansings of other residents. The corridor was all gloomy tones of brown, and the excremental colour and smell of this dingy byway went with the bathroom, which had stains on the walls like old maps and blotches more repellent in the toilet-bowl where something seemed to have happened with Condy's Crystals. The cracked wash-basin was a mess of squeezed-out toothpaste tubes and rusted bobby-pins, and the final sordid touch was a framed printed sign screwed above the ringmarked bathtub which said, GUESTS ARE POLITELY REQUESTED PLEASE NOT TO SHIT IN THE BATH. 'Politely' was the bit I liked. It was hard to believe that this had been set up in type, in Bodoni Bold, and printed.

When I went back to the musty bedroom I said hopelessly, 'We should have looked around more. We should have tried for something better than this dreadful bloody dump.'

'It's cheap,' she said, not pointing out that the Princeton had been my choice. 'It will do for a few days while we sort out. When you get a job we can look around for something else.'

'Someone said it was used as a kind of leave place for the troops, GIs mostly, a brothel, I suppose, more than a residental,' I said as if this was a mitigation. 'Put toilet-paper down on the seat first,' I warned.

Cressida went to a window so opaque with city grime that it seemed as if a wartime black-out screen was still pasted over the glass. 'Well, at least it's in the Cross,' she said, as if she could see out. 'It's a pretty street. There's a flower-stall over there. And we don't have to sit up here. We can always go out.'

She turned away and sat on the edge of the bed and wiggled her toes. 'I think I'd better tell you now,' she said evenly. 'I'm going to have a baby.' The expression on my face made her laugh. 'It's hardly surprising, darling,' she said. 'I suspected it a while back. Now I'm sure.'

'But are you sure?' I said stupidly, hardly hearing what she said.

She laughed again. 'I'm a very regular girl. Yes, darling, I am quite sure.' She came across and put her arms around me. 'It's all right,' she said. 'It's not anything to worry about.'

'It is something to worry about.' I tried to fight down a flurry of panic. 'I'm not divorced. We can't get married.'

'Who said anything about getting married? I haven't said anything about it. We love each other, don't we?'

'Yes, but ... You see ... Well, listen, this is serious. I mean, do you want to ...'

'Get rid of it? Oh, no, I don't want to get rid of it. It'll be our baby. I want to have it.' She didn't seem frightened or worried or excited, just serene and calm.

'Well, that fixes it,' I said. 'We're going to get out of this bloody terrible dump! You're not going to have it here.'

'Crikey, I hope not,' she said, and flung herself back on the bed, hugging her laughter into herself. 'Nor am I going to have it for quite a long time, darling,' she added after a while, her mouth twitching. 'So while we're waiting why don't we get dressed and go down and have some coffee at the Arabian?'

Coffee in cramped dim cellar lounges and the soft play of branch- and leaf-shadow in the autumn streets, as much as the emotional and physical raptures of 'a love still sublime even in the sleazy room of the Princeton, have been the palliatives of this uneasy arrival time of the last few weeks. There really are flower-stalls in Kings Cross and the one run by old fat Maggie has become *our* flower-stall, and we now have *our* tobacco kiosk where Cressida has charmed an old dragon of a woman into letting her have under-the-counter cigarettes, so we no longer have to save the tobacco from our used butts to be rolled up into airmail paper or smoke those terrible South African things that smell as if they are made from wildebeeste dung. And we have our own coffee-lounge where we can hear *our* songs on the juke-box, 'Laura' and 'It Might As Well Be Spring' and 'The Breeze and I' and 'Deep Purple' and 'Night and Day'. And in the evenings we can walk through light-dazzle and cacophony under the bronzing leaves, and nobody takes any notice of us or cares who we are, although heads turn wherever Cressida walks.

Kings Cross is a little spurious and more than a little self-conscious, and its air of cosmopolitanism is an awkward masquerade, but there are misfitting foreigners about and odd eccentrics, and a raffishness has persisted, and it is better than Melbourne, and better than the rest of Sydney, which is even more war-scarred from its self-inflicted injuries. A coarser, tougher city, poised on the edge of violence. A cocky, callous place ...

There was a big crowd on the safety-zone and the trams, as usual, were banked up halfway along the street. Near me stood a nervous little European refugee—the odd round shape of the hat and the long coat and the briefcase and thick-soled shoes testified his origins—and as the line of trams began to move again he turned to the man next to him, a tall rawboned type with a trap mouth and jutting chin, and asked in a heavy, thick accent, 'Iss zhis, z' next one, for z' Bellyview 'Ill?' The rawboned man looked at him with sidelong contempt and snarled, 'Why don't you reffo bastards learn t' talk English!'

I still don't know what made me react the way I did, but I had him by the shoulder almost before I realised what I was doing, and I threw a wild punch at him and began snarling myself, 'You wait until *you're* in Prague, you rotten uncouth bastard, and you're asking directions in *your* impeccable bloody Czech!' And then we had bumped through the crowd and were lurching across to the gutter, flailing at one another and brawling and

swearing, knocking over newspaper billboards, and the little refugee scuttled aboard the first tram that came along, whether it was for Bellevue Hill
or not, but by this time a red-faced policeman had us both by our jackets
and was snarling too, 'You break it up, you two bastards, or you'll both be
in *real* trouble!'

Coming back to the Cross, I smarted with humiliation and anger—anger
with myself, mostly, that I had allowed myself to become trapped in the
snarling violence and vulgarity of the place.

George Johnston, *Clean Straw for Nothing*, Collins, London, 1969.

Dorothy Hewett

Dorothy Hewett (1923–), poet and playwright, was a Communist Party
activist in the 1950s. At this time she worked in factory jobs and lived in
poorer areas of Sydney.

Embracing the working class

Sixty-five Marriott Street, Redfern, in the Cold War fifties—my very own
Wigan Pier. This is a card house with a difference. Dying asparagus ferns,
dead pot plants and chamber pots, hanging baskets draping a dismal curtain, three stands of rusty barbed wire looped along the front fence, it is a
fitting memorial to Miss Donithorne and her maggot. The maggot is love,
both spiritual and carnal. I have embraced the working class, and the
symbol is this decrepit brick corner house where we squat one dark night
with our two pink blankets, amongst the chocolate boxes, scent bottles,
rice-coloured face powder and laddered silk stockings. The newspapers
under the balding lino date back to the thirties. We are pulling up the giant
weeds, throwing out the cracked chamber pots, the wire baskets and the
mountains of buried tins.

A thin man, with no teeth, in a beanie, two muzzled whippets straining at
the leash, stops by the front fence. 'There's six dorgs buried in that front yard,'
he tells us mournfully. This is the Red Belt, where house-proud working-class
housewives sweep the pavements, blacken the front doorsteps and polish
the brass doorknockers until they glitter, but the poor, the old, the homeless,
the mad, the alcoholic, the subnormal, the disabled, the petty crims and the
Aborigines exist behind tattered blinds, boarded-up shop fronts and two-
storey terraces with the staircases burnt up for firewood.

The air is breathless with soot and smog. The knock-off whistles from
the brewery, the print factory and the glassworks punctuate the day ...

The two front rooms are large, with an autumn leaf dado. The kitchen is
painted a dreary railway fawn. An ancient Early Kooka stove, with one
burner and a missing leg, lists drunkenly in the corner. There is no sink, so

we wash up in the pitted cement tubs in the wash house; an old bath in one corner and a bricked-up wood copper in the other. The second bedroom has abstract wet blue patterns crisscrossing the wall, furred with mould in the winter. The kitchen looks like a giant spider web. We have so many electric cords running off the central bulb that we are always blowing the power lines. The man from the electricity department turns up, scratches his head and laughs.

'What's this, mate?' he says.

'Bunnerong!' (Bunnerong is the main Sydney power station.)

Richardson and Wrench, the housing agents, send round a lard-faced, heavy-jowled man in a grey double-breasted suit to bang on the front door, yelling, 'I know you're in there,' while I huddle in the hall or slip out the back to wander the streets till the coast is clear.

When winter comes we wade in the freezing streams in National Park to collect the coal that washes down the hills from the mines. When we burn it in the little black grate in the front room it spits out clinker, frightening the stray black cattle dog that has come to live with us.

Under the autumn leaf dado we type up the stencils, and print hundreds of illegal leaflets on the flatbed out in the shed. We are 'the centre' for the South Sydney section of the Australian Communist Party. There are no books or paintings in our house until we start a lending library of what we call 'working-class classics'—*The Ragged Trousered Philanthropists*, the novels of Howard Fast, Eleanor Dark and Katharine Prichard, *The Socialist Sixth of the World* by the Red Dean of Canterbury.

Dark figures knock on our front door late at night, picking up their copies of *Tribune* (the Communist newspaper) for sale at branches and factory gates. I have a *de facto* and a new baby, but we hardly spend any time alone. Our lives are devoted to the betterment of the row on row of little semis surrounding us, whose inhabitants neither know nor care.

The people next door hold a wild party every Saturday night. When the piano belts out 'The Old Piano Roll Blues', it is a signal for a punch-up—yells, broken glass and crockery, bodies thudding against the common wall. Once, passing the house, I see smoke and flames pouring from their car parked outside and run in to warn them. A week later, a skinny-faced man with crossed eyes sidles up to me in the lane and passes me a bolt of dress fabric, mumbling toothlessly out of the corner of his mouth, 'For your trouble, Missus.'

Across the street live a bevy of beauties, ageless, black-haired and lithe—grandmother, mother and several grown-up daughters. They swan around the front porch or hang over the front fence like birds of paradise. The father, a tall, silent seaman on the Suva run, comes home occasionally, bringing exotic silken kimonos 'for the womenfolk', who all have lovers. Their parties are legendary—bottles whizz down the front hall, shadowy figures skid out on to the pavement, pulling up the wooden fence posts and belabouring each other across the skull. The sounds of broken glass shatter the night. Next morning they leave for a week or a fortnight, coming back when the coast is clear with lowered heads and subdued voices, until they have built up their reputations again ...

Our back room is packed full of illegal literature, and when the referendum to ban the Communist Party looks as if it will be won, we realize we will probably go to jail. We spend hours burning the dangerous stuff in the back yard. Ash floats over the roofs of Redfern. Nobody takes any notice. By the afternoon, when most of it has gone up in smoke, the referendum is lost and we breathe again. But when the news breaks that the Section secretary has gambled all the secret funds away at Thommo's Two-Up School and the Labor Party representative on the Referendum Committee has stolen all the profits from the grog sold at the referendum party, the Redfern Communists are under something of a moral cloud. We have always been regarded as anarchists, or worse, by the Centre—Marx House—in the heart of the city. Everybody knows about the Redfern comrades in the Council elections who vote several times, trying on the shoes of all the dead still left on the electoral rolls.

Snowy has done time in Long Bay jail; Carol Jackson, her black bodice stuck full of pins, is the local dressmaker. Her son Eddy, covered neck to buttocks in lurid tattoos that rock seductively as he walks, is a genius. He taught a Party class on political economy when he was only twelve. Pat Gale is a Party sympathizer. She lives with her son Red Siddy in a battered semi under a loquat tree with Frankie Laine belting out 'I must go where the wild goose goes' on the record-player and a whippet dog they race at Harold Park 'for an interest'. Her twinnies smile like street-wise cherubs from the sideboard, their naval caps cocked provocatively over one ear. 'I've spent nights in Hyde Park in the Depression wrapped in newspapers against the cold, Red Siddy at the breast,' she tells me.

Joe the anarchist is an ex-American seaman, blackballed on the San Francisco coast. Bill is a tall, balding ironmoulder who sits in the kitchen drinking endless cups of Lipton's tea. Harried from town to town by the cops during the Depression, jumping the rattler, he has never settled long enough to marry. Now he has been put out to grass with a job in a peanut factory. 'It's no job for a man,' he tells me bitterly.

My friend Gwen met her husband Jimmy Shipton in the orphanage. They have a star boarder in the back room. One night, in a drunken confessional, he is unmasked as Gwen's lover and the father of the two children Jimmy Shipton always thought were his. Both men dump her to fend for herself with the two unwanted children. When I protest, Pat Dale grows philosophical: 'No man wants to be lumbered with another man's kids,' she says, turning up 'Mule Train' on the record-player.

Dorothy Hewett, *Wild Card*, McPhee Gribble, Melbourne, 1990.

Sunday Telegraph

A beat-up story that tapped into one of the city's deepest fears.

Centipedes used in fight against funnel-web spiders

Two brothers are using centipedes to combat deadly funnel-web spiders which infest the front garden of their home.

The brothers, Harold and Bill Ring, of Norton Street, Ashfield, have caught more than 200 funnel-web spiders in the past two years.

They have discovered that centipedes are natural enemies of the spiders and usually kill them in a fight.

Even when bitten repeatedly, the centipedes seldom die.

There are no funnel-web spiders in the Rings' back garden, where many centipedes live.

The brothers are moving centipedes from the back garden to the front garden, hoping they will wipe out the spiders.

Mr Harold Ring has four children—aged between 21 months and three years and nine months.

He has forbidden them to use the large front lawn, which is riddled with spider holes.

'We have to be on guard all day long because there is little hope of a child recovering from the bite of a funnel-web,' Mr H. Ring said yesterday.

'Almost daily the children run into the house crying "funnel-web, funnel-web"!

'Most people think that funnel-webs exist only in the North Shore area, but there are certainly hundreds of them in Ashfield, and probably in neighboring surburbs too.

Yesterday, State Entomologist Musgrave said that funnel-web spiders existed all over the metropolitan area.

'But there is no particular cause for alarm,' he added.

'Since 1927 there have been only five deaths in Sydney from funnel-web spider bites.

'Funnel-web spiders seem to favor sandstone country, but they have been found even in Darlinghurst.

'I have never heard of centipedes eradicating these spiders, and I think the matter is problematical.'

Sunday Telegraph, 4 February 1951.

Adrian Dixon

Adrian Dixon was brought up in a suburban Methodist family, found his sexuality at university, and discovered the camp bar underworld of 1950s Sydney.

Sydney's gayest bars

In the early 1950s Sydney's three gayest bars mid-week were the Carlton, Ushers, and the Long Bar of the Australia—close together in Castlereagh Street between Martin Place and King Street. Between 5 and 6 o'clock each week night, but especially on Wednesdays and Fridays, these bars swarmed with what was unquestionably Sydney's most smartly dressed collection of young men. Formality was the keynote. Fashion decreed well-cut, single-breasted suits, mostly in charcoal grey with narrow silk ties, and olive green or grey Trilby hats predominated. More audacious dressers occasionally affected pink or even mauve shirts. Open-neck shirts were unthought of! On the occasion of my first visit I was innocently unaware how far my College grey double-breasted suit fell below Carlton standards. The regulars—and most of them were—belonged to exclusive little cliques, each occupying a regular area from which it critically surveyed and appraised members of other groups. Conversation was generally shallow but sparkling with witty quips: 'My dear, she's so stupid she thinks oral sex is just talking about it!' 'She shouldn't, she's been down on everything but the *Titanic!*'

The regulars understood the fairly well-defined social status of each clique in the social hierarchy. Successful professionals, haute-couturiers, interior designers, actors, and business executives all belonged to the top-ranking groups. Shop assistants, hairdressers, and junior clerks drank in groups less socially prominent. Social interaction between the groups was usually limited to polite nods and smiles of recognition, although sex was the infallible social catalyst between apparently incompatible cliques. The beginnings of an affair between members of two socially disparate groups signalled a bewilderingly swift revision of attitudes. In no time at all honeyed smiles replaced icy Patrician indifference. Most groups clustered around a tacitly acknowledged leader—usually someone whose financial position enabled him to maintain a house or apartment of his own where he could hold large parties. Just about everybody in Sydney's gay society answered to a 'camp' name. Prominent 1950s hostesses included Faye, Hilda, Mary, and Nora, each of whom owned premises large enough for lavish gatherings.

> Adrian Dixon, 'Adrian finds his Avalon', in *Being Different* (ed. Gary Wotherspoon), Hale & Iremonger, Sydney, 1986.

Penelope Nelson

Penelope Nelson (1943–), novelist, was the daughter of two journalists. Her mother, Micky McNicoll, was the social editor of the *Daily Telegraph*.

Micky's girls

The old *Telegraph* premises were made up of several buildings between
Castlereagh and Elizabeth streets, shackled together with interlinking doors,
three uncoordinated lift systems, floors of overcrowded offices, rickety fire
escapes, hallways with torn lino floors, a basement noisy with metal printing presses, steep staircases and landings with grimy old louvred windows
that neither opened nor shut. I thought it was the most glamorous place in
the world.

Micky's office, known as 'Social' to everyone in the building except
her—she called it the 'women's section'—was on the fifth floor of the western building on the Castlereagh Street side. The lift on that side was so
ancient that it needed an attendant to work it. Even so, it often overshot the
mark, missed a floor or refused to start. The alternative was to use the stairs,
but females seldom used the stairs near the lower floors, the domain of the
compositors. The cartoonists had a room a few doors along from Social
near the bathroom (cracked mirror, naked light bulb, cold water only). The
people who produced the *Women's Weekly*, known in those unabashed
days as the *Weekly* girls, were on the sixth floor. Two flights below the fifth
floor was the infamous canteen, a snack bar in the wall presided over by
Miss Daniels, whose dandruff was a big talking point on Micky's floor.
I never actually saw dandruff fall into the vanilla slices as Miss Daniels
scratched her greying hair and made cheerful remarks about the viruses
going round these days. But Micky's staff—inevitably 'Micky's girls'—swore
to it. I couldn't believe the other things they said about the canteen, either.
They didn't like the food. What was wrong with them? How could anyone
not like meat pies, sausage rolls, passionfruit-icing-topped vanilla slices,
white bread sandwiches and best of all, cornucopias, huge pastry horns
filled with jam and artificial whipped cream and dusted all over with icing
sugar? There were actually women on Social and the *Weekly* who settled for
a Granny Smith when they went to the canteen. Then washed it under the
one cold water tap.

As women's editor, Micky was responsible for a page of 'News for
Women' on Wednesdays and Fridays, a five-page 'Magazine for Women' on
Thursdays and a seven- or eight-page magazine on Sundays. Hence her
long hours in the office. I spent long afternoons in Micky's office, too. I'd
arrange to go into town to have my hair cut at the T&G building in another
vain attempt to get my fringe to sit like Raewyn's, and afterwards would
hang about in the Social outer offfice until Micky emerged frrom the bare
wooden room where she subbed copy, chose photographs, took telephone
calls and arbitrated on all manner of things.

The Social girls, all lowly paid cadets or D grades, had to scamper from
one event to another, notebooks in hand, photographers in tow, looking
presentable wherever they went. To this end they had a few props to enable

them to pass muster with the city's best dressed women. Most celebrated of
these was the Office Dress, a shapeless black number that, accessorised with
the office scarf, belt or string of beads, made its appearance at one cocktail
party after another. The brightly smiling gynaecologists' and wool buyers'
wives who starred in the Thursday and Sunday women's pages knew it at
fifty paces. Because 'grooming' was a legitimate topic in the Social section, it
was not considered frivolous to spend spare minutes fixing up a manicure or
trying new make-up. The outer office and the bathroom at the end of the
corridor often reeked of acetone nail varnish remover and Yardley's English
lavender talcum powder. The hair spray era had not yet arrived ...

Bizarre colour adjectives and an occasional gibe enlivened the formula
writing of fashion notes, social jottings and photograph captions. Early in January 1952, for instance, Micky queried the colours chosen by Princess Elizabeth for her forthcoming tour of Australia. Advance publicity announced that
the Princess would base her wardobe on Tudor cream, Pacific yellow, Edinburgh rose and wildflower blue. The *Telegraph*'s 'Magazine for Women' was
not impressed. 'Tudor cream is a light champagne shade; Pacific yellow is a
sunny, acid yellow; Edinburgh rose is a new name for vieux rose; wildflower
blue is best described as a deep baby blue.' The *Telegraph* reported that
Sydney fashion experts gave this selection the thumbs down. 'The unanimous
decision was that favoured materials for formal occasions during the Royal
visit would be bengaline, faille and taffeta—in quiet greys, blues and black.'

Later the same month the 'Magazine for Women' announced that Sydney
women were clamouring for tiaras for Royal tour functions. However, following the King's death in early February, the whole tour was cancelled.
Undeterred, the *Telegraph*'s fashion notes found mourning clothes news-
worthy. Court circles were in full mourning dress. 'All black ensembles for
women in court circles, with little or no jewellery. (Diamonds only are
excepted. It was noted that the new Queen wore diamonds on the lapel of
her black coat when she returned from Africa.)'

There were strong conventions of language and form in the women's
pages. Micky frowned on women who wanted to be known by their own
first names or retain their maiden surnames: the form was Mr and Mrs Male-
name Surname. ('Sunbaking on the beach are Mr and Mrs George Falkiner.
They alternate between their Palm Beach house and the surf and their
lovely cruiser, *J'attendrai*, moored in Pittwater.' 1 January 1952.) Women
photographed alone or in all-female groups waved their husbands' first
names like flags unless they were divorced. ('Playing with her Christmas
present, dachshund Theresa, on the terrace of their lovely Palm Beach
home is Carolyn Copeland. With her is her mother, Mrs Alan Copeland.
They have one of the loveliest views of the beach from their home.')

Penelope Nelson, *Penny Dreadful*, Random House, Sydney, 1995.

Midget Farrelly

Bernard 'Midget' Farrelly (1944–) was Australia's first world male surfing champion.

A beat-up paddle board

... [O]ne day when I was down on the beach at Manly I came across a really huge, beat-up paddle board sitting on the sand just a few feet from the water. It was a monster: about seventeen feet long, twenty-three inches wide, and six to eight inches thick through the centre. It had no rocker in it, and was shaped like a big cigar. There was no one around at the time, so I took this thing and dragged it around and pushed it out a tiny way into the surf and tried to catch a wave with it. I didn't do very well the first couple of times, but then I managed to catch a wave standing up. I guess I must have been pretty stoked—I took that surfboard home with me!

Next day, when I came down to the beach, I asked at the surf club who owned the board, and all I learnt was the nickname of some fellow who didn't care about it. It was the thing in those days if you had an old surfboard you didn't want just to leave it there on the beach in case someone else wanted it. So I took the board home again, painted it, and patched the holes in it, and from that day on I've been on a board just about every day of my life. I still go body-surfing sometimes, and I like fooling around with skis and belly boards and all that, but board riding is really what counts with me—it's got something that nothing else in the world has.

I had that old cigar board for a couple of months, and I really learnt to ride on it. I used to take it down to Manly every chance I got, push it out through the soup, and catch as many waves as I could. I can still remember flapping in towards the beach, stuck way up on the end of this huge board and all the older surfers laughing at me. It was a lot of fun.

I was pretty small in those days, even for my age—it was about this time that I picked up the nickname Midget—so after a while I began to leave the board at Manly to save the drag of having to lug it down to the beach every time I wanted to use it. Then one weekend it was smashed up in a storm, and I thought the end of the world had come. But my parents had realised how keen I was on surfing, and they helped me to buy a racing-style board that was built specially for me. It was about fourteen feet long and twenty-one inches wide—a beautiful board with plywood decks, cedar rails, a shining stainless steel plug and stainless steel tail-hook.

This Surfing Life: Midget Farrelly as told to Craig McGregor, Rigby, Adelaide, 1965.

Thomas Keneally

Tom Keneally (1935–) ran for his school and the hope of praise from one of the convent girls watching. Keneally was brought up a Homebush boy.

Down on the mark

On starter's orders, we walked up to our graduated marks. Ahead of me, in lane four, I could see Gaffney of St Joseph's College in his pink and lavender, dancing on the spot and waving and jiggling his hands. I always wondered why runners jiggled their hands. It implied that the race brought with it the chance of wrist injuries. Whatever its purpose, I made sure I did it too.

Down on the mark. We all knew how to take the posture, few of us knew how to use it to drive away with the fore and aft leg once the gun went. Peter McInnes knew. But you couldn't prove your seriousness as an athlete to people like the Currans unless you could manage a crouching start. Different matter for the mile, of course. You could begin the mile with a standing start. Explosion was not necessary—or even the gesture toward explosion I was making as I crouched.

I got a good start, at least a fair imitation of an explosive one. A runner can tell at once, going into the first bend, whether he is running above himself, in time with himself, below his best. That day, owing to some amalgam of physical and psychic causes including the presence of Curran, I was above myself. I gained two yards on Gaffney in the outer lane. I knew I had Rankin beaten, the other St Pat's kid who ate sugary food even in Lent. Not an ascetic like me. A Celestial. A breeze from the south-west of the great continent of Australia, from the interior, swept up and nudged my shoulder as we entered the back straight where Curran and her sister sat. *Give it a go!* it implied. I was Curran's dream athlete envisioned. For her sake I took Gaffney on now with so little effort, shoulder to shoulder. Then out into open air, that lonely space in laned races, that ice-cold, blazing eminence, that kingship under threat. Running in first place, representing Curran, St Pat's and GMH: Keneally.

I could see a little ahead of me the limed lines which marked the start of the 220 yards, and I pounded across my 220 yard line, sensing but as yet ignoring the first aches of breathlessness and muscular failure.

They speak of the wall in the marathon, but the 440 yards or 400 metres has a wall as well, about the 320-yard mark. Those who have been foolish enough by too much flamboyance in the back straight to invite the wall can all at once hear the thunder of their enemies from behind. To the observer it is as if the failing lead runner is being held back by the shoulders. The head goes up or down, a confession of distress, the shoulders begin to waver. In the final bend I could see Gaffney's lavender shirt from the corner of my eye. It went past me like a man-sized spinnaker onto a wind I could not even get a whisper of.

At the turn into the straight, he was five yards ahead of me and of course uncatchable. This was a good time to perish, to cease upon the hour. Of course, Joey's boys like him were generally boys from the bush. One of our standard primary school essays: *Is it better to live in the Bush or in the City?* Gaffney, the child of some country chemist or solicitor or farmer, was demonstrating the natural superiority of bush cunning and lung capacity.

Cripes, Rankin on my shoulder! Sugar-eater. Girl-fondler. The infrequent visitor to the confessional. The slapdash votary. The fellow who liked Mathematics II better than he liked novels and had never heard of GMH. He came up in the last half-yard and nudged me by inches.

Thomas Keneally, Homebush Boy, William Heinemann Australia,
Port Melbourne, 1995.

Clive James

Clive James (1939–), television documentary maker, novelist, critic, and writer of the verse 'The Book of My Enemy has been Remaindered and I am Glad', has lived in London since 1962.

Praying it would end

Even at its best, Sydney Tech was simply a waste of time. But even at its worst, it mainly just got me down, rather than driving me to despair. Had it been a boarding school I would probably have been in real trouble. As things were, most of my agonies were self-inflicted through an excess of inward-turned imagination. Unfortunately misery is not relative. For some reason the school prided itself on its achievements in rugby union. It always finished high in the CHS competitions and occasionally fielded a team which could beat the best of the GPS teams, although Sydney High always remained the unbeatable enemy. For most of my school career I was obliged to play House football, which was a joke. The very idea of dividing the school into houses was another joke. I was a member of Williams House. Nobody seemed to be bothered by the fact that no building existed which could be described as Williams House or even Williams Hut. In fact Williams House consisted exclusively of the yellow singlets its members wore during athletics competitions. Dyed at home by the mothers commanding various techniques and materials, the singlets covered the range of all possible yellows from fresh butter to old urine. Wearing mine, I came third in the heats and second last in the finals. Once I had been a fast runner, but that was before I started to shrink.

House football took place in a park only a few miles' brisk march from the school. As a cold wind whipped across the grass, the two teams would position themselves in expectation of the opening whistle. The start of each half was the only time when the eye could detect even an approximation of positional sense. The moment the whistle blew, thirty small boys would gather around the ball, forming a compact, writhing, many-legged mound which during the course of what seemed like hours would transfer itself at random to different parts of the field. I was somewhere in the middle, praying it would end.

But there was worse to come. On days when a Grade football team had a bye, its members would be brought to our parks so that they could practise dodging tackles. They ran down the field while we tried to tackle them. It went without saying that they were bigger, faster and more skilful than we were. The real nightmare was when the First Grade side turned up. The star of First Grade was Reg Gasnier, already tipped as the brightest schoolboy rugby prospect in years. Indeed he toured England the following year with the Australian Rugby League side. Merely to watch Gasnier was to die a little. He was all knees and elbows. His feet scythed outwards as he ran, like Boadicea's hub-caps. There seemed no way of tackling him without sustaining a compound fracture. Up and down the field he steamed while we ran at him from different angles, only to bounce off, fall stunned, or miss completely as he side-stepped. He was beautiful to watch if you weren't among the prospective victims. The way he shifted his weight in one direction while swerving in the other was a kind of poetry. Regrettably it was also very painful if experienced at close quarters.

I can well remember the first time I was deputed to tackle Gasnier. He was three times as heavy as I was, although, density having the relationship it does to dimensions, he was only twice as high. There were only a couple of hundred people watching. Gasnier appeared out of the distance like an express train moving unhampered by rails. I ran at him on a despairing collision course. Casually he put his hand in my face. My head stopped while the rest of me kept going, so that I spent a certain amount of time supine in mid-air before falling defly on my back. While I was being resuscitated on the sidelines, Gasnier kindly materialised in my blurred vision and explained that the thing to do was to keep my head low so that he could not palm me off. The next time I tackled him I kept my head low. Side-stepping with uncanny ease, he put his hand on the back of my head and pushed my face into the ground. So much for the friendly advice. When they picked me up, or rather pulled me out, there was an impression of my face in the turf that you could have made a plaster cast from. It would have looked disappointed but resigned.

Clive James, *Unreliable Memoirs*, Jonathan Cape, London, 1980.

John Pringle

J.M.D. Pringle (1912–), a Scotsman who came to Sydney in 1953 to edit the *Sydney Morning Herald*, left in 1957 and returned in 1965 to edit the paper again.

The three winds

Sydney is ruled by three winds, which command the city in turn like the chiefs of an invading army. The first is the north-easter, the prevailing wind of summer. It is a fair-weather wind, a lazy, languorous wind, which comes in from the long reaches of the South Pacific heavy with moisture and sticky with salt. This is the wind which drives the great Pacific rollers on to the open beaches before leaping over the narrow barrier of land, making the pines at Manly sing as it passes and ruffling the calmer waters of the Harbour on the other side. On Sundays the crews of the eighteen-foot yachts catch it as they round the buoy for the long run home, and push out their bellying spinnakers which lift the small hulls out of the water until they seem to be flying.

The north-easter is a sea-breeze and is out of its element on dry land. As soon as it reaches the brick-and-concrete towers of the city it begins to flag, though it still has the strength to rustle the skirts of the palm trees on Macquarie Street and to fan the foreheads of the drinkers squatting on their haunches outside the pubs in Balmain and Woolloomooloo. A few miles inland it fades away altogether, daunted by the size of the continent before it. To the western suburbs it brings no relief from the heat, but to the more favoured eastern suburbs it is a source of pride and joy; and the wealthy citizens of Bellevue Hill and Point Piper set their houses to catch it like the yachts on the harbour set their sails. But the north-easter is not an unmixed blessing. If it brings coolness, it also brings the humidity which is the curse of Sydney's summer.

The north-easter has a rhythm of its own. It starts gently in the morning, the merest sea-breeze, and grows stronger all day until by six o'clock in the evening it is blowing half a gale and sending the more timorous yachtsmen in for shelter. Then it dies away as the sun goes down. Sometimes, too, it seems to grow stronger each day, while the temperature climbs steadily and Sydney swelters in sticky heat. Then suddenly it drops and there is a great calm. In the city the heat seems unbearable. Women sit outside their terraced houses in the inner suburbs and lean over their cast-iron balconies, unwilling to go indoors. Pale-faced children play languidly in the streets. But the men look to where great clouds are building up in the south or turn on the wireless to listen for the weather forecast. They know that the time has come for the north-easter to give way to the second of the three winds—the southerly.

The southerly comes with a rush of cold air and a splatter of rain. The Sydneysiders call it the 'southerly buster', because it arrives with a banging of doors and windows like a train coming into the station. It can be fierce for a few hours, bowling over the yachts in the harbour like ninepins and dexterously removing loose tiles from the house-roofs; but it is a much-loved wind in summer, bringing down the temperature with a bump, cooling the sultry streets and sending fretful babies to sleep. Generally it blows itself out in the night, and Sydney wakes up in the morning to blue skies and brilliant sun as the north-easter resumes its sway over the city. In winter, however, it may blow for days, bringing cold Melbourne weather and a hint of snow to pampered Sydney.

The third wind is the westerly, a gusty, dusty wind blowing from the heart of the continent. It is an unpredictable wind, following no rhythm and obeying no laws, but it is always unpleasant. In winter dry and bitterly cold, in summer dry and hot as the blast from an oven door, it pounces on the city and worries it. It is an uncomfortable, penetrating wind, which gets through clothes and windows, forcing dust into the eyes and nose. Like the sirocco of the Mediterranean, its extreme dryness seems to irritate people, making the easy-going Sydneysiders nervous and bad-tempered. In winter it may blow for weeks on end, but in summer, fortunately, it rarely lasts more than a day or two—fortunately because it is only when the westerly is blowing that Sydney gets truly hot. The temperature climbs into the hundreds; the tar melts on the roads; and those who go down to the beaches for relief find that they cannot run bare-foot across the burning sand to the water. Worse still, it is the bush-fire wind. If you look up at the sky during a hot westerly, you will see a curious reddish-orange haze on the horizon. This is the smoke of bush-fires burning beyond the city boundaries. On a bad day, when the city is ringed with fires, the sky is half obscured with smoke and the angry sun glares down on the city like a blood-shot eye.

I have described these three winds which rule over Sydney not only because they set the rhythm of the city's life but because each one seems to represent the conflicting elements which shape Sydney's character. The north-easter is the Pacific wind, and while it blows it tries to make Sydney a South Pacific city. Under its warm and humid breath men slow down in their daily tasks and dream of the islands to the east. Work is hard; pleasure is easy. Young men and women go down to the beaches of coarse but golden sand, which stretch for miles to north and south of the city, and spend the long days of summer basking in the sun or swimming in the surf. City typists take their sandwiches to the Botanic Gardens at lunch-time where they lie on the grass above the blue waters of the harbour before going back, a little late and a little sulkily, to their hot and dusty offices. And if the men who are working on the roads or digging drains in the streets pause rather more frequently to lean on their shovels and wipe the sweat from their brows, who can really blame them? The temperature is eighty-five and the humidity not less than eighty per cent. And who can blame them if, when work is done, they crowd into the pubs and swill down pints of the cold, strong beer which is their greatest pleasure?

The southerly, on the other hand, is the voice of conscience, the voice of home and England, even though it comes from the Antarctic. While it blows life resumes the brisker tempo of the northern hemisphere. A man can work hard without getting too tired or can sit indoors and read without longing to be out in the sun. It is a Puritan wind, which scourges the city for its laziness.

But the westerly is the voice of Australia. This is the true aboriginal wind, hard and lean and dry as the bones of dead sheep. Like the continent itself, it seems hostile to the white man who has swarmed on the sea-board. It hurls itself down from the mountains of the Dividing Range as if it would blow the city into the sea or burn it down with its fierce bush-fires. It mocks the efforts of suburban gardeners, withering their dahlias and roses in a single morning and turning their trim lawns brown no matter how they try to assuage its thirst with hoses. It is a nagging reminder of the great dry continent which stretches away beyond the Blue Mountains so clearly out-lined on the horizon.

Sydney, then, is a compromise, a mixture of these elements. It can never quite decide whether to be a thriving, bustling, Anglo-Saxon boom-town, a new Birmingham or Chicago, or a happy-go-lucky South Pacific city, an Australian Rio de Janeiro or a Buenos Aires. And always the Australian con-tinent is warring against both these alien conceptions, insisting on its rights and making the city hard and bare and violent like its own nature. It is an inconsistent city, where men in blue serge suits jostle against other men wearing nothing but a pair of shorts or a linen suit and a tropical shirt. It is a gay, pagan, boisterous, raffish city, full of oysters and beer and pretty girls in summer frocks and white sails on the harbour, but full also of hard-faced business-men and angry policemen shouting at street corners and traffic jammed in narrow streets.

John Pringle, *Australian Accent*, Chatto & Windus, London, 1958.

Penelope Nelson

Penelope Nelson, a little older, on the joys of Royal Sydney Golf Club.

The Matrons' Ball
I remember one formal dance from that year with something approaching disbelief. The Matrons' Ball at the Rose Bay Golf Club [Royal Sydney Golf Club] belonged more to the Edwardian era than to the year before 'I Saw Her Standing There'. I went without Roger, for the invitation list was solely in the hands of the 'matrons', upper-class married women whose husbands belonged to the club. Micky [her mother] had a childless friend from the

country who was determined that some lucky young person should go to this highlight of the social calendar, as her protégée. She wasn't even a close friend of Micky's, but that seemed to intensify the gratitude that I was supposed to express for the opportunity.

I had some reservations about the golf club to start with because one of my fellow sub-editors, who came from a Jewish family in Dover Heights, had told us how she had walked across one of the outer fairways, defying the club's restrictive membership rules …

It was a program dance. Each guest carried a small card with a little tasselled pencil. On the card were the numbers 1 to 12 with blank lines beside them. During the early part of the evening a kind of cocktail party, the equivalent of a Jane Austen Pump Room promenade, took place, in which we ladies circulated, engaging the gentlemen in conversation, hoping that at least a dozen of them would respond to our hopeful smiles and enquiries about their cars, golf games and accountancy courses by asking us for a dance. The experience gave me a new respect for the women of the eighteenth century and the heroine of *Persuasion*.

There were enough gallant young men around for me to succeed in filling all but one or two of the blank lines. I have dim memories of the pleasantness of some of my partners, and of a live band, but the vividest recollection is of the one dance I had to sit out. Not wanting to be a wall-flower, I went into the bathroom. The pong of smelly sports shoes dominated the rows of olive green lockers outside it. Near the mirrors, a melange of scents—Femme, Arpège, Airwick—teased the nostrils before being drowned out by the stink of hot feet. Gayle Galbraith, at the mirror already, raised her left wrist with its tasselled card tied to it as she kept dabbing on Love Pat with her right. She had an expressive comic face with large brown eyes. She rolled these eyes up in an expression that said something like *One day we'll boast about enduring this anachronistic crap*. She sniffed theatrically at the golf shoes …

At about the same time, I missed out on what was supposed to be an even greater social opportunity than the Matrons' Ball. A friend of Micky's, an effusive member of the Black and White Committee know as Petal because of her habit of calling everyone else 'Petal', asked me if I'd be a jockey at the Black and White Ball. 'All the lovely young things,' she said. 'All jockeys! I've known you all since you were babies. Isn't it exciting?'

Exciting for her; another dilemma for me. I asked for more detail about this ceremony. It appeared the jockeys reeled in some sort of wooden horse, winding string on wheels. 'Such a lot of fun. The horses are auctioned, and we make a lot of money for the blind. And the jockeys look just wonderful, all in black and white of course.'

Penelope Nelson, *Penny Dreadful*, Random House, Sydney, 1995.

Ruby Langford

Ruby Langford (1934–) was born on the north coast of New South Wales. She has lived and worked both in Sydney and in the bush.

Corroboree

When we first moved into Ann Street, Surry Hills, we survived on my endowment and any casual work Lance could get, but it only covered food. I took the kids to the Smith Family to get outfitted and with the eight of them we took up two fitting rooms. They got to know us well and we'd go home loaded up with brown paper parcels and cardboard boxes of tinned food. One morning they approached me at home and asked if they could take photos of the kids for their Christmas appeal. Somewhere in their files is a picture of me with a beehive hairstyle sitting on the front step of Ann Street nursing Pauline, who was two, and Ellen (four) sitting beside us.

Lance was working on the Water Board and I got a job around the corner at Silknit House making trousers for Reuben F. Scarf. I asked my cousin and his wife to stay and they saw the kids off to Cleveland Street School each day. Things were looking up. We bought a Ford Mainline ute and went to Paddys each Saturday for food, then we took the kids swimming at Coogee. ...

The kids were going to Sunday School round the corner in Commonwealth Street. The place was run by Central City Mission and was also a soup kitchen for the needy. They gave the kids bread and pies and cakes to bring home when we had no food. The Brown Sisters came to our rescue, they were called Our Lady of the Poor and wore brown habits.

I'd heard about the Aboriginal Progressive Association and I decided to go to the meetings. Charlie Perkins was there, and the Bostocks, Eadie and Lester, also Bertie Groves, Charlie and Peggy Leon, Joyce Mercy, Ray Peckham, Helen Hambly, Allan Woods and Isobel McAllum whose father was Bill Ferguson, a member of the Aborigines' Protection Board. We elected Charlie Perkins spokesman—he was still at university—and we met at the Pan Hellenic Club rooms in Elizabeth Street. Charlie organised that because he played soccer for the club. I was elected editor for our newspaper *Churringa* (meaning message stick). Ever since school and the long stories I'd wanted to do some writing, so I was happy.

It was about 1964 when we formed our first Sydney APA. We heard some dancers were coming down from Mornington Island to perform a corroboree at the Elizabeth Theatre in Newtown. At the next meeting we decided to apply for concessions. I'd never seen a corroboree or been in a big theatre before. Our seats were upstairs overlooking the stage.

When the lights went out we could see the glow of a fire on centre stage, with bodies huddled around it, and we could hear a didgeridoo in the background and clapping sticks and then the chanting. In a while the whole stage was aglow with the light from the fire, and the corroboree began.

A narrator talked over a microphone, explaining the action as the dancers performed. After each performance we clapped and clapped. Something inside me understood everything that was going on. I had tears in my eyes and I could feel the others in the group were entranced like me.

One story in particular made me sad. It was about a tribal family—man, woman and child. It told how another man came and took the woman away, and left the baby to die. The father searched and hunted until he found the man and speared him. His wife threw herself over a cliff and died. The final scene showed the father burying his child, and it was the most moving part of the corroboree. It showed him digging the earth up with his hands and placing the bark-covered body into the ground, and, as he was covering it with earth, he'd smite himself across the chest and wail for the loss of his child and cover more soil over the body then smite himself again, and this went on until he had it completely covered. I was crying by then.

Afterwards, we asked permission to visit them backstage. It was strange because they were dressed in khaki overalls and they were so tall, big rangy warriors all over six feet. Only one of them could speak English, a bit pidgin, and they were wary as they looked at us, until the one who could speak explained that we were part of them, and then they gave us big toothy grins and we were shaking hands all round. I can remember almost every detail from that night.

I went to a meeting of the APA on National Aborigines' Day in Martin Place. The Governor General and several other dignitaries (black and white) were going to speak. I wore a fur stole over my dress. I put my stilettos on and did my hair up. At Martin Place I met up with the others and found a seat. The Police Band sat behind us. A man on the dais was singing in the lingo and I listened closer. It was Bundjalung language, words and sounds I hadn't heard for a long time. It was an eerie feeling in amongst the skyscrapers. ...

I came home after an APA meeting one night about nine or ten and Lance was standing on the balcony calling out, 'Why don't you stay home and look after the kids instead of running around to meetings,' and so I had to give up my political work before I'd edited the first issue of *Churringa*.

Ruby Langford, *Don't Take Your Love to Town*, Penguin,
Melbourne, 1988.

Patrick White

Patrick White (1912–90), novelist and playwright, was rumoured to be a recluse—one of the quaintest of Sydney's urban myths. His letters of the 1960s, casting a cold eye on life and society, are a feast. David McNicoll (1914–) was editor-in-chief of Frank Packer's *Telegraph* and *Sunday Telegraph*. Nola Dekyvere (1904–91), socialite, also wrote a column for the *Sunday Telegraph* in which she attacked *The Ham Funeral*. Murray Rose (1939–) was an Olympic swimmer and actor. Joern Utzon (1918–), a Danish architect, designed the Sydney Opera House. The Baillieus are a prominent Melbourne family. Rudy Komon (1908–82) was a Sydney art dealer.

One of the lowest places on earth

DOGWOODS, 24.vi.62

TO GEOFFREY DUTTON

… The rehearsals of *The Ham Funeral* are going well, I am told. I am keeping well away from them as I don't want to be interrupted in my present work. One thing disgusts me, and that is the publicity that is being put out about the play. It looks as though they are trying to sell it as a 'spicy evening', and in doing so I feel they are going to put off a lot of the genuine supporters without bringing in more than a few of the morons at whom the publicity is aimed. I suppose one would have to expect an attitude like this in a place like Sydney. It is really one of the lowest places on earth …

DOGWOODS, 18.vii.62

TO THE DUTTONS

Dear Nin and Geoffrey,

… I expect you heard something of the launching of *The Ham Funeral* from Beryl Pearce. It was a wonderful night from my point of view. I was well bricked up in a pillar of alcohol, and watched from the back row of the circle. I don't think I have ever been in such a full theatre in Sydney, and the audience was with the play. (We had a most depressing dress rehearsal audience, which laughed in all the wrong places, and sent us home to bed in a state of despair.) Since then houses have been very good on the whole, and I am wondering whether they will extend their miserably short season. The *Herald*, *Sun* and *Mirror* all gave excellent reviews. The *Telegraph* panned it, but that was to be expected, and the semi-literate, exhibitionist gossip females like Mrs Dekyvere and Andrea are doing their best to keep people away. Certainly I snubbed Mrs D. on the first night by refusing to be photographed with her …

DOGWOODS, 30.viii.62
TO BERYL PEARCE
John tells me there is a big drive for dinner jackets and long white gloves. I have a 30-year old dinner jacket which has been shut up in a suitcase since the outbreak of War, and which has probably turned to lace by now; I daren't look at it. I have my 5-year old black suit which I intend to wear—it is very presentable—and if that is not formal enough I can lurk at the back of the theatre—I would anyway. I don't want to wear a dinner jacket again in my life-time. Sorry if this sounds bloody-minded, but you know how I appreciate you all without my telling you.

Yours
Patrick

DOGWOODS, 18.ix.62
TO WENDY DICKSON
Dear Wendy,
Thank you very much for the telegram. The first night was another of those strange dreams. Everybody was there, including the Governor, who was heard to whisper when the dogs began to bark and the little girl ran on at the beginning of the play: 'Ah, THE WIND IN THE WILLOWS!' The Governor's Lady was in 'donkey brown', we read ...

DOGWOODS, 8.iii.63
TO DESMOND DIGBY
Dear Desmond,
... I managed to get to the Luncheon on Monday after a dreadful Sunday night, when I started a kind of bronchial complication and vomitted up everything besides. However, I took everything. Manoly took me to Parramatta and I went in by train, looking like a waiter going on duty, as my only presentable and cool suit was a new black one I had bought to wear to the theatre and concerts in the summer. There was quite an amiable atmosphere in the Sydney streets for once, and I hung about the Circular Quay for a bit waiting for Them to approach. Finally they did, standing up in a very leisurely car. She was all in blew, he in a kind of tweedy number the colour of dry cowshit. After a bit I approached the yacht in fear and trembling, and ran into the Utzons, who had received a summons in the air on their way from Tahiti, and had been rushed straight from the plane. In our nervous condition we ganged up quite a lot, and he promised to show me over the Opera House. His wife is of that plain, dank-haired mermaid kind one sees from Denmark, very pleasant. As her English is a bit vague, she smiles. Then we went on board, up a red carpet, with sailors slapping their rifle butts, and were received by I don't know how many members of the household: a tall, toothy, elderly man in a lounge suit, and glamorous young Navy and Army equerries among them. The Army equerry, who was Australian,

appeared to have read some of my books, and told me that other members of the household were 'very interested'. In fact, he said, the copy of *Voss* had disappeared mysteriously. (I should think the Juke had probably thrown it out the porthole after reading half of Chapter 1.) The guests were very oddly chosen indeed, and I couldn't think for the life of me why I had been asked. I had imagined there would be other artists of various kinds, but Doris Fitton and Murray Rose were as close as we got to that—with of course the Utzons as a last minute inspiration. Otherwise they were all business tycoons (that Kirby, looking like a purple fig about to burst, Warwick Fairfax, Hallstrom), civil servants, and an admiral and general or two. We were lined up on either side of the saloon for the introductions to Ma'am and the Juke. There were drinks before and after, good stiff ones too, and one needed it. Mary Fairfax was tottering and using her smelling bottle before the drink was produced, and the headmistress of Cheltenham High, a nice hearty old thing with whom I had conversation, confessed that she was petrified. Doris, of course, was in her element, doing all that *grande dame* stuff she'd learnt in rep, tremendous curtsey while Lady This and Lady That were tottering and nearly falling under their chiffon hats. Lunch was really very good—rolls of smoked salmon with scrambled egg at the side (it's worth remembering), tournedos on foie gras with a salad, and *profiteroles* with chocolate sauce. I have never sat at such a long mahogany table. There were some rather gold urns down the centre, and vases of yellow and white flowers. They sat on either side, and I was at the lower end, so could look right down and observe. I was between Murray Rose, who is a most civilized young man, able to talk about things, and a Mrs Parbury, a youngish woman with heavily loaded eyelashes, who is niece of the Duchess of Gloucester. She came out here originally to be with her auntie, and fell for Parbury, a tall dark handsome Australian of family. I used to know his great aunt (now dead) and aunt (now crazy, but at large— she was always a thin spinster drifting from park to park, for no wrong reasons, just to pass the time, and now poor thing she is so mad she no longer knows which park she is in.) My mother used to know the Parburys in her youth on the Hunter, and I can remember her telling me in shocked tones that whenever the Parburys wanted to go for another trip they sold off a paddock. I used that in connexion with the Goodmans in *The Aunt's Story*. However, I couldn't tell the Hon. Mrs Parbury any of that at the luncheon. I couldn't find out any of her interests, only that she has two children whose education is worrying her. I told her to send them to the ordinary schools, but she is afraid they will develop split personalities. I told her I had developed one at the best of schools. That didn't get us very far either, nor the fact that one of her relations is one of my oldest and closer friends. After lunch we stood about in the saloon again for coffee, and I spoke to Admiral McNicoll and his wife. He is the brother of that bastard on the *Telegraph* who is one of the leaders of the opposition to my books. I think the admirals would show themselves to be of the opposition also if the politenesses were down, but we were soon led up to Ma'am, who began to discuss with McNicoll the oiling of stabilisers. She is fed up because the stabilisers in *Britannia* are apparently of an old-fashioned variety, which have to be taken out for oiling, while the latest can be oiled in position. After they had been through all this another lady who had been led up, all coffee lice and chiffon hat, spoke about the Barrier Reef, so I thought I had better put in a word as obviously a word was not going to be put to me. I told Ma'am she must make a point of seeing Fraser Island one day, and about the interesting wreck which had taken place there, and of the Nolan paintings which no doubt she had seen. At which she gave a shriek, or as close to a shriek as she could come, and said 'Ohhh, yurse! The Naked Lehdy! We saw one in Adelaide'. Poor girl, she might loosen up if one took her in hand, but as it is she struck me as being quite without charm, except of a perfectly stereotyped English county kind, and hard as nails under the Little-Thing-in-Blew appearance. I suppose it's just as well that she's tough. One wasn't led up to the Jokey Juke—he approached, and I think he made up his mind early on that he was going to keep well away from anything that might be an intellectual or an artist ...

DOGWOODS, 15.iii.63
TO DESMOND DIGBY
To-day Utzon showed us over the Opera House. Of course I really only went because you would have been so shocked to hear I hadn't found time for it, but how infinitely glad I am that I did. It has made me feel glad I am alive in Australia to-day. At last we are going to have something worth having. If only they had got going on the whole thing a few years earlier, so that we could be certain of having a part in it! I was particularly glad to have been shown over by Utzon, a kind of Danish Gary Cooper, although his English is a bit woolly at times, and difficult to follow. How shocking to think of those miserable little aldermannish devils attacking such a magnificent conception from their suburban underworld. Funnily enough as we were walking up and down all those steps in such a very contemporary setting I kept thinking of Phaestos, Mycenae and Tyrins. It occurred to Manoly too, without our having discussed it. I suppose the contemporary and the ancient do have a lot in common; it is the in between periods which went astray under the mass of detail ...

DOGWOODS, 24.v.64
TO GEOFFREY DUTTON
... Further: Expect you heard from Ursula about our funny evening at Hannah Lloyd Jones'. Apart from a conversation with Sid on the veranda,

with the moon coming up behind some tall gums, and a good gossipy gin-up with Ursula herself at the end, it was a bloody awful evening, full of Baillieus looking like their bulls. Dinner was all little tables, and I seemed to get stuck at the wrong one. The other man opened with: 'Well, Mr White, I hope you will consider returning to live among us.' I answered feebly that I had been doing just that for the last 17 years. I had beside me Hannah's very bedroomy niece Mari (Livingston) ,Gibb, an ageing blonde, who looked as though she would oblige quickly under the stairs [not her reputation]. On my other side was rather a rigid young woman in blue, from Adelaide, a Gosse or a Hay—Dull, but to be trusted. People who read the Sunday papers tell me that this party was the social highlight of Show week. Wadda-ya know! Still, I like old Hannah when she stops having the social jitters, and one can get down to talking about a few new lines for the shop. Ursula, I have discovered, is a Geminian, which explains that certain empathy.

How this letter has drawn itself out. I think I am staving off the evil moment when I start answering some dirty ones.

20 MARTIN ROAD, 18.iv.65
To PEGGY GARLAND
We have almost been through the ten days of hell which the Sydney Royal Agricultural Show brings to people who live in these parts. It is only a stone's throw from the showground, and we have floats, trailers, trucks and caravans parked all down this street for the duration. During the day the cars of the showgoers are added to these, often literally on the pavements, and in front of our garages in the back lane so that we can get neither in nor out. One is a prisoner for ten days, except for the breathers of Sunday and the night of Good Friday. Of course it brings a lot of life to the neighbourhood, and some of the inhabitants obviously flourish in it: ladies who normally stroll listlessly around the block and back start spanking twice round the block, and our next-door neighbour sits on her terrace at an iron table in her pastel bubble-nylon nightie, I suspect when her husband (to whom she isn't speaking) is out. One starts speaking to neighbours one had never addressed before, and I wonder whether one will speak to them again before the next show. It's all probably like the war in London.

20 MARTIN ROAD, 28.xi.65
TO THE DUTTONS
… Oh, I had forgotten—Rudy Komon asked us to lunch one day at his house, a decrepit looking semi-detached brick villa on the waterfront at Watson's Bay. Inside there are paintings to make a thief's eyes fall out. Dobell minia-

tures and drawings by the dozen, things one didn't know existed. A Conder in a frame made by Conder himself out of what looks like the woodwork from a stable. Little masterpieces by several painters I had always tended to dismiss. One of the best of Williams's abstract landscapes. A most unusual Blackman of a schoolgirl looking like Thea Astley surrounded by phallic drums on a very yellow beach. Where Rudy goes wrong, I think, is over Molvig—whom he considers 'possibly the greatest, certainly the most misunderstood Australian painter.' We ate a mass of delicatessen and drank several bottles of wine, but it was the paintings which made me drunk.

20 MARTIN ROAD, 26.iii.67
TO GEOFFREY DUTTON
… We had drinks recently at Admiralty House, the Drysdales also there, and Clem Semmler. Manoly discovered the latter has exactly the face and head of a grasshopper. I quite like him, though. When we were leaving Maie embraced Tass. She said: 'I don't know why I always kiss Tass and never Maisie.' Maisie replied: 'Let's keep it heterosexual, shall we?' Maie rang the day they were flying up to open the Show. She was unhappy at having to make a speech about the scones, because 'there's nothing you can say about a scone.' I told her everyone concerned would be satisfied to hear the scones were extra dainty this year. She could probably give herself quite an amusing time camping her way through official functions, and nobody to understand the language …

20 MARTIN ROAD, 24.iv.67
TO HAROLD HOLT
PRIME MINISTER OF AUSTRALIA
Dear Mr Holt,
I have felt all along that we Australians are ill-informed on the origins and conduct of the war in Vietnam. A few months ago the enclosed booklet came my way, and I am sending it in case it isn't known to you. It is worth reading and thinking about.

I'd like to add that I have always voted Liberal but can't go along with the war-in-Vietnam policy, nor can I stomach the invasion of Australia by the United States, although I have nothing against Americans in their own milieu.

Yours sincerely,
Patrick White

20 MARTIN ROAD, 18.ii.70
TO TOM MASCHLER
Dear Tom,
… About *Portnoy*, I hardly know what to advise. I think it is one of the wittiest books I have read, and you can repeat that if you want to when publish-

ing in Australia. I'm doubtful about Adelaide as a launching place. One is inclined to think of the Adelaidians as being advanced because of a handful of progressive intellectuals one knows, but the majority are terribly starchy and reactionary. Sydney is the most emancipated city in Australia; I'm not saying that because I come from it; there is much that I detest about it. On the other hand, I'd like to see Portnoy come in the Adelaide Establishment's eye!

Yrs,
Patrick

20 MARTIN ROAD, 19.vi.70
TO GEOFFREY DUTTON

Yesterday was the day of the great Rally and I now feel alive again after living in a peculiar kind of nightmare for the last couple of weeks. Now that I have addressed a multitude from the top of a lorry in Centennial Park, led a march, and made a second speech in the Town Hall, I feel I could face almost anything. People tell me my speeches came over all right, but you never know: they may have been speaking out of kindness. In the Park the other speakers were Harry Miller, Vincent Serventy the bird-man, and Jack Mundey. I think the latter will probably be our saviour; he announced that the monster will not be built where proposed, and as he represents the Building Labourers Union he's in a pretty strong position. In the Town Hall the speakers were Neville Wran, Leader of the Opposition in the Legislative Council, Kylie, a girl called Anna Katzmann who is Captain of the Girls' High School threatened by the Moore Park scheme, and Mundey and myself again. There were also four rather deadly (but most necessary) mayors, all of whom want the sport complex in their suburbs.

In the meantime the Government has appointed Walter Bunning to make an independent inquiry, and have put off announcing their decision till December. I dare think we have won! But we shall have to continue throwing an occasional bomb during the next few months. I heard that bastard Lewis being interviewed the other day: he sounds the most shifty kind of thick-voiced politician, full of lies, and downright stupid.

Patrick White Letters (ed. David Marr), Random House,
Sydney, 1994.

Oz

Oz magazine, edited by Richard Neville, Richard Walsh, and Martin Sharp, was to some extent modelled on London's *Private Eye*. On the basis of this article a stipendiary magistrate found this issue of *Oz* to be obscene. The three editors were sentenced to jail. However, with John Kerr QC as their counsel they appealed successfully.

A gas turn

Methodist Minister Robert Bush has been seen lately on Sydney's northern beaches armed with a tape–recorder to conduct his own sociological survey of teenagers' habits, morals, etc. *Oz* reproduces below a replica of a fairly typical conversation anyone can hear at the Newport Arms (nerve-centre of the party-crashing clique) on any Saturday night. It is not the sort of thing the Reverend Bush will be playing to his ABC listening audience, however. If you read this in a guttural, awkwardly, emphatic monotone, then you will enjoy a more accurate understanding of our beach boys' habits than a hundred ABC programmes could supply.

The word was flashed around the Arms that there was a GAS turn up at Whale Beach Rd, so we piled into the Mini Coopers and thrashed over and y' know what the old man of the bird who was having the turn said we couldn't crash—so Dennis belted him and we all piled in and there was a helluva lot of grog and plus th' tin tubes the fellas brought up from the Arms we all managed to get pretty pissed—there were a few KING birds there but they were holding hands with these fairies—so Dennis belted them and we all got on to the birds and Frank got one of them so pissed she passed out, so we all dragged her out to the garage and went through her like a packet of salts—KING! Then the old lady of the bird who was having the turn said she'd ring the Johns so Sid chucked all over her and she got hysterical so Denis BELTED her and Paul did this King hambone on the kitchen table and ran around the house in the raw—ripping the gear off all the birds—god he's KING! And then the little dago crap told Phil to leave his bird alone so Phil got Dennis and Dennis SMASHED him—God Dennis is a King fighter and a KING bloke—he really is and it really was a gas turn and I had a KING time and Sid was the funniest bloke I know kicked in the TV set and chucked in it god it was funny.

Oz, February 1966.

Roseville Chase Garden Club

The late 1960s might have been turbulent elsewhere, life went on unchanged at the Roseville Chase Garden Club in the green heart of the North Shore.

Our Christmas meeting

A fitting finale to a successful year of Garden Club activities.

> 'So join us in the singing,
> Have lots and lots of fun.
> Then when the party's over,
> God go with you everyone.'

So ended the opening number, written specially for the Children's Choir by
Evonne Grub, at our Christmas Meeting on 13th December 1967. The Children's Choir, consisting of 12 voices, gave a performance, which would
have excelled in any company. Such numbers as:—'Twelve days of Christmas', 'Away in the Manger', and the selection from 'Sound of Music' and
'Mary Poppins' were heard with the rare richness, simplicity and the sweet-
ness of a high class Children's Choir. As one member remarked even Julie
Andrews would have been impressed. Varied first grade entertainment followed the Children's Choir.

Wendy (Mrs Wenban)—lost!!?—Then found 'Waiting at the Church'—with
a note! rendered her item as only Wendy can. Mr Harmour with his mandolin
gave his usual classical numbers in true artistic style. Our thanks to Mr Hall of
the West Pymble Garden Club, who with Garry Shelley at the piano, and his
dancing puppets added variety to the programme. The trained voice of Else
Catheart delighted all. Else is an experienced singer, who gives up most of
her spare time entertaining the Senior Citizens. Diana Butler, of the children's
choir, with poise and confidence, captured the appreciation and admiration
of all, with her singing of 'My Treasure', and her encore number. The performance of the senior choir was par-excellence. With added voices their numbers were expressed in really masterly style. 'Silent Night' sung by the
combined senior and junior choir impressed all. Our thanks to Alderman
McLean, who, at short notice, carried on as compere, in place of Mr Bullivam,
who owing to illness regretted he was unable to be in his usual place on
stage. Special mention of our pianist, Mrs Thompson, without whose help
and encouragement throughout the year, the concert would not have been
possible. Congratulations to the ladies' committee, who worked as a united
and happy team, cheerfully missing part of the concert to make sure supper
arrangements were well in hand—the supper and service were excellent. The
choice of coffee or tea was appreciated by the record attendance.

Thinking back over the years, I would place our Christmas party of 1967
towards the top of the list of successful cultural functions, it has been my
pleasure to attend over a period of many years.

Ralph H. Law, *Journal of the Roseville Chase Garden Club*,
January 1968.

David Foster

David Foster (1944–) trained as a scientist before becoming a novelist.

A Balmain wake for Martin Luther King

Ain't No More Cane is a chain gang song. Now what in God's name could
have prompted Michael Ginnsy to have brought this tape along tonight? Is

he mad? Even given there were white men in chain gangs. Was it no more than a desire to impart his enthusiasm for the music? Or can it be he perceives, with Aristotle, the primary importance of musical education. Either way, it is music not vitiated by a cynical, urban *Weltanschauung*. It is pure Mississippi mud.

Ain't No More Cane is, we should say, a song from *ante-bellum* Arkansas and we're listening to it, rapt. It is of course The Band, The Hawks, recorded in the basement of Big Pink, their house at West Saugerties, New York, sometime between June and October of the previous year, with a single mike on someone's home recorder, and their Southern twang is unmistakeable on this, an Australasian premiere.

Ain't No More Cane is a *work* song. 'Rock music', writes the urbane Allan Bloom, whose views I find, on the whole, congenial, 'has one appeal only, a barbaric appeal, to sexual desire. Young people know that rock has the beat of sexual intercourse.' Spoken like a true Chicago Jew. With respect, this is the comment of a man who never swung a hammer at a dogspike. There is more to rock than the pelvic thrust, Allan. Mars swaggers off to battle to its beat and Hermes keeps its rhythm on His datestamp. Rock is the rhythm of our hearts, the rhythm of jogging, the Four Seasons. *Solvitur saltando*, dancing is the answer. We are wired for rock as we are for language, and that's the problem.

'*Listen!*' orders Ginnsy, and the people listen though the sound is very faint. They listen, because these people are open to experience, and though the evening is supposedly a wake for Martin Luther King, the black April victim of Southern white oppression, no one has a problem in sitting back to listen to white Southern boys making music, because it's great music, and Aussie, like Dixie, was beaten to begin. By no person present is Ginnsy's gesture, in providing this music on this night, misconstrued, for ain't no such thing as taste, now the alchemical solvent has begun work. Taste is in reformulation, answers are being sought, instincts are being heeded and acted on: Bliss was it in that dawn to be alive, But to be young was very heaven. Sure beat the nineteen fifties.

We are on the corner of Cameron Street, Balmain, where the 441 bus turns left, in a two-storey building that was once a corner store, with a residence above it, for the storekeeper's family. The verandah, in such a state as to provoke uncertainty in passers-by glancing up, is cantilevered out over the footpath, and contained only by some ornate wrought iron, of the kind that made its way to the colony as ships' ballast in Victorian days. The cornice is an entablature, with finely tuck-pointed brick piers, in lieu of caryatids. Over the verandah, the bullnosed sheets of rusting, corrugated iron grow more restless with each passing breeze and piss into a guttering that could be removed in minutes by a five-year-old boy, using his bare hands. At street level, the entrance is secantial to the kerb, and both the antique sandstone steps below the French doors are worn as the kerb itself; the same, weary beslippered feet that trod the kerb often as not went on into the shop, but by '68 the shop is become a residence, and the shop windows are hung with heavy curtains, and in the cracks between the curtains can be seen at night sometimes the glow of candlelight.

A symposium has been scheduled by Barbara Byng, one of the shop-house residents, to protest against the assassination of the Rev Dr Martin Luther King Jnr, shot dead in Memphis, where he'd planned on leading a dustmen's strike. It is hoped to explore means by which white Australians can express solidarity with adulterous clerics and black American dustmen. Keynote speakers are bound to include Barbara, who has a particular interest in Blues music and civil rights, Nisi Papadimitriou, who has just finished reading *Soul on Ice* by Eldridge Cleaver, and Nisi's new friend Monica, who was raised in Alabama, and has seen plenty of negroes.

There has been a disappointing roll-up, according to Barbara, who must have been hoping they would spill onto the footpath. Certainly, the shop is full, and the music from the shop hi fi can be heard blocks away, at the police station. The music contains a strong West African element (excessive *portamento* in the vocals, the search for the ever-so-slightly flattened third, which here misses by a country mile), but the blues harmonica has the poignancy of oboe, and the rhythm guitar is a Gaelic strum. It's your Jewish one-man band, the boy from Duluth, Minnesota, 'where'—to quote from the jacket notes of *Planet Waves*, '74—'Baudelaire lived, and Goya cashed in his chips, where Joshua brought the house down!'

Too soon for *Hurricane, They Killed Him, George Jackson*—songs written with the Black Civil Rights Movement in mind—but well in time for *Oxford Town*, inspired by James Meredith, and *Blowin' in the Wind* is an anthem of the sixties, and it is on the disc being spun now, over and again, *The Freewheelin' Bob Dylan*.

These are the battle hymns of the Revolution. Cain't you hear that slave boy holler in his hut?

David Foster, The Glade within the Grove, Random House,
Sydney, 1996.

George Johnston

George Johnston (1912–70) had just returned from living on Greek islands where the local women wore black.

A very short white dress
'Look,' he had said, intending to make some point, 'I'm thirty-five,' and Cressida had smiled across at him and said, 'Already?' and this checked him

on the point he wanted to make and raised a small laugh among some of the others, that sort of approving laugh like a tick made on a formal questionnaire that went with the smart anachronism of a Queen's Birthday holiday party in a tweely restored little mid-Victorian cottage in one of the in suburbs, drinking red wine out of flagons and watching Ginna, his continuity girl, stirring the minestrone in a plastic apron over a miniskirt that showed white net stockings to eight inches above the knees.

It was very much that kind of a party, and I remember thinking it could never have happened in earlier years. Not in this part of world. Cressida wore a Mary Quant thing, black and white with a hood that made it look a bit like an academic gown, and her net stockings were black, and Sue wore tights and a very short white dress made up out of a crocheted Hong Kong table-cloth and Edda a Marimekko shift, and Martha tight pants and ruffled shirt in a kind of batik. There was a hint of flagrancy about their sophistication. They were all married women, or had been, although some of the present associations were not quite clear, and there were two late-arrived babies, desperately conceived, rolling on the hairy rug where the Siamese cat stalked mewling. All four women dressed just a bit younger than they really were. But smart with it. Attractive women still. They all wore interesting rings on their fingers, original rings, not acquired hurriedly, rings denoting distinct experiences, cosmopolitan travel, peaks of admiration.

I had not met Martha since London, over seventeen years before, when she had been a top mannequin there, and she still had all the style and the looks and was threatening more than half seriously to get out on the catwalk again in her middle forties, and show the young ones. You felt she could, too. Edda was from Trieste, and she too had been a model in London, and a notable beauty, but that had been after Cress and I had packed up and gone off to Greece. One of the babies on the floor was hers, and she was married now to Steve, who was trying to get rid of a cattle property he had up north in the brigalow scrub and talked, as he had talked for years, of writing a novel.

The men were all smart too in a casual holiday way, checked shirt and hacking scarves and sweaters and fine socks—Giovanni from Alitalia dreaming of white and cubic towns spewing down the hillsides in Reggio Calabria, and Harry who dealt in old houses, restoring them with sandstock brick and white paint and filigree balconies of cast-iron, and Peter the grazier who had once stayed on the Greek island with us and who dreamt melancholically of selling everything up and going back to Europe to live. He had in his middle fifties fathered the other baby on the rug, but there had been no solution in this and he no longer lived with Sue of the Hong Kong tablecloth-dress, although they continued an intermittent social rapport among their friends. He drifted around art openings and film society shows and lived, alone and dispirited, in a beautiful beach house twenty-five miles up the coast. He had recently built a darkroom into the house where he developed and enlarged his photographs and made his own colour prints of his one long and hopeless sojourn abroad. Earlier the emptiness had left his eyes when he had been talking of trying Ibiza or buying a small vineyard on the coast south from Barcelona. A year before it had been the Dalmatian coast, a year before that a Greek island.

George Johnston, *Clean Straw for Nothing*, Collins, Sydney, 1969.

Keith Martin

Keith Martin (1930?–82?) worked as an industrial rounds journalist for the *Sydney Morning Herald*. Folklore says he was the first Catholic to be employed in the *Herald* newsroom and that on his first day he wore a sports coat. The chief of staff, a woman, publicly reprimanded him: 'Mr Martin, *Herald* gentlemen wear suits.'

The second Moratorium

The expressions on the faces of Sydney shoppers and office workers emerging into King Street on Friday evening, September 18, were something to behold. Fear mingled with disbelief. Here, in cosy, safe King Street, hitherto the scene of nothing more violent than the occasional bargain sale, groups of bodies were wrestling on the pavement, police caps were rolling across the roadway, and above all rose a virulent chorus of hatred against the forces of law and order. This was Sydney's second Moratorium—and what a contrast to the first one.

I have set it all down because I believe it should be done, and because I believe some lessons can be learned from the errors on both sides.

My Left wing friends have asked me if I saw police brutality. My answer is that I saw a few policemen being brutal. My Right wing friends have asked whether I saw professional agitators at work. I replied that I saw a small number of agitators who, if they were not professionals, were doing pretty well as amateurs in encouraging demonstrators to disobey the police.

In the previous Moratorium in May an estimated 20,000 demonstrators sat down on the roadway and footpaths outside the Sydney Town Hall to make their point of opposition to the Vietnam war and conscription. This time they were not allowed to go to the Town Hall, or to get on the roadway, and that is where the trouble began. The plan was for groups of demonstrators to march in during the early afternoon from the universities, from North Sydney, Kings Cross and other points. After that, the crowd was to march down George Street to the Town Hall for the sit-down in the street.

The marches to Wynyard Park were relatively uneventful, except for the arrest of the draft evader Mike Jones and a few others on the march from the Sydney University. I followed the march of about 400 secondary students and teachers along George Street. The marchers kept to the western footpath, obeyed traffic lights and were watched by a string of police at the kerbside who made no attempt to intervene.

At 2 o'clock what seemed an interminable number of speeches began in Wynyard Park, during which there was a floating population in the park which I estimated at about 8,000. Many of the audience drifted away periodically into pubs and milk bars. The NSW Moratorium organiser, Ken McLeod, told the crowd he had been refused police permission to take an amplifier truck into the park. Nevertheless, he was using an amplifier and most people in the park were able to hear what was being said, although whatever merit the interspersed folk singing had was totally lost in the poor amplification. During the speeches police massed at either end of the park.

About 3.30 p.m. the convenor, Ken McLeod, told the crowd that police had moved into the Sydney University marchers and arrested Jones. He said the police had arrested people even though they were obeying orders and marching on the footpath. (This did not tally with the account of a colleague, who was an eyewitness and said the marchers had tried to march on the roadway.) McLeod's statement was greeted by boos and hisses directed at the police.

Although the demonstrators, according to their own programme, were due to leave the park between 3.30 and 4 p.m., neither the Sydney University group nor the University of NSW group had arrived at that time. The speeches and singing continued.

The first arrest I saw occurred about 4 p.m. I saw several police conversing, apparently earnestly, with a young man and a young woman carrying a sign. After what appeared to be a quiet conversation, both were led to a police waggon and placed inside.

At 4.45 p.m. McLeod declared the rally closed and called for no violence. A large number of the crowd then began gathering on the roadway in York Street outside the rear entrance to Wynyard Station. At this stage I had heard no actual orders from McLeod or any of the other organisers that the roadway was to be occupied. About 200 police massed in this part of York Street, then marched towards the crowd. A man called: 'Everyone relax. No fighting whatever happens.' The impact of the police swept the crowd backwards. I saw a youth struggling violently with several policemen. Whether he or the police started the fight was impossible to tell. As the police cleared the roadway shouts of 'pigs', 'Fascists', rang out and many in the crowd gave the Nazi salute to the police.

Several Moratorium officials were still standing on the microphone platform in Wynyard Park and one of these, a bearded man who appeared to be in his middle or late twenties, took the microphone and declared: 'It's all provocation at this stage. Just walk around them.' A few seconds later he said: 'Go through the Wynyard Arcade to George Street. Be orderly at all times. Move south and east from the park.'

I walked through the park towards Margaret Street and suddenly heard in this direction continued loud banging, not unlike the noise from a panelbeating shop. As I got closer I could see the noise was being made by the rear doors of police waggons being thrown open, and the struggles of demonstrators as police forced them into the waggons. I crossed the roadway and took up a position outside Pfahlerts Hotel, where I could see the scene clearly. I saw that about one quarter of the police on the roadway actually involved in making arrests or moving demonstrators from the roadway were not wearing their numbers.

The struggling crowd made its way into George Street, where police reformed outside Wynyard Station in a line across the roadway. But the crowd, which by this stage had gained considerable momentum, flowed around and through them. At this stage the police appeared to have momentarily lost control of the situation, at least in this section of the street. The police then seemed to change their tactics and instead of trying to block the march, concentrated successfully on getting the marchers on to the footpath.

At the intersection of George and King Streets demonstrators found themselves confronted with a solid wall of police on both sides of the street. A senior police officer called out 'Move in, move them and keep them going. Arrest any pedestrian loitering.' Then began the concerted police effort to divert the marchers up King Street, which led to the worst incidents of the day.

Many of the marchers, apparently intent on following the original plan and marching down George Street to the Town Hall, refused to budge from the King Street corner, which quickly became a packed mass of struggling humanity.

A middle-aged man in a fawn raincoat shouted at the few demonstrators obeying police instructions to go down King Street: 'Stop, you can't go this way. Back to George Street.' A young girl near me asked her companion: 'Is he a marshal?' but the boy did not know. The crowd hesitated and a series of fierce fights broke out between police trying to push the crowd up King Street and those resisting or trying to cross to the other side of the street. At one stage at least a dozen groups of police were struggling with demonstrators. I saw a wildly struggling youth grabbed by the hair by one of several policemen who were putting him in a waggon. Another policeman swung an uppercut at a demonstrator struggling with other police, and in another incident I saw a policeman knee a youth in the groin as a group of police forced him back to the kerb. These were the only instances of deliberate brutality I saw.

By this stage many of the demonstrators appeared wild with hatred against the police, shouting and screaming at them but not initiating any violence. A new pattern then formed, with police plucking out of the

crowd the most abusive of the demonstrators and putting them in the waggons. This operation was carried out violently and efficiently. Sometimes a
single policeman would thrust into the crowd to grab a particular person.
Within split seconds half a dozen more police would be at his side to
ensure that the prisoner was subdued and that none of the other demonstrators were able to stop the arrest. Near me a youth remarked loudly and
sarcastically: 'Who would help the police?' A young constable said: 'That's
offensive to me,' and immediately arrested him. Another constable challenged the person who had been calling him 'pig' to step forward, but
there were no takers.

By 5.30 the demonstrators had given up trying to cross King Street and
began moving up King Street. At the Pitt Street intersection they found
another force of police preventing them from moving south in Pitt Street. A
marshal with a loud hailer announced: 'Form up in Hyde Park and re-group
to commence the march to the Town Hall.' The marchers then went to
Hyde Park without further incident.

In Hyde Park, McLeod told the demonstrators there were two courses
open to them—to wait in the park for people already at the Town Hall to
join them, or to go to the Town Hall. Most of the voices favoured going to
the Town Hall, and the march resumed. Near me I heard one young man
say to another: 'Let's get them running,' and both set up a chant, 'Run to the
Town Hall.' Within seconds the crowd was streaming across the park and
across Elizabeth Street, bringing traffic to a standstill.

At the corner of Elizabeth and Park Streets the demonstrators were confronted by another solid wall of police. It was now 6.15, almost two hours
after the time scheduled for the sit-down opposite the Town Hall, but the
numbers of demonstrators seemed as large as ever. Many of them forced
their way into Park Street, but were unable to get further than Castlereagh
Street, where another large body of police had formed up. Police grabbed a
youth and a screaming girl who was hanging on to his arm and forced them
into a wagon. I asked another youth who had been standing alongside him
what had happened, and he replied that the youth called a policeman a
'fuckwit'. At this stage police appeared to be pushing and shoving without
much plan, and a girl fell through a plate glass window, apparently without
serious injury. Gradually the crowd began to melt away, and by 7 o'clock
most of them were on the march, not to the Town Hall but to Victoria Park
near the University, where a second rally was held, only to be washed out
later by rain.

The violence of this latest Moratorium in Sydney, with 173 arrested, con-
trasts strangely with the peace and order of the last, when only seven were
arrested. The violence seems to have stemmed from two things. In May the
demonstrators were allowed to march on the roadway; this time they were
not. Again, in May, they were allowed to get to the Town Hall; this time

police made an extremely determined and successful effort to see that they did not get there.

In the spate of charges and counter charges it is difficult to apportion blame. Each side claims the other was not sincere and accuses it of lack of co-operation ...

Keith Martin, 'Moratorium march' from Nation (ed. Ken Inglis),
Melbourne University Press, Melbourne, 1970.

Edmund Campion

Edmund Campion (1933–) is a priest and writer, perhaps best known for *Rockchoppers: Growing up Catholic in Australia.*

An easy mark for developers

My homecoming horizons were widened when, after a few years as chaplain to Sydney Hospital, I was put in charge of the parochial district of Woolloomooloo. Many of its houses hadn't been much to start with; by now, they were dilapidated and askew, an easy mark for developers who were, I soon found out, slavering to get their hands on the 'Loo. Well, we stopped them. I have told that story elsewhere but, in the telling, I did not say enough about the allies we made then. Libertarians, old members of the Sydney Push, products of Professor John Anderson's circle, the original Sydney think-tank whose aim sometimes seemed only to think, never to do— here were idealists I would not normally come across. Our focus was domestic and limited to the little lanes and streets of our own neighbourhood; whereas they saw a bigger picture, as wide as all Sydney, and after one battle was over with they moved on to other fields. Coming from different directions, we met at the Wayside Chapel in Kings Cross, in the coalition of resident action groups and across the pages of the little publications that sprouted then. They have paid for their temerity in challenging the developers, especially at the hands of those overpaid hirelings, the lawyers. But they raised the alarm about what was happening in our city, and that will be their glory.

As well as them, living at the cathedral meant you got to meet a range of Sydney's walking wounded you would remember always. There were harassed women with children who came, always at weekends, wanting fares to impossibly far places like Melbourne or Wagga Wagga. There were homosexual victims of basher gangs who would limp in late at night to get a clean shirt and the fare home. They would have picked up a boy in Hyde Park who decoyed them into the Domain where they were rolled for watch and wallet before being beaten up. There were the wretched refuse of other shores who babbled glottally and consonantally, their brains eaten away by war or alcohol, but who still called the cathedral home. There were suicides, drunks, visionaries, dropouts, conmen, naggers and cranks—life's victims, all of them.

A young woman went off her medication and spent the afternoon raving in the cathedral. Persuaded to leave peacefully, she asked could she use the presbytery lavatory. Once inside, she started to strip. Shirt, skirt, knickers, bra came floating into the corridor. It was nearly teatime. Would there be a naked confrontation with Cardinal Gilroy? Just in time I managed to get her dressed and drove her home to Balmain.

Edmund Campion, A Place in the City, Penguin, Melbourne, 1994.

Rosa R. Cappiello

Rosa R. Cappiello (1942–), novelist, came to Australia from Naples in 1971 and worked in clothing factories. She has since returned to Italy.

Slaves of the dollar

My job? What could I do other than blow up. At the A.&D. factory where I'd been working for a week or so, the women workers were blessed with worn-out arses and addled brains. During menopause, widows, sluts, old maids in search of husbands, were capable of having plastic surgery just to convince the marriage brokers that they were born again. The manager—a short stocky Friulano, unhappily married to a wrinkled asexual Australian woman some fifteen centimetres taller than he was. The supervisor—an extremely thin Calabrian dwarf madly infatuated with the ever-lustful short guy. The manager assigned me twenty-nine as my payroll number. He bestowed it upon me as though it were an order of merit, accompanying it with a wink and pinch on my arm. Then, standing at the far end of the row of sewing machines, he kept miming the number with his fingers, two four five, two nine, two nine, twenty-nine, twenty-nine. In Naples said number is synonymous for prick. The short stocky guy mimed it to me continuously with his lips, with his outstretched hands. For a while it was great fun. The dwarf, fearful that I might reciprocate the manager's advances, was very kind to me. It was the first time in my life that a woman paid me court so that I wouldn't steal that half man of hers complete with his tooth decay. The dwarf would look at me from afar, a thoughtful glance, then she would come forward, with a waddling walk like that of a pregnant duck, the packet of material for sewing in her arms, and she would almost bow, almost kiss my backside—with us being *paesane* because pride and dignity dictated that we should help each other. I let her carry on. It was to my advantage. I was philosophical and pliable.

The married workers were not well-disposed towards the single ones. The superiority of having a pair of pants for company, even if the pants were empty; even if you saw those women at dawn running like hell with sleepy toddlers hung about their necks, whining, so that you'd really feel sorry for them. Children looking more like bags of rubbish than fruits of love. This is the female factory worker, wife of the modern coolie and coolie herself, who has got down to a fine art the act of tying her baby to the bed or to the downpipe of the kitchen sink so as not to forego the happy hour on Friday which is pay day. Slave of the dollar, she sends her newly-born babe to relatives in Egypt, Yugoslavia, Spain, Greece, and after a few years back it comes like a postal package by sea or by air ...

Redfern, like Paddington, Surry Hills, Chippendale, Haymarket, Darlinghurst and lots of other suburbs, seems designed like a cemetery. They remind me of the grey avenues of Poggioreale cemetery, but without the addition of well-kept flower beds. The fossils which live there begin to fatten, their stomachs swell, like satisfied worms. In each of these hovels at least a dozen bodies are crammed and kicking, tenants and children, owners and children, singles. A Tower of Babel ...

After the Sunday afternoon nap, rested, washed and deodorized, I sit on the pile of bricks in the Portuguese family's yard, anxiously awaiting Lella, so we can go and have our usual cappuccino at Maman's café-brothel in Newtown. Record players blare maddeningly nearby offering me music and sound at full blast for free. A small group of people, gathered together in the open air, drink straight from the can and nibble on potato crisps. The men sport long hair and reddish beards, the women have a slovenly look about them, the consequence of a low degree of self-confidence. Some of the group are painting à naïf the front of the house where they live all together. Violent colours which hit at the anonymity of the lane like a punch in the eye. The Turk's child is squatting naked against the wall, shitting. On the corner the pub reigns supreme. Tough fellows in shorts and white singlets, brimful glasses in their hands, restore the energy expended in training in the park, cracking jokes and laughing loudly. There's the newsagent, the takeaway, the stench of fried fish and and rancid potatoes, the laundromat, the delicatessen which sells continental delicacies. This is my kingdom and I fit in like a gardenia in a dandy's buttonhole. I'm sorry I'm not a painter. If I were I'd express through my painting the trust this street inspires in me and the privilege of being able to live here. I'd paint the wretched gutter where the cat slakes its thirst, the unkempt woman who in the morning, already drunk, pops out in her filthy dressing gown to collect her bottle of milk. I'd paint the pretty Lebanese poofter with the misty eyes and the sincere smile on his lips when he says 'hello' to me. I'd paint the mothers with their little children dangling from their breasts who, without having brushed their teeth, run still sleepy to their work, the sound and the fury of that precise moment when they rush out into the street, spurred on by the chaotic hurry to free themselves of their offspring, blood polluted by cents when boiling over with pride and boasting, guts tangled in the machinery, tears without salt, faeces constipated because of a sedentary life, hands which give bitter caresses, the absurd words which they exchange when they gather together for their meal. I'd paint the feverish race for gain. The impulse which turns simple people into their own executioners. I would generate the song of songs in paint. The Apocalypse with an alarm clock in its hands. There would be no other canvas, pictures or displays at my passing. I'd mutate the flesh of workers into paper money for bank reserves, their sweat into the ribbon which ties it, their feverish eyes into diamonds and gold nuggets as big as pin heads. With their fatigue and their suffering I'd paint the side dish to accompany their plate of minestrone, on a yellow canvas two metres by three point four.

Rosa R. Cappiello, *Oh Lucky Country*, University of Queensland Press,
St Lucia, Qld, 1984.

David Ireland

David Ireland (1927–), novelist, had a variety of occupations, including working in an oil refinery, before becoming a full-time writer. The pub in this extract was past Parramatta.

The study of drinkers

Next time I saw Sibley alone I asked him how his investigations were going.

'I'm finding all sorts of things,' he said cheerfully. 'This is another dimension here,' looking round the Southern Cross.

'Questioning non-drinkers, too. Do you know, Lance, how many non-drinkers have never held a social conversation with a drinker? Or know no drinkers by name. Or have never visited a drinker's home, or have no drinkers among their personal friends. Do you know the percentage of non-drinkers that belong to an organisation for the assimilation of drinkers?'

'No, Sibley. You've got me there. But what do you mean, assimilation?'

'That's my aim, the aim of the thesis. To investigate means of assimilating the drinker into the main body of society.'

I thought a bit. 'Sibley, maybe you shouldn't say too much about this. The guys round here are likely to be pretty sensitive about thinking of themselves as another race, or having to be assimilated into the rest of society. I reckon they feel they *are* our society, and the thought of having educated people stooping to lift them up, well, they might take it hard.'

'Don't worry, Lance. History is on my side. Research and quantitative analysis will bring a solution to their problems.'

I shook my head. His eyes followed the crack up the back wall where it pointed to the clock. It had spread a bit.

'My opinion at the moment is that drinkers should be encouraged to join local organizations, be part of the community.' He fished in his pocket and brought out papers.

'These are opinions from non-drinkers. I'll read a few to you. Eighty-seven per cent said they'd feel uncomfortable if a drinker sat next to them in public transport or a theatre. Similar percentages said they have nothing personal against drinkers, but they could never be friendly with one and they thought their appearance was unattractive. Similar numbers said drinkers try to get more for nothing than non-drinkers, that there's always trouble when you let drinkers into a nice neighbourhood—they give it a drinking atmosphere. And here's some hard figures. Drinkers are pretty much alike: ninety per cent. There should be restrictions on them to protect others from drinkers' lack of responsibility: ninety-four per cent. The two cultures can never merge: ninety-four. Drinkers probably prefer not to mix with non-drinkers: ninety-nine per cent.

'Where did you get these figures, Sibley?'

'Round here, in the Mead. Oh, I see what you're getting at. Yes, over on the North Shore, where there's no chance of drinkers buying land or houses or keeping up with the rates, the percentages are low; they're on the drinkers' side in droves. Very liberal, very humane.'

'Very remote.'

'Exactly,' he said pleasantly. 'People can't act outside their own frames.'

Sibley and I chatted on a bit and this time he put a few down him. Some of the other guys must have watched us for a while, and got interested. They'd been telling Sibley to piss off lately, never mind his free beer. I guess they wanted to ask *him* a few questions.

'What's the strength of you, Sibley,' the Great Lover said. 'Why study us? What's it all about? Who's going to see all those answers?'

'It's his thesis,' I said.

'His whatsis?' said Mick.

'My thesis,' said Sibley proudly. 'For my PhD.'

'What's that when it's at home?' said Serge. He didn't usually ask questions, unless you thought a brief 'Outside' was a question.

'His doctor's degree,' I explained. But Sibley wanted the floor.

'The study of drinkers,' he orated, 'is the study of a dying race.' He'd had too much to drink. 'Hopefully, the results of my surveys and questions and calculations will illustrate the dimensions of the drinking problem. And I mean hopefully. It is entirely possible that all drinkers can be helped from total reliance on alcohol to independence of the drug. For it *is* a drug problem. Society has a good number of well-educated, well-qualified, well-disposed humanitarian people who will be prepared to give time to help, to raise up those who can't kick the habit by themselves, to reform the drinker, to absorb him into the main body of society, to integrate and assimilate him into the mainstream of Australian culture.' Digging his grave with his tongue.

'What's so crook about grog?' said the Great Lover. Love of alcohol oozed from every pore.

'Alcohol oppresses you all. It ties you in to this way of life.' Sibley waved a thin arm round to indicate the slopped red bar, the decrepit chairs that so often doubled for weapons, the punched door, broken glass, the cracked glass doors at the back of the pub, the hills and hollows in the pub yard, the browned paint on the rafters and high ceiling of the saloon bar, the sight of Alky Jack bent over his glass and Danny playing football in some corner of his head that still worked.

'What will your whatsit do?' asked Mick politely.

'It might be published,' Sibley answered. 'My analysis of you could be read everywhere.'

'Yeah, but what will it do to us?'

This was Sibley's chance. Never before had they shown so much interest in what he was doing. Perhaps he was getting through. If he could have this effect on them while he was a beginner, then when he had his doctorate and he worked on other social evils, he might find he had powers, personal powers, that made his choice of vocation more than just chance. It might be his destiny to change men's lives. Abetted by the beer he saw himself a public figure, the sort of guru who is asked to pronounce on society's ills by all the media.

He decided to try out these powers. He would persuade them, help them to see a better way, show concern, lift them up.

'If I am successful,' he said, his eyes glowing with persuasive intentness, 'and others join me to help drinkers all over the country—all over the world—then the whole way of life of drinkers will be changed. Changed for the better, changed irrevocably.'

He watched their faces. The King was looking away, maybe through the windows, no expression on his face. Maybe Sibley had got him looking already at his way of life. Serge looked at a spot at the side of Sibley's jaw, Mick at his chest and slight shoulders like a butcher guessing the dressed weight of a carcass.

'You won't even look at your beer, won't even stop at the pub on the way home—'

'Won't look at a beer!' said the Great Lover incredulously.

'Won't look at the stuff,' Sibley said firmly. 'You'll never have to congregate in surroundings like this, you won't have to listen to that racket—' the races weren't on, but Sibley's eyes went up to the loud-speakers. 'My effect will be to take you away from gambling, from wasted time, wasted lives, from poverty, to constructive pursuits, educational interests, work that is for the benefit of all, to helping the unfortunate and oppressed of other lands.'

Sibley paused for breath, and Mick asked me, 'Any chance of this happening, Meat?'

'Well,' I said. 'I don't know. If he's right and he gets a lot of other people interested, he might make an effect. These things sort of grow, maybe if he gets governments interested, they might make things tough for drinkers. Maybe. I don't know.'

Sibley knew. 'I can do it, I tell you. You can't go on living like this. Putting effort into things that are a waste of time and money and all your abilities. If I get the support I hope for, then a certain amount of compulsion may be necessary.' He smiled a tolerant smile. 'I hope it won't be necessary, of course. But when you try to do things for people, things for their own good, you sometimes have to *make* them see that what you have in mind is right. If drinkers could be raised up to the standard of life of those more fortunate, if these conditions and ways of life could be blotted out, poverty and oppression could be replaced by happiness, prosperity, solid goals in life, worthwhile things that give life a quality drinkers never dream of. I'm not alone, you know,' he said defiantly. 'There are great numbers of enlightened men and women of all professions, able and willing to give time and help to the assimilation of the drinker. All he needs to know, to get him on the right track, is that there are well-disposed people who feel for him and want to help and want to see him raised up to the level of the rest of society.'

Sibley was good for another fifteen minutes of this, but he had no audience. Without a word, the other guys turned and walked away back to their places at the bar.

I heard a voice say something like '... I'll give the cunt well-disposed.' In a very cold tone, it was. Might have been Serge. Or Mick. Or the King, who hadn't said anything before.

I persuaded Sibley to stuff his papers back in his pocket and go home. 'Write up your findings, do something, but get out of here.'

He didn't understand, but he'd had enough and the beer had reduced his statistical ability. He went ...

... I hadn't seen Sibley for a while and no one mentioned his name.

I don't know why I mention him now though I miss having him round, him and his coloured pens and bits of paper. Maybe he's living-in at the university, working his test results up into a book.

The publican came round asking if we'd seen one of his beer barrels. You know, the stainless steel kegs the breweries lovingly send with our nourishing brew tightly enclosed.

'Was it full?'

'No. Nothing like that. Just an empty. But I'm one short. Have you seen it, Danny?'

'I might have emptied it. After that I've got no use for it. Long as she keeps coming through the pipes.' He went on talking, but it wasn't to us.

'Where'd you leave it?' Mick said.

'Out the yard, with the rest.'

'Some kid's pinched it and sailed it down the creek.' Kids rowed canoes down as far as the first weir.

After that, they took no notice.

Sibley should have been on somebody's stocklist. They'd have missed him, too.

David Ireland, The Glass Canoe, Macmillan, South Melbourne, 1976.

Helen Garner

Helen Garner (1942–), novelist, lived in Melbourne most of her life but has moved to Sydney.

Our ride to Sydney

A huge wheat transport picked us up as dark and cold fell just outside Holbrook. It bore down on us in the remaining light, brakes shrieking. Grace clung to my leg and screamed with fear; I stepped back in panic on to the grass verge. But Javo turned to me with a laugh of triumph.

'Come on, Nor. It's our ride to Sydney!'

I slept a little on the hugely vibrating sleeping-shelf, which shook my bladder and gave me indigestion by disturbing a hamburger I had eaten at Gundagai.

'I'm going to stay awake *all night*, till the morning comes!' announced Grace, sitting up like Lady Muck behind the great gear stick. Three minutes later I glanced over and saw her head droop and her eyes close.

At three o'clock in the morning the truckie dropped us at a blighted all-night café thirty miles out of Sydney. The girl serving us was bare-armed in a cotton dress. Two coppers stood drinking coffee in the kitchen. The fluorescent light turned us into corpses.

Gracie added up brightly at the laminex table and ate a fruito; Javo wolfed down a plate of baked beans on toast. We were not looking at each other. Outside the café we started walking towards Sydney. It was a bitterly cold, icily clear night, with a sky miles high and light coming from somewhere far away, the stars perhaps for there was no moon. A dog barked from a driveway. The cops stopped in a black maria and brought us to Liverpool station: in the back of the van Javo grinned at Gracie's round eyes but pretended I wasn't there. I was too cold to care. At the station he clowned with Gracie on the turnstiles while I crammed myself with my book into the ticket-puncher's booth. The first train came through at 4.20. It was full of shiftworkers huddling themselves inside what was left of their body warmth from bed. We were the most wide-awake people on board.

Outside Central Station at six o'clock. Javo foul-tempered again, Gracie tired and frightened. I have to keep us together somehow. Frozen and miserable,we trudge along the colonnades looking for a taxi. Grace whinges and at last I pick her up and lug her on my hip. Javo is always twenty steps ahead of me. I can't keep up. At 6.20 the cab drops us outside Peggy's place in Annandale. Cold sky, dark before dawn. I tap nervously on the front window. Peggy opens up, brings us in quietly, insists that we take her big bed, and moves into the spare room. In the bed still warm from her body our limbs thaw and we fall asleep, not touching.

Helen Garner, *Monkey Grip*, Penguin, Melbourne, 1978.

Jessica Anderson

Jessica Anderson (1916–), novelist, was born in Brisbane but has lived most of her life in Sydney.

A good place to bring up children

Sylvia went to David Jones's corner by bus, then walked to Wynyard down Market and George Streets. Here she was again away from the polyglot population of the Cross and among people from all the suburbs. But she had learned long ago not to strain after an impression of a people. One must simply let it happen; and she now supposed, when nothing much happened, that the freshness had been taken from the human scene by her familiarity with Sydneyans abroad, whose mostly Hogarthian presences had run like a thread of varying thickness through her life, forming unforgettable knots on the tourist coaches. So today only the bold new towers made their mark. Set back from the old building line to provide broad paved areas, they sometimes tolerated nearby little old buildings with toy turrets or balconies, which made her wonder if what the developers meant to destroy, they first painted in humorous colours.

Yesterday she had travelled from Platform 3. Today she waited on 4, which was the other side of the same platform. When she first went to

London, and she had been asked about the Australian classless society, she had not known what to reply, but later she was able to say that though there were no divisions of the complexity and rigour of the English classes, difference of income, sustained through two or more generations, was often visible and audible in the people, and that, she supposed, could be called class. And as she had spoken, there had always hung in her memory the curved walls of this tunnel, from the floor of which rose this platform, like an elongated box, onto which people arrived together by climbing the broad steps from below, but on which they divided into two, and stood back to back—the westbound on 3, and the northbound on 4. And on each side there were those whose habit it had once been to stand facing the other way.

From the upper deck of the train as it crossed the bridge she saw, through the flashing girders, the main harbour and, in the stream, solid as a building, the Stoldt ship spoken of by Rosamond. For Sylvia, water was the only convincing element of division. On catching sight of the familiar little church steeple, dwarfed by the sweeping north approach of the bridge, she physically felt the crossing made, the North Shore reached.

Janet Holyoak, hearing Richard and Sylvia talk of the North Shore line, had visualized a train line winding around all the intricate bays and points of the north shore of the harbour. She even said she saw a little Puffing Billy of a train, with a whistle that went toot-toot, but that was only to dramatize her disappointment on learning that after crossing the bridge (though a few miles of meandering did give an occasional glimpse of water) the North Shore line settled to a course, varying from north to north-west, through dry and rising country. Janet was also interested to learn (she too having heard of the classless society) that if you spoke of the North Shore, and left train lines out of it, you meant only the eight inland suburbs from Roseville to Wahroonga, though Roseville was disputed nowadays as being too mixed.

Stewart would have called the North Shore definitely good stuff, grade B, for in financial terms the best stuff was still on the harbour shores and hills of the eastern peninsula. But in the post-war years the newly rich adventurers who felt no misgivings about buying in the east were often daunted by the North Shore, because when its residents called it good they also meant seemly; it was spoken of as 'a good place to bring up children'. After Sylvia had left both her homes and taken a room at the Cross, it occurred to her that its seemliness was helped by its inaccessibility to the north-easterlies. The big damp southerlies blustered their way through, as did the galling winds from the western desert, but from the sensuous salty north-easterlies, which on summer nights could saturate the eastern peninsula, the North Shore was removed, so that the children of the residents were not tempted out at night to roam the beaches or to pile all together into a car and drive away anywhere. Perhaps this knowledge, even if hardly conscious, was implicit in the comment that it was a good place to bring up children; and if a few of the newly rich adventurers did penetrate, it was usually because their wives wanted their children to be different from themselves, and so moved to this 'good' district, knowing that though they would be unlikely to be accepted, their children were likely to be. That, Sylvia had always taken for granted, was Greta's reason.

For Janet's amusement, and their own, Richard and Sylvia had pronounced the word 'good' in all the ways of its residents: the innocently factual, the unctuous, the respectful, the finical, the sophisticated wry, not forgetting to add that there were those who never used the word at all. Janet (and Geoffrey Foley, who had come into it by this time) said it sounded a bit like the Home Counties; but Richard and Sylvia, extending the joke, shook their heads and said that the North Shore was incomparable. When Janet came out in the sixties and stayed with Richard's parents at Pymble, she was disappointed to find what she called only a few rather pretty middle-class suburbs; but Richard added a postscript to her letter to say that she had failed to appreciate the mystique of the North Shore which, besides, had changed, the wild arrogant moneyed kids of the sixties having been let loose everywhere.

From her high seat on the train Sylvia saw little change. As the line progressed she looked more and more often down on the crowns of trees, evergreen and in spring flower. At Roseville station there were still roses, and at Killara beds crammed with spring annuals. The line now ran on a ridge from which spurs thrust into the bush as headlands do into the sea. On these spurs and the more accessible slopes were the 'best' streets. Though not visible from the train, Sylvia saw them in memory, radiating away from the central ridges, getting quieter and quieter as they went, the trees taller, and the ancestral notes of spring and autumn—the tender greens, the reds and golds—making strange and melancholic the grey-greens and umbers of the bush valleys below. Sylvia's memory of this was so positive that she had to struggle to reach the later information (from Greta and the Holyoaks) that new roads now plunged down to the floors of the valleys, and that housing estates, hardly accessible by foot, were laid out on their slopes. Joining and leaving the train were girls and boys of an adolescent bloom enhanced by the severity of their school uniforms, and whose released voices thronged the air. Travelling one afternoon from her room at the Cross, Sylvia had seen Hermione in a group like one of these, and had noticed for the first time her lack of modernity, the biblical quality of her beauty.

A number of these boys and girls got out of the train at Wahroonga and preceded her as she set out for Orlando Road. New fences bisected many of the gardens of the big houses, and new houses stood in the rectangles of land thus detached. The rectangle was less insistent than at bare Burwood but, in spite of trees and the hilly terrain, it did prevail. Hot from walking,

Sylvia took off her jacket and hooked it by one finger over a shoulder. The boys and girls were slipping into gates. A car passed; a David Jones delivery van stood at the kerb; a man walked behind a motor mower on the footpath.

Jessica Anderson, *The Impersonators*, Macmillan,
South Melbourne, 1980.

C.C. Catt

C.C. Catt was a contributor to an anthology of short stories, *State of the Art*, edited by Frank Moorhouse. The subway has been cleaned up: the graffiti have gone.

Graffito spy

You might have seen it if you've ever walked through the tunnel under Railway Square. I know there are a million there but its right between 'PUNK SUCKS' and 'SOMEBODY, WHERE ARE YOU?' And anyway, it stands out so that people can hardly go by without being forced to look at it. I've seen people reading the blurb on the other wall or talking, and then as they get to it their heads seem to jerk around to it as if they know they are missing something.

It's funny how it started as just something to write. I walked out of the party at our flat with a mug of rosé and sat on the front wall. We're right between street lights and there was no moon, no stars, no cars, no lights from open windows. I could have been a bit drunk too so I sat there in pitch black for a while, sipping by feel and spilling a bit, before I started to see the shapes of things. Like the footpath. I wondered how old the cement was. It was cracked and crumbled enough to be hundreds of years old, except for a new strip across the path where someone had dug to fix some pipes. I remember moving the beer mug around in front of my face to try to catch the light gleam in the rosé but there was no light or my eyes weren't working. So I looked at the new cement because it was the lightest grey around, and tried to absorb the light into my eyeballs.

I just happened to find the lipstick in my overalls pocket and the thought of lipstick and mouths made me think of him and the next thing I knew I was kneeling on the cement with an empty mug and writing with the soft lipstick on the rough cement. I don't know how I thought of it. The cement seemed to eat the lipstick, crunch it, and as I finished, the metal case was scraping with each downstroke. The funny part was I couldn't remember what I'd written.

I had to rush back inside and scream out for a torch. Of course no one had one and they kept asking me why I wanted it. I grabbed some guy's lighter and I could see that he was going to grab it back but then he decided that it would be sort of cool to lend his cigarette lighter to a drunken chick. I heard them saying that someone should go with me because I was worse than they thought but I ducked out the door and behind the wall before they had argued over who should go. The guy must have decided to worry about his lighter because he came out for a look. But he went back when I wasn't around.

I know it's taking me a long time to explain it but I wanted you to see how unpremeditated the whole thing was when it started out. Here I was, a bit under the weather, stumbling around with a cigarette lighter in the blacked out street and trying to find a bit of new cement in the footpath. Then as soon as I flicked the lighter and saw the first line it came back without the need to read it.

> I MET HIM
> I LIKED HIM
> I LOVED HIM
> I LOVED HIM
> I LET HIM
> I LET HIM
>
> I LOST HIM

I think you can see it, even if it's only on the page instead of the cement. It's sort of banal I think but still it's incredibly poignant; has a certain sorrow, pathos. Piquant. A little raunchy too. My own little revelation. Epiphanies, Brenda calls them.

Graffiti is highly contagious apparently. The next day when I went outside someone had written 'ANARCHY SUCKS' with white chalk right beside mine. Everything seems to suck around here.

There were at least a dozen blurbs on the footpath by the weekend but I wasn't concerned with the graffiti generating process. I was only concerned with what I had written. Crumpled paper lay all over my room where I'd written it at least fifty times, fifty different ways, trying to make it better, I tried:

> I SAW HIM
> I MET HIM
> I LIKED HIM
> I LOVED HIM
> I LOVED HIM
> I LOVED HIM
> I LOVED HIM, LOVED HIM, LOVED HIM
> I LET HIM
>
> I LOST HIM

I thought that might accentuate how I loved him but it looked bit overdone. I tried:

I MET HIM
I LIKED HIM
I LOVED HIM
I LET HIM
I LET HIM
I LET HIM
I LET HIM
I LET HIM
I LOVED HIM

I LOST HIM

I thought that one might show a bit of the feeling of throwing myself into him, completely letting go, discarding everything, diminishing everything except the physical need.

But the original probably expresses the spontaneity that I'd felt and I decided that was how it should stay. The trouble was, the lines sort of filled me. It was as if I'd written them on a long sheet of paper and then folded it in a circle and kept revolving it in front of my eyes. The lines just kept rolling and I began to lose the beginning and the end. I'm like a teletext, I thought. World headlines flashed on a skyscraper. I knew it couldn't just end on the footpath.

Railway Square tunnel was the place. Empty. Hollow. Shuffling feet and transience. The graffiti—contemporary epigrams. The place echoed the forlornness of my lines.

The size of the letters worried me. Too big or too small could have ruined it. I also agonized a bit about whether to take one of the girls with me. Brenda would have come and I almost asked her. I fought against it even though I needed the moral support. It had to be done alone, I decided.

Strangely, I felt little as I scrawled on the pale yellow tiles with the black pen, hands slightly shaking. There were footsteps echoing but I didn't know if they were right beside me or way down the tunnel. I shut them out as a presence and made them into just noises.

I forgot the full stop. I just left.

I think it's better without the full stop anyway.

'PUNK SUCKS' was already there when I wrote mine in but 'SOMEBODY, WHERE ARE YOU?' came later. It had to be a response to mine.

Don't you think?

Even on that first night I had to go back and walk past it.

Echoes are endemic in the tunnel. A fug of echoes.

I just walked up and down the tunnel slowly to read all the graffiti. There's too much there to read all at once and a bunch of guys started annoying me so I left.

Nearly every night I go there now. If there's a busker near it I can stand there without attracting attention. Some people stop to listen and they invariably start reading between songs.

Or I just walk slowly till the faster walkers go past and then I turn as if I've forgotten something and go back. People don't notice.

Facial expression is what I look for. In the tunnel I feel sort of dead. Like some of my senses are anaesthetized. Then I watch as someone reads it and I get an incredible buzz. I can almost feel them physically. It's a real jolt. I even saw a group of musos with a couple of guitars sitting underneath it and trying to write a song. It didn't have a chance because they tried to fit my words into their music. They reckoned that they had something but I could have told them it was hopeless.

Well I haven't heard it on the radio yet, have you?

I suppose you're wondering who I'm writing this to. At first it was for him but after the first page or so I realized that I'd been thinking so long now of a 'him' that I don't think of him any more now as a 'you'.

There's just the lines now, not him.

He even came back to the flat one night. The other girls called me to the door and he obviously wanted to get back together.

'Can I see you?' he said.

'What for?' I asked him, trying not to sound hurt and realizing just then that he didn't hurt any more.

'I thought we could talk.'

'There's no need to talk.'

'I'd like to explain.'

'No point.'

'Look, I came to see if you could understand ...'

'If you want to know what I understand, go to Central Railway tunnel.'

'What?'

'Go take a walk along the tunnel.'

'Don't talk ambiguities.'

'And when you get to the end keep going up on to the platforms and jump under the first train that comes along.'

He patted the air with both hands. 'Okay,' he said, 'I'm not going to push it.'

I didn't even bother to watch him walk down the steps.

Even at that stage watching was becoming important. Seeing the effect of my lines. Some people have a printout on their foreheads. Their brains are so vulnerable. I can see the stifled whimpers and I know that they are fuller people from reading it. I know they understand.

Even the shrieks from the other end of the tunnel don't jar my nerves. They could be laughter or a rape. From this distance it's all the same. Like I said, I get kind of in a trance and I'm only responsive to people's reactions.

Leaving it is the biggest problem. I don't like to leave it with the possibility that some bureaucrat may stab his pen in a sheet of paper and send people down with paint brushes or cleaners.

So I wrote it on my bedroom wall.

It seems more fragile on its own.

It needs others around it. What I had to do was transfer that living tapestry off the tunnel wall to my bedroom. I've studied each one minutely to get the detail just right. I've adopted the same method they use to rebuild historical structures. They number every brick and stone to make sure that it fits together just as it did originally. But it's just not the same with graffiti. I don't know why.

I've just thought of a camera, too. If I shoot all of them and blow them up I can fit the photos together.

Then I'll have it there at any time, along with the others.

But I'll always go back to the tunnel. It's the faces that I need. The endless traffic of strangers to read the lines and give off their little facial epiphanies.

C.C. Catt, 'Graffito spy' in *State of the Art: The Mood of Contemporary Australia in Short Stories* (ed. Frank Moorhouse), Penguin, Melbourne, 1983.

George Papaellinas

George Papaellinas (1954–), novelist and short-story writer, was born in Sydney of Cypriot parents. He has worked at a variety of occupations, including taxi-driving and teaching creative writing.

The welder

Christos should be welding.

Come on, Christos. What's your story. It's your turn.

The Armenian, that one, the one with the overalls open to the waist—you can see that he's a single man. No wife, that one, as many holes in his overalls as a bachelor has opportunities, eh, Christos?—anyway, the Armenian screams.

'Eeeh, Christo ... come on, bastard!'

You can see him, can't you, Chris?

Silenced in the sponge of noise, the Armenian turns to wave his gun at Christos, the welding tip glowing.

'Fucken' ...' he mouths, 'fucken' black-eye bastard ... fucken' wog old bastard ... come here!' and he turns back as a car rumbles closer. Fourteen welding lines, up, up and up and one down, a long straight one now ... and he turns again to yell soundlessly at Christos and then again, up and up ...

Anyway, that's our Chris' story. He can't hear him. There's nothing to be said 'cause there's nothing to be heard.

Christos counts smudges on concrete. He's on his break, one an hour. A stretch and a sip of coffee and a sit-down away from the line.

Christos. Your posture. The stool sits taller than Christos does.

The noise.

His head.

Christos' head is down, he blows into his cup and swirls imaginary coffee. Clever bastard knows his break's over. Five minutes, mate, and you should know the measure of five minutes by *now*. A cup of coffee is finished in three and then you stretch your arms! Off the stool! Sitting around's what you get your holidays for.

Come on, Christos! Think of your mate.

Poor bastard's been taking care of your welding for eight minutes, that's fourteen lines and that's hard on the arms and the back too. You should know that. You've been at it long enough. Come on, he has to travel a whole car ... Look, Bill the Scot, he's already on his stool with a mouth full of coffee and Argiris is back at work.

Get up! Swing your arms! Get the blood into them. The ache'll go away, stretch your back. And anyhow, it's easier when you're working, you don't feel it.

Get up, will you, Chris. There's work.

Look at him.

Head in his coffee cup, blowing into it and hot air is all that's in it by now, for sure. Christos is manufacturing minutes.

Five minutes for five. Nothing for nothing.

Give Garbis his.

Christos looks up. Is five minutes up, is it?

What's wrong with the Armenian? Not a bad boy, though a little too loud with stories of last night's breasts and thighs. Why all this? Why all this jumping around and mouth under his goggles as pale and straight as a welded seam? The waving gun? Don't point it at me!

Chris cups his free hand, taps it on his skull and turns it to the sky. The ceiling. Are you mad? Hole in the head?

'Whatsa matter with you, *pousti?*' Christos queries all this with a tilt of his head! This drama.

Well what do you expect Christos to do? Five minutes aren't up, are they? Couldn't be. Clock's wrong.

The Armenian spits hard on the concrete. Saving his breath. He waves his gun between the car that's coming and Christos.

Christos swipes at the heat and the Armenian. Hand like a breeze.

'*Gamo tin panayia sou!*' Why this jumping around! Find trouble last night? Who'd you visit? The Virgin? Fuck her too!

Christos isn't going to take any of this. Been around here thirty-three years now. He doesn't have to take any of this! Boy's fit. At his age, he welded and welded with no bloody breaks at all.

Boy!

Fuck 'im, Chris.

Look at him jump.

Christos brings his cup up to his mouth, drinks deep, tastes nothing and smiles with the enjoyment of it.

He bends, stiff at the waist, stretches over to the urn and pours another cup. You can hear the creaks. Old bloke, Christos. He waves it at the Armenian. There's your coffee. By the urn.

'*Ate, then, pousti* ... coffee ... for you, pooftah,' and he's on his feet, he's at the brink, here's Christos at the red line, swing your arms, Chris, rub your back and he's rolling his eyes at the Armenian, outta the way, 'C'mon ... c'mon,' and Christos tests his gun, ssst, sst, he sets his goggles and here's a car, noisy and here's Garbis, he's a boy, he's *still* here, look at him, he holds that gun like a girl, not like that, like this, look, like this and shit, outta the way, the boy's in the road and there's a car coming! Outta the way, Christos shoulders Garbis outta the way! Go and sit over there.

The boy brackets his gun, Christos' back to him, his gun weaving, a line, a line, a line, the boy's got five minutes, half a one already gone. Why is he standing here?

Garbis hugs his arms, relieved of the gun's weight and brittle. A little muddled by the ringing and more than a little by the echo of his own screams in the din, he drags at the stool to bring it closer to the urn. The bolts hold it still in concrete, as they do every time he tries the same. He sits. Fuck 'im, he decides as he tosses the coffee, already cold and greasy. Fuck 'im. And he pours another, his low whining as unheard in the pumping of the assembly line as he now accepts his screams must have been.

Fuck 'im, anyway, he decides and checks the clock.

George Papaellinas, *Ikons: A Collection of Stories*, Penguin,
Melbourne, 1986.

Sandra Harvey and Lindsay Simpson

Sandra Harvey and Lindsay Simpson are journalists who covered the Milperra bikie massacre trial in 1984.

The clubhouse was his castle

The first Sydney clubhouse for the Comancheros became an integral part of Jock's power base. His domain was the western surburbs, and the clubhouse, although small and unattractive, was his castle. It was a fibro building wedged among the smoking chimneys of Granville, an industrialised suburb lying almost 28 kilometres to the west of Sydney ...

The houses in George Street, with their empty yards, corrugated fences and dogs chained to kennels, formed a dismal backdrop ...

Engineering companies and milling specialists sprawled on either side of the four-lane F4 Freeway, which swilled cars westward from the city. Graffiti on cement walls facing the highway read: 'Vote Socialist Workers for a Labor Government with Social Policies.' It is doubtful Jock ever read this graffiti. Despite his working class background, the group of men he now surrounded himself with were not men who aspired to following a socialist leader ...

Jock's self-appointed title was the Supreme Commander. On his leathers, he fastened army badges to symbolise his strength. He told his men he was a former member of the crack squad to enhance his reputation for being ruthless. Most of his followers believed him, others dealt with his idiosyncrasies by ignoring them.

Inside the clubhouse he erected a Nazi flag. With the appropriate solemnity, all new members swore allegiance to their Supreme Commander and to the Comanchero Motor Cycle Club. Military parades were set up when each man was awarded his colours and became a full member. A strict code of laws was pinned on the wall and his men were forced to obey them.

Jock ruled on the principle of divide and conquer, encouraging animosity and competitiveness between his club members, who as a result would squabble among themselves.

He set up a strike force—his army elite. They wore a special patch on the front of their leather cut-offs displaying a dagger with a lightning bolt running through it, the words 'Strike Force' written across it. Sheepskin, JJ, Tiger, Leroy and Foghorn were the chosen members of this inner sanctum. They were his most loyal subjects, men to 'take care of any trouble' if it developed with other clubs or organisations ...

Jock's favourite magazine was *Soldier of Fortune*. He was proud of his notoriety and conquests, keeping newspaper clippings of his skirmishes, including one which spoke of a rock band called Grand Junction who developed a deep fear of the Comancheros. One of their roadies was beaten up, and a patron in the Bateau Bay Hotel, where they played, was thrown through a plate glass window.

A banner was erected to dead Comancheros inside the clubhouse, giving them full battle honours.

'To Lost Brothers' it read.

An eagle sat on top of a yellow shrine, which had a gold cotton fringe on the bottom. On one side were the names of Lost Brothers, brothers who died in bike or road accidents. The list in 1982 stood at three. Bull Spackman, Johnboy and Spoon.

Once a member joined the Comancheros, he was a member until death. All nominees signed a photocopied form pledging their bodies to their brothers. Families had little place in the funeral rights.

The form stated:

'I, being a nominee of the Comanchero Motor Cycle Club, do hereby being of sound mind and under no mental or physical pressure, agree that in the event of my death, regardless of circumstance, the following will be abided by:

1 I am to be taken to the Palmdale Crematorium;
2 Transported by sidecar attached to a Harley Davidson Motorcyle;
3 The Cortege is to be made up of my fellow Comancheros, as laid down in the Comanchero tradition;
4 I am then to be placed in the Comanchero garden along with my other brothers.' ...

Snoddy began to consolidate the first Australian chapter of the Bandidos ...

No heroin is allowed in the club, instant dismissal and a bashing if anybody is caught using it or associating with anybody who uses heroin.

Everybody's woman is to be treated with respect, as you would want your own woman to be treated.

No woman is allowed in the clubhouse unless her old man is there. (This is to stop dissension among members so nobody roots anybody else's missus.)

If a fight occurs between members, the offending member is suspended for a period which is worked out by other members at the general meeting.

If a member is set upon or becomes involved in a fight with an outsider any member who does not back his brother will be bashed and thrown out of the club.

If a member wants to become involved with another member's missus or girlfriend, and the woman's old man agrees, the member and his brother in question may decide if they can go together.

If another member's old lady or girlfriend puts it on you, tell her old man and let him deal with her, otherwise severe punishment is dealt.

The new rules were noted in the minutes book at the first Bandido meeting.

Sandra Harvey and Lindsay Simpson, *Brothers in Arms*,
Allen & Unwin, Sydney, 1989.

Glen Tomasetti

Glen Tomasetti (1929–), novelist, short-story writer, and folklore collector, lives in Melbourne. She has frequently worked as a folk-singer, playing her own songs on the guitar.

My Sydney

… She was sixty-five at the time and I fancied I knew her. A few months later, she went on an ocean cruise and returned with several small canvases.

'There was a great choice of activities on board,' she recounted, 'and first-class people to lead them. Your father took golf lessons and I joined the painting class. Something unexpected happened after the first morning. The tutor, a professional artist and a very lively girl, held this one up for all to see, and what do you think she said? "There's talent for you!" That's what she said!' Emilia conveyed pride and modesty rolled into one.

For her next birthday, I presented oils, brushes and palette. Apparently charmed, she did not bother to use them. I began to think about her arrangement of rooms. Given time, she made unlikely spaces, with awkward features, look graceful and welcoming. I thought of her father, the early photographer, and of her own photography, her developing and printing when first married. Now, I had faith in her to see in a painting what I did not, and to articulate it.

At the Gallery, I proposed a wheelchair. Standing in one spot tired her more than walking. With excellent eyesight, at eighty-five she had a persisting tendency to carry on beyond her strength.

'A wheelchair? Oh, what a good idea! You are on the ball!' exaggerated Emilia.

Recently, I perceived her constant praise as a reflection of deserving more herself, and was less irritated than when it seemed an automatic inflation of her children, inviting them to perpetual pubescence.

We arrived at the suite of rooms through which one passes from initial European attempts to depict life on this continent, to contemporary ventures as limited in the scope they, as a whole, represent. More than halfway in time and space, we stopped.

'There it is,' I announced. '*Cahill Expressway* by Jeffrey Smart.'

'Is that Sydney?' Emilia asked in wonder.

'Yes.' I was bright. 'The tunnel runs from a point on the city side of Kings Cross to near the bridge. Cahill was a Premier of New South Wales.'

Fingers spread, she placed her right hand against her right cheek. She tucked the little fingernail between her front teeth and speculated. Silence ensued.

'Mmm.' From Emilia, this sound expressed a large range of responses and without the danger, encountered in family politics, of words. Here, it suggested measured interest.

'What strikes me first,' she said, 'is that luminous curve of wall. The sky is grubby and everything on the ground cleaned up. I think of the contrast as being usually the other way round.' She paused. 'The statuary above the tunnel gives an idealised view, something heroic and forward looking, though we see only the back of the masonry and an indication of figures. Vertically below,' she became animated, 'is this rather pathetic character, an underworld figure perhaps, and standing at the entrance to another underworld. Is it the Premier?'

Not knowing and wishing I did, I said nothing.

'Just propel me forward, dear ... Yes, I see ... He's lost an arm. The victim of a war? Very overweight and not at all healthy. He turns to the light whilst there's an absence of hope in his face. Let's move back ... A somewhat mysterious painting, isn't it? I wouldn't say the mystery is promising.'

'In the execution, there's a fine appreciation of tone. Colours, if not the theme, are harmonious. A quite brilliant technique.' She looked up at me. 'It doesn't make the viewer want to give three cheers for the Cahill Expressway as a feat of human ingenuity. That's all I can tell you, I'm afraid.'

'That's terrific. Thanks.'

'Oh, one more thing ... It's peculiar that the set-up painted, I mean the road, buildings and builders' gear, fence, lightpoles, railings are every one of them made by humans and yet the total environment is dehumanised, barren. Yes, barren.' She gave a tiny shiver. 'What else?'

'I'll show you something different,' I offered, and took her round the partition to see Grace Cossington-Smith's painting of the Sydney bridge under construction, shortly before the great arc was joined overhead.

'Ah!' Emilia sighed relief. 'This artist caught a moment that reminds one of achievements of the spirit. Her shades and texture are of the period, too, when we used cretonne for covering chairs and making curtains.'

We headed back in the direction of the Charles Conder beach and Box Hill paintings.

'Stop, stop! There, to our right!' Her voice was full of happiness. 'Now, there's something to feast the eye upon!'

'Do you mean the big Streeton?' There were two. 'Of Sydney Harbour, 1907?'

We gazed. Emilia drew a breath and spoke her satisfaction.

'That's *my* Sydney!'

It was my Sydney as well for, in childhood's empathy with the parent. I first saw the place partly through her eyes and felt it through her feelings.

The canvas before us was more than a canvas. It was re-entry to the vast yet intimate blue of the harbour viewed from a bushland shore towards North Head. The air shimmered with sunshine and vapour, and it was the air when Streeton painted the picture, the magic of this form of permanence containing the air of 1922 when Emilia started her years as a bachelor girl and her long, transferable love affair with Sydney.

'Beautifully painted.' She was reverent. 'Look at the colours in the plants amongst the undergrowth. And, of course, he captures the dazzling depth of blue and the bays, the whole thing that adds such zest to the business of living.

'Who's the painter? Streeton. Oh, Sir Arthur Streeton! I thought he was one of the has-beens. Well, not in my book. I take off my hat to him! In future, whenever I want a whiff of Sydney and can't get there, I can come here. Dead easy.'

We went to further riches for Emilia and me. She sat wordless before Conder's *Coogee Bay* (1888). Finally, she said, 'I lived at Coogee, you know.'

'Yes, I know.' In energy output, I tiptoed. So deep her reluctance to give details of her youth and so keen my desire to understand through information, I learnt late how to be still and wait.

Rapt in contemplation of Streeton again, she left the wheelchair to look within wide frames around three small horizontal paintings. At *Sydney Wharf*, she exclaimed, 'Isn't that perfect? Though the warship is out of date, you can just hear a ferry pull into the jetty. Down goes the gangplank and we're off.' She peered closer. 'To Taronga Park Zoo, do you think?' She laughed at herself and sat down carefully.

'That's enough for you, isn't it?' I asked.

'It certainly is! Do you suppose we could find a cup of tea?'

'Let's try the Treble Clef, round by the river.'

For the walk from Gallery to café, I asked the attendant on the exit door whether we might take the wheelchair. He bent the regulations and we moved out into the sun. Fresh-leafed plane trees lined the pavement. As warm and windless as any woman could want for a new outfit and blow-away hat, Cup Day '88 almost emptied the city to Flemington Racecourse. The few who strolled in the arts and gardens oasis south of Princes Bridge had an appearance of selective leisure. Emilia and I were alongside the grassy hillock between the theatres building and Concert Hall.

'My godfather!' she muttered. 'Do I actually see a couple copulating in public?'

'You do,' I confirmed.

'I'm enjoying myself too much to let it worry me,' she insisted. She could not, however, resist a judgement. 'Sheer exhibitionism!'

'Well, when you come to think of it,' I said, 'the entire Arts Centre is an exhibitionist area.' My joke amused only me.

'Your tolerance is either a pose or it does your intelligence no credit.' It was argument rather than reprimand. 'You know how bad it is for them to be demeaning the act of creation.'

'They're probably drugged and temporarily reckless, poor kids,' I said.

'Oh, how pitiful! That didn't occur to me.'

In the Treble Clef, Emilia, a great one in her day for knocking up a batch of light scones, agreed to risk the Devonshire tea. Waiting for it, she scrutinised the platforms of Flinders Street Station across the river. Shrubs and the near bank hid the water.

'This is very pleasant,' she remarked, 'but after the waterways we've seen in the Gallery, it might be as well that we can't look upon the muddy Yarra.'

Born in the country, Emilia gave to a city no more loyalty than preference for what she found there.

'When we had the flat at Elizabeth Bay,' I said, 'for that first family holiday in Sydney, do you remember looking out the window and seeing me talking to a man on the jetty?'

'No. Tell me.'

'He was old and he was fishing. I stood watching him and he asked where I lived. I said, "Melbourne" and he said, "What do you want to live in Melbourne for? Melbourne's no good. You've got no bridge in Melbourne and no harbour." I thought hard and declared, "We've got St Kilda Road!" On instinct, I turned and, from the other side of the little park in front of the flats, you were rapping on the inside of the upstairs window and beckoning me to come. I came. Don't you remember?' I was laughing at the paradox of shared experience, forgotten by one, crucial to the other.

'Not a thing. You always had a fantastic memory.' She made it the slightest of rebukes, as if I might remember too much and seek to interpret it.

'When I came upstairs,' I continued, 'you were cross with anxiety and you said, in one of your rare scoldings, "You must *not* talk to strangers like that! I could hardly believe my eyes! Really, I don't know what kind of future you'll have if you talk to strange men! You are *far too* venturesome!" I had no way of saying I was defending my home city.'

'You all loved that holiday, didn't you.' She meant Dad, Mick and me.

'But you did, too, surely!'

'Oh, yes, I did,' she murmured, smiling. 'Sydney always does something for me.'

I connected this gladness with the season of independence before she married, and three of us eventually came from the eggrack.

'You took Mick and me to afternoon tea at Prince's or Romano's, I never know which.'

'Romano's,' she put in promptly.

'I remember long white tablecloths, a pastry called a match and an orchestra, but the best thing of all was seeing people dancing in the afternoon. "This," I thought, "is Life." It was marvellous!'

'How old were you?'

'Ten,' I answered. 'January 1940.'

'Precocious little thing! I don't know what I was thinking of, taking a child of mine there at such a tender age.'

Perhaps she wanted to go there herself and if she needed an excuse, a treat for us was a good one. Not saying this, I returned to watery Sydney. The Devonshire tea came as I talked.

'Of course, put-putting round the harbour in that outboard motorboat Dad hired, and landing in bays for lunches you packed ... It's unforgettable. At ocean beaches, he taught us to surf. I'm grateful for good instruction about outdoor physical things, and about not being frightened to get up and go, as if seeing the world is everyone's right.'

Emilia appeared doubtful. It had nothing immediate to do with me.

'What huge, doughy-looking scones!' she lamented.

'You were both great travellers, weren't you?' I encouraged. She cut a scone with caution, as if it might reveal something nasty. 'You know,' I went on, 'Dad's surfing directions are clear to this day. He told us, "When you see sand in a rising wave, it's a dumper. Take a deep breath, face the oncoming wave, and dive under it." I wish I could apply that as easily to other life situations.'

Her thoughts were elsewhere. She always belonged under pergolas and parasols more than in sea and sand. Eager to tell her of other indelible impressions left by Sydney, I recalled the occasional big, middle-aged man in dark glasses, seen basking during the week at Bondi or Manly. In my Melbourne district, proper fathers, and all men were fathers, went to work on weekday afternoons, so how did these big, sleek men earn a living? I could see they were not poor.

Ignoring the kind of money that reproduces itself, Emilia accounted for basking by pointing out that much of Sydney life arises from climate.

'Maybe,' I co-operated, 'but Dad warned us, also on that holiday, that Melbourne people need to be careful when doing business in Sydney. Sydney business is sharp by comparison. I now think there's continuity through a few generations since the convict days, hence a formal outcry and easy acceptance of crooked dealings. The first time I did a freelance job in Sydney, I was paid with a dud cheque by a company that went into liquidation the day before the cheque was written: sharks to match the ones in the water round Pinchgut Island.

'You told us, as we circled the island in the motorboat, of prisoners left there for extra punishment. True or false, it was really the introduction to our history.'

Emilia often said that living with a focus on history is like travelling in a car and looking out the rear vision window. She now changed the subject.

'Tell me, in your opinion what could be the reason for choosing to paint the Cahill Expressway under a sullen sky, instead of the beauties of Sydney?'

My reply was history again without the name.

'Since Streeton and Conder made those pictures, there've been two world wars and a massive depression. To some, pretty scenery became trivial. They thought about poverty, destruction and suffering. Personal pain is identified with mass pain. Art for art's sake denoted, in some circles, an immoral indifference.'

'I don't understand,' protested Emilia. Then, 'That's not true. I do understand.'

'In Nazi Germany, Brecht wrote, "A harmless word is absurd." You can see why. I've been with lots of people where, if you spoke of your enthusiasm for the beach and harbour paintings, and even if you said you lived there, you would hear a scoffing "Oh? And what would a privileged person like you know about the tough side of Sydney?"'

This brought her out.

'Quite a bit I could tell them! When I stepped off a train alone at nineteen, I was no privileged person. I fended for myself and I had no parents behind me. I can only say I believe a guardian angel was watching over me. Whatever I went through, however, did not blind me to surroundings of immense grandeur.' She grew more vehement. 'And within everyone's reach, I might add, for the price of a ferry ticket! I only had to use my eyes.'

Driving Emilia home by way of Alexandra Avenue, we soon left the greenery for Swan and Church Streets, Richmond. Her forebears lived, worked and prayed at sites I discovered along the margins of these streets. They furnished the city with significance. I did not draw Emilia's attention to them, for they gave her no joy. She carried a curious avoidance of preceding generations, whereas I bore Enid Bagnold's curious tenderness for my unknown ancestors. Emilia broke our silence, saying, 'My eyes and mind are refreshed by all I've taken in this afternoon. I know Sydney is no longer as Streeton and Conder painted it, nor as I knew it in the 1920s. Dear, raffish old Sydney ...'

We turned east on the crumbly intersection from Church to Victoria Streets. Rumour attributed the shoddy pavings of Richmond to a tradition of crooked local councils.

With Emilia in the car, I found myself singing a snatch of 'The Last Time I Saw Paris'. It went,

> 'No matter how they change her,
> I'll remember her ... that ... way.'

Associations to pull it from memory were obvious. She liked to play and sing that song at the piano. The words echoed our separate and linked attitudes to Sydney. Less obvious was a touch of prescience that I might not have Emilia's company again like this for an outing.

Off and away from the railway lines that keep domestic life possible, she showed a self otherwise protected out of scrupulous habit.

Glen Tomasetti, 'My Sydney', in *Expressway: Invitation Stories by Australian Writers from a Painting by Jeffrey Smart* (ed. Helen Daniel), Penguin, Melbourne, 1989.

Gay Bilson

Gay Bilson (1944–) is a chef and restaurateur.

The Mardi Gras Opera Gastronomique

Pier 13 is an artless structure of concrete, steel and glass which functions as an alternative passenger terminal for ships arriving in Sydney when the more glamorous Circular Quay Terminal is unavailable. Its sparse shell conjures up images of the mass immigration of a past era, all paperwork and little human welcome. Its very soul-lessness and emptiness, its lack of character, in fact make it a perfect space in which to produce theatre uninterrupted by irrelevant decoration ...

Waiters led the diners down from the balcony to the northern entrance of the hall which is accessible only through a huge garage-like doorway (our proscenium arch) and impending drama was announced by the metal door being rolled up by pulling on a marvellously, loud, heavy chain.

Thus the diners entered as one crowd, but were held in that entrance by Synergy's drums, a second aural curtain. If the icecream's entrance remains the over-riding visual memory of that dinner, then the tension and precision of Synergy's taiku drums remains as an extraordinary auditory memory.

Before any food, or the tools of eating appeared, one more act, if fleeting, was witnessed. Once the diners found seats, a child was carried to the table, coated and dressed as a kind of white bird, and having been set down on it, she ran the length of the cloth (her feet not touching the ground!).

This was an act of invitation and defiance against the mores of polite eating: 'Look! you have been bought up not to put your elbows on the table, yet here is a child using it as a floor and a stage. What else may we offer you now that we have upset, and will upset even more, your preconceptions of a festive meal?'

Tongue in Cheek, the first edible course, made by Janni Kyritsis, was the witty and edible realisation of a verbal phrase phrase: pigs' cheeks wrapped around veal tongues, and wrapped in belly pork and poached in a fine stock. It was served cold, a slice of moist and pork-sweet terrine, accompanied by a slice of jellied pigs' ears, fine strands of sliced, poached ear set in aspic, the cartilage providing a wonderful bite.

Although a salad of black truffles would have been more fitting (a reference to the humble pig and the glorious, expensive truffle which attracts the pig as gatherer because of its pheromones), their expense precluded their use and pickled walnuts were substituted. This provided a legitimate acid contrast to the sweet pork flavours. Loaves of bread with good crust were broken at the table.

A 'tableau vivant' of references to *Tongue in Cheek* had been installed inside the rectangle: a woman in black sat knitting one stitch and tumbled about her, piled in a large basket and fallen onto the ground were hundreds of pigs' heads, each wrapped in muslin (as a gesture to possible shock of their raw state).

The supposed sophistication of the urban elite who are familiar with 'haute cuisine' on the plate was addressed by reminders of where the edible had come from and by what means—death. And with the first glass of wine and the impossibility of not looking the pig in the eye, they listened to David Pereira play some of J.S. Bach's Suite for Violoncello in C Major— music composed in an ordered world before the French Revolution.

There are many valid analogies between dining and dramatic theatre. One of the major ones is the sheer energy used in the preparation and cooking (direction and rehearsal) before the food (the play) is presented to the diner (the audience). The food eaten (play watched) disappears in only a fraction of the time it took to prepare.

Implicit in the planning of this dinner was its theatre and in the case of *Tongue in Cheek*, the meaning of its visual symbols. The perceptions of the audience of diners probably varied from puzzled laughter to a possibly over-complex reading of what the cellist and 'tableau vivant' represented but, as in any theatre like this (there was some connection with installation art), all that mattered in the end is that it was noticed.

The main course, Act 3, entitled *Fish out of Water*, was a perfectly poached Tasmanian salmon and crayfish 'boudin'—a sausage of smooth light texture, fat and pink, with pearls of sago in its sauce. It was prepared by Damien Pignolet of Claude's Restaurant with all his fanatical attention to the details of quality and perfection.

Fish out of Water was preceded by a *Mezzo up a Ladder*. Suzanne Johnston sang an aria from Puccini's *Gianni Schicchi* from the platform of a crane, and from her raised stage, her unamplified and glorious voice reached even those seated furthest away.

And so to the entrance of *Ball and Chain*, a giant, medieval, spiked weapon crafted in edible materials in order to disintegrate, melt in the mouth, not to kill.

To record the designing and building of *Ball and Chain* is, in the end, irrelevant to its immediate theatre. The fact that Searle and his acolytes spent somewhere around 500 hours to produce 6 minutes of glorious theatre is irrelevant to the lickerous pleasure of its short public existence. We do not need to know that over 2,000 eggs were used, over 90 litres of cream, over 45 litres of milk, although we may wonder over the statistics. The fact that the icecream weighed over 200 kilograms does not make any more substantial the Unbearable Lightness of Being.

As I record this dinner, I am listening to Tony Buck's record *The Piston Song*. One side is titled *The Piston-Lubricated Mix* and a voice has just stated 'let me explore you with my mouth'. It is a tired expression, but it is refreshed by appositeness in the case of Searle's icecream and the whole of our *Opera Gastronomique*: *Ball and Chain* disappeared in the act of eating, and the eating proved it wonderfully edible.

Tony Buck's *Piston Song* is the musical equivalent of Fritz Lang's film *Metropolis* and it has an inexorable, heavy beat with an edge of fucking. The entrance of Searle's icecream held the same edge and tension, exaggerated by Buck's *Piece for Ball and Chain*.

The music, by ball and chain, and performed behind the closed end of the long table, drew the icecream towards its proper demise. Twelve naked, but clay-smeared bearers, hands in silver-sprayed mittens because the carrying frame was as cold as the icecream, bore the icecream slowly down inside of the rectangle, spotlit and surrounded by billows of machine-made clouds. The biscuit spikes (filled with raspberry sorbet and vanilla icecream) were tipped with silver leaf and turned the vanilla icecream ball into a weapon of war.

Waiting at the end of its glorious path were gloved servers who broke the cones from the core and placed them on 220 plates, as the bearers returned the frame to its starting point ...

Ball and Chain—its heraldic entry conjuring images of ritualism and religion as well as debauchery and libertarianism—was Art, and succeeded in representing the cerebral, the creative and the fleeting; it was transporting and illuminating almost in the same way that great music is.

Gay Bilson, 'Opera Gastronomique', Oz Arts, Issue 6, 1993.

Neddy Smith

Arthur 'Neddy' Smith (1944–), is a thief, stand-over man, and murderer.

I ripped the red phone off the wall

It was about a fortnight after I teamed up with Bill [Sinclair] that six of us— the guys from Double Bay—decided to see *Rocky*, a new movie that was receiving plenty of publicity. It starred Sylvester Stallone as a tough, street-smart boxer on his way up. Everyone was raving about it. We went to the afternoon session. It was Monday, I know, because it was settling day. The movie turned out to be a top show; it had everyone hyped up. I think it was the music that did it. I know the music got my adrenalin pumping.

After the movie we all retired to the Oak for a few quiet ones. Everyone was in a good mood and having a good time. A few guys went on to the Golden Sheaf; I stayed a while longer for settling at 6 p.m. Neville Biber stayed with me. Settling out of the way, we went to the Sheaf to catch up with the others.

When I arrived, everyone was yahooing and having a good time—so I joined them.

The place was starting to pack out—Monday was always a big night at the Sheaf. We always congregated in the corner near the juke box and they kept playing the theme from *Rocky*. Now and then we got a little out of hand playing up, but we never bothered anyone else. We always kept it in our own group.

Kenny was there with his girl. He was out of his head on coke and the drink wasn't helping any. The boys started to play up a bit, still continuously playing the *Rocky* theme. This friend of mine, a television journalist named Grant, decided to hop up on to the bar and then dive off into my arms. I was supposed to catch him. The only thing was that he forgot to tell me. I was standing watching Grant, not knowing what he was about to do, when all of a sudden he dived off the bar straight at me. I tried to catch him but had no luck. We both ended up on the floor, but not before we managed to knock over a few guys' drinks.

It was all done in good fun, so we got up from the floor laughing and went over to the three guys that lost their drinks and offered to buy them a new round. We were in the wrong, so we thought: 'Why not buy them a drink?'

The three guys were only average-sized guys, but they had huge mouths. Straight off they started to abuse me. 'You fool,' one of them said. I tried to tell them we were only having a bit of fun, but no matter what I said they wouldn't have a bar of it.

The theme from *Rocky* was playing in the background and these guys were getting aggressive. Maybe it was the music, I don't know. Anyway, one of them decided to take a swing at me. Silly move.

I was all hyped up with the drink and the music. I was also as fit as a Mallee bull at that time. He missed but I didn't. The first guy went down and out. I didn't give the second one a chance, I hit him flush on the jaw before he could make up his mind what to do. Down went number two for the count. The third one backed out of range so I chased him a few steps and stepped into him as well. He wanted no part of it. Bad luck, he was with the other two so down, but not out, went number three.

The manager, Peter Ryan, came over.

'Ned, I saw that. You weren't to blame. If you had been I would have barred you for life.' Then he escorted the three guys out of the pub.

That shook a few people up, so they drifted off. Not us.

We all went upstairs to Julie's Bar where it was a 12 o'clock finish. Kenny started to play up. Standing at the bar was this guy and he wasn't one bit impressed with Kenny. He called Kenny a loudmouth.

'Who is he, Ken?' I asked.

'That's [we will just call him Joe Bloggs]. He's a karate champion, just won some sort of world title.'

We continued to drink. Bloggs and Kenny were glaring at each other. I could see that it was a special to be on any minute. The guy told Kenny to get outside. Them's fighting words. Well, out they went to the landing at the top of the stairs. Kenny was shooting off his mouth instead of cutting straight into the guy. Big mistake. The guy put Kenny on his arse with a single blow. I never saw the punch—it was too quick. Then this guy turned to face me. He was probably going to ask me if I wanted to do anything about it. No way, Bud. I don't give starts. Before he got a word out, I hit him flush on the jaw with a left hook. He went down, but not quite out.

There was no way I was going to let this bloke get off the floor. No way. I kicked him in the head a few times and, just to make sure that he wasn't getting up, I ripped the red phone off the wall and smashed it over his head a few times. Full of money, it weighed a ton.

While I was bashing Bloggs about the head, the girl who ran the bar, Julie, tried to drag him out of harm's way. Well, I was not having any of that. I took hold of his legs and started to kick him in the balls. There was no way I was going to even consider letting this guy off the floor. I was not silly! That put a scare into all those drinking there, so they left and the place was closed for the night. I went home to sleep it off.

Neddy Smith, Neddy: The Life and Crimes of Arthur Stanley Smith,
Kerr Publishing, Balmain, NSW, 1993.

Daphne Guinness

Daphne Guinness is a Sydney journalist with earlier experience covering English society for Fleet Street.

Truly posh

The social scene is in its last gasp. Pretty well dead, except in the minds of some. 'The question whether or not it exists only comes up when people like you start constructing lists,' as a Bolshie posh put it. There were no landed gentry at the Black and White Ball. One reason is they have 'gone to God'. For instance, Lady Kennedy, wife of Clive, the horse-racing patron, who always referred to 'renovation time' when she had her hair done, died last year. The Stevens and Knoxs are not seen at the Black and White any more: an explanation is that there must be a whole bunch of society entertaining itself at the Queen's Club or at the Golf Club (Royal Sydney, of course). Another is that they are past it: they did Romano's and Prince's and all the glittering balls in their youth; now there is nothing they would sooner do than curl up on the chaise longue with bangers and mash.

If we persist with this game, however, and acknowledge a Sydney aristocracy, whom would it include? Just for fun, of course, such a list would go back to the grand old country families such as the Macarthur Onslows and the Wentworths, while newcomers like the Falkiners of Haddon Rig and the Whites command respect. They made pots of dough but they made it through enormous working empires and employed hundreds of people. James Fairfax would be included. His was a big business that kept going (albeit without him). His friend, the architect Espie Dods, must be considered. His first cousin once removed, the late pediatrician Sir Lorimer Dods, was a gent and the sort of person no-one was surprised had a knighthood. The whole rise and fall of the Lloyd Jones family illustrates that, so yes, they would be in the running. Then there are the Graces, they qualify. 'Would you consider Lady Marjorie Pagan?' someone asked, sotto voice.

'Is it true she and Sue Du Val are Sydney's number one hostesses?' Don't whisper, they are. So bung them in. Sue Du Val can get anyone to her parties from Gough Whitlam (not aristocratic) down.

The Earl of Portarlington is a good name, as is his brother the Hon. John Dawson-Damer. Their title is old, their motto, 'Virtue is the way of life', quirky; they are true-blue aristos. To broaden the base, any member of the Australian Club would certainly think he was aristocratic, ditto the Royal Sydney. When they talk about the golf club, that is what they mean. They are not referring to Bonnie Doon at Eastlakes on the edge of the ICE Botany site, which is boring beyond belief with not so much as a molehill to conquer.

It is also aristocratic to belong, by extension, to the Rose Bay Swimming Club. Members of the Australian Club think members of the Union Club are common. Some members of the Union Club would prefer to belong to the Australian Club but cannot. Big occasions during the year at the Australian Club include Fathers and Daughters Night.

The Cabbage Tree Club and the Palm Beach Surf Life Saving Club are related. You cannot become a member of the Cabbage until you have served your time with the Surf. It is men-only at the Cabbage. Wives qualify as members of the Pacific Club where they live in a world of their own. Very jealous of rights and privileges. The late Judge Tom Reynolds once took his son, Simon, to one side and said he must become a member of the Surf Life Saving Club to qualify as a member of the Cabbage Tree Club or he would regret it late in life.

Those who yearn to become a nob do themselves no harm being involved with the polo at Warwick Farm. The Royal Sydney Golf Club is the mecca for people of the eastern suburbs and some are members of the Elanora Country Club.

For the yachting fraternity the Royal Sydney Yacht Squadron, in addition to the clubs they belong to, is the passport to grandeur. And no-one seeking aristocratic infiltration should knock back the Sydney Cricket Ground, especially with the upcoming installation of its posh new $4 million lavatories.

Daphne Guinness, 'Spectrum', *Sydney Morning Herald*,
10 September 1994.

David Malouf

David Malouf (1934–), novelist and poet, was born in Brisbane.

City of water, light, and air

To live in Sydney is to live as much in light and air as on land—an effect of the great body of water that touches the eastern shores of the city, separates its northern from its southern half, and reaches fingers into its many suburbs. Even when it is not actually visible through a window or at the end of a street, the harbour leaves such a reflection of itself in the mind, hangs such a mirror of itself in the upper air, that its light strikes off every surface, changes every scene.

Open to seaways that lead outward to the world, Sydney is the most outgoing of Australian cities. It faces away from the landmass, breathes the open Pacific, and the fluid element it lives in has created a style of being here, of feeling and seeing, that is also fluid. Restless, buoyant, genial, in love with movement and with shifting images of reflection and change, it can seem, at first glance, superficial, but looked at closely, as does Kenneth Slessor, the poet who speaks most strongly for the harbour and its mood, it has depths:

> Darkness comes down. The Harbour shakes it mane.
> … Lights appear
> like thieves too early, dropping their swags by night.
> Red, gold and green, down trap-doors glassy clear.

That picture of wavering lights on water is a familiar one to Sydneysiders. It can be experienced on any night from the northern foyer of the Opera House, where it is mirrored in John Olsen's grand mural evocation of another Slessor poem, 'Five Bells', or from the Wharf Theatre at Walsh Bay, or the Ensemble Theatre on the other side of the harbour at Kirribilli, or, after a performance of the Australian Opera, or in the Concert Hall or Drama Theatre, from the covered walk along the water's edge between Bennelong Point and Circular Quay. The physical life of a city inevitably affects what is produced there. It also changes, however subtly, what is brought in from elsewhere. To hear *Pelleas* at the Fenice in Venice is not the same as hearing it in Brussels or New York. We bring to the occasion, and to our reception of it, something of the watery city we have just stepped out of; the work is acclimatised, changed. So too, coming from an early evening walk round to the Opera House, Mahler, a composer Sydney has made very much its own, no longer belongs entirely to the Central European world his music so poignantly evokes. The mixture of cracked sentimentality and noble doom, of stoicism and savage irony, has developed a new set of references, found a new home. Mahler is not the first composer one might think of in this unbuttoned and sometimes raffish city, but he suits it just the same; he speaks in an unexpected way for its uneasy mixture of grandeur and thin, rather anxious allure. This is a nervous city; a lot of its energy is overwrought, its glamour, as Slessor knew, a surface over depths. Painters like John Olsen and Brett Whiteley also know it. Lyric grace and the line that contains it is never far in their world from unease and the opening of the two-dimensional on to a void. One of the most revealing experiences Sydney offers is to stand in front of the works of these artists in the State Gallery and to catch at the same time, through plate-glass walls, a glimpse of the wharves at Woolloomooloo, and beyond, in mid-harbour, the little fort of Pinchgut, sunlit and romantic-looking but with a history as dark as any the Old World has known. Air and water are the elements these pictures point to, and the darkness that is inherent in them, along with the most vivid light. It is, quite strikingly, the Aboriginal paintings in our galleries that evoke most strongly the heavier element of *earth*.

This is a water city, a port; it deals in changes. Bring in a Mahler symphony, or a Shakespeare play or a play by Ibsen or Chekhov, and it has first to pass a customs barrier. When it gets to the other side it has developed an accent, begun to express itself in a new idiom. The mechanicals of *A Midsummer Night's Dream*, the rustics of *As You Like It*, become local types, the spaces of Holy Russia reconstruct themselves as the spaces that lie between our own scattered cities. It is an Australian distance that opens up between Chekhov's characters and creates the void they pock their billiards balls into or dance across and see yawning beneath their feet.

Inevitable, perhaps, that in a city that is so vividly aware of the body and its precarious moment, a city where you can swim for nine months of the year at harbour and ocean beaches, the art that is most immediately expressive of it should be the dance. Graham Murphy's Sydney Dance Company, Paul Mercurio's Australian Choreographic Ensemble, The Aboriginal and Islander Dance Theatre, Stephen Page's Bangarra, the One Extra Company, all work out of Sydney and express something of its exuberant joy in the physical, its cheeky humour and sly, understated wit. It is here that the 'pagan' style of the city, its apparently mindless devotion to the physical moment, comes up hard against its own limitations and, while remaining true to 'the body's world', finds an inner grace and power in which the physical is both supremely present and at the same time transcended.

Lights on water, lines of red, gold, green against the night skies of summer—to steal another line from Slessor, 'The fiery paintbox of the body's world'. Nothing characterises more clearly Sydney's public style than those popular outdoor occasions, New Year's Eve, Jazz in the Park, Opera in the Park, Symphony Under the Stars, that end with a spectacle against which even the great southern constellations look pale—the splendid but transitory brilliance of fireworks. The showers fall, red, gold, green, and are seen twice over, once in air, once in the water. The depths open downwards, as Slessor observed, but are also opened upwards, and the crowd's breath soars to fill them. Something is spoken for here, some joyful commitment to transitory beauty, to 'the fiery paintbox of the body's world', that is essential to the place, a statement, a light and popular one, of what can be glimpsed, if only momentarily, in a world of eternal change and transformation, but is still worth sighing or reaching for, and seems all the more precious perhaps because it can never be caught.

David Malouf, 'Sydney: City of water, light and air', Australian Opera News, 27, Summer Season 1994.

Roger McDonald

Roger McDonald (1941–) has written novels, poetry, short stories, film scripts, and non-fiction as well as working as an editor.

Dolphins came in close

Each day he walked farther south along the coastal path slammed by the sea. When he came within sight of Waverley Cemetery he turned aside, put his head down, and tramped a maze of suburban streets …

He went to a rocky headland and stared at the sea. Just the sea.

He had seen the sea rarely as a boy. Just once from a plane bringing him down, the tiny Cessna beetling through cloud canyons and frightening foxes over tussocky knolls …

It was late July, the coldest time of year cutting in. Wind lifted the wave-tops into white peaks as he walked to a point south of Bondi and stared at the sea. The stormy crash and counterflow of the breakers carried his gaze farther out until he fixed on an eddy, a patterned patch of smoothness in the rough. It was like the flattening wake of ship except there was no ship to be seen, only heaving half glimpsed half submerged shapes. He saw what they were. Dark whales in the ocean swell wallowing past sandstone caps, rising, blowing, sinking from sight. Nobody else saw them. Walkers went past with their eyes on the wet path ahead in a belief that wonders were elsewhere. It was a wild day. Five of them exploding like burst pipes in a steam factory and then gone. He tracked their resurfacings until they left him alone. They came in his sleep after that, with marbled eyes regarding him.

A day later, calm, a single whale with a rectangular platform snout appeared. It cruised along chunky as a barge. Still nobody saw it but him. His feeling was a gift that he held in his heart for as long as he could. That night he dreamed of the whales in the depth of their dive, shadowing away to darkness.

The following morning was calm and dolphins came close in. Nine of them. He counted them. Later the shadow of a stingray. Then a container ship balanced on the horizon, bulbous as a galleon. Finally an aircraft carrier rising from under the horizon, planes on deck with wings folded back cicada-like. It was a vision of ignorant strength and destruction and unknowingness rising from the sea.

Roger McDonald, *The Slap*, Picador, Sydney, 1996.

David Marr

David Marr, journalist, is Patrick White's biographer as well as the editor of his letters.

The irresistible city

This unruly, corrupt and beautiful place is so big now: half a dozen cities in one, sprawling west all the way to the mountains. Big cities are exciting: in the simple mathematics of these things, four million people are much, much better than one. Sydney is these millions of people. The mood of the place is their mood. There is fear, worry and anger here, but this is a city that believes in its bones that the future is good. When pollsters try to measure optimism levels around Australia, Sydney goes off the dial. Not that we care much for comparisons. Sydney laps up flattery, but doesn't really give a damn what other cities really think. The rest of Australia lies somewhere over the mountains and we sit on the edge of the Pacific looking east, but not much further out to sea than the last line of breakers. In Sydney's imagination, this is a city without a hinterland, all of Australia wrapped up in one and a great city of the world.

The truth isn't crucial here: this is how we *feel* about Sydney.

Despite all there is to be ashamed about in this town, Sydney has never been keener to celebrate itself. A couple of weeks ago you could spend a morning walking from the exhibition of Francis Greenway's architecture (much of it lost) at the Hyde Park Barracks down Macquarie Street to the Mitchell Library where they've gathered in one room all the best engravings of early Sydney (mostly buried under office blocks) and then still round the corner to the Museum of Sydney to see plans and photographs of the buildings (some already demolished) that won the Sulman prize for architecture. This rolling round of applause continues across the Domain where the icons of Sydney are always hanging in the Art Gallery of NSW: von Guerard's Sydney Heads bathed in innocent sunlight to Brett Whiteley's opium visions of a blacker, dangerous town.

A great city's sense of itself is fed by rumour and gossip, paintings and novels—surprisingly few good novels of Sydney—by family legends and scraps of history remembered from school, by morning radio and evening television—and by newspapers. For over a century the *Sydney Morning*

Herald has been crucial to Sydney's picture of itself as a respectable but disorderly town, erratically democratic, not quite secular, tolerant but with an undertow of old hatreds. The focus of the picture shifts and changes over time but from the first there's been a sense in this paper and this town, that hanging over Sydney there's always been a smell of money. Money means optimism and curiosity.

Money has made Sydney the first destination of new ideas, new vices, new fashions, new people and yet more money. Nearly a quarter of the nation lives in Sydney and most immigrants want to settle here—despite the realities they find in Cabramatta and Liverpool. Tourists make Sydney their main port of call and despite these visitors showing an odd taste for opals and Darling Harbour, their presence confirms Sydney's high opinion of itself while feeding the city's coffers. That's a very Sydney arrangement—all the more so because it wasn't meant to happen.

Sydney is a city of mean motives overwhelmed by its own good fortune.

Every town has a reason for being that works like a window into the soul of the place. Sydney is only here because of the harbour. But the British didn't have a clue it existed: Cook sailed right past. The penal settlement of Botany Bay might have been just another abandoned settlement around Australia but for the sheer good fortune of Captain Phillip finding, a few miles up the coast, 'one of the finest harbours in the world, in which a thousand ships of the line might ride in perfect security.'

What was meant to be a dumping house for British convicts flourished through lucky break after lucky break to become a great port, then a great city. Nothing much was planned. The prevailing instincts of government have always been to scrimp and save. In this town, luck has been everything.

The site is so beautiful its shrugs off what would ruin a dozen cities. The land lies under us with a kind of aboriginal resignation, never accepting the worst it's suffered and never admitting defeat. One of Sydney's great assets is the sense we have that after all that's happened here, we might still get it right. Perhaps that's pitching it too high. Maybe it's just a crazy confidence we share that even after so much has been lost and given away what's left will still be wonderful.

From the moment Phillip dropped anchor, Sydney has been given away, slice by slice. It's probably the oldest continuous tradition of government in NSW, from the first plots to army officers round Sydney Cove to the 24 hectares of showground delivered to Rupert Murdoch. Governments treat this town like Norman Lindsay's Magic Pudding: however much is taken, there's always a full bowl left of beef and beer.

> Onions, bunions, corns and crabs,
> Whiskers, wheels and hansom cabs.

This is the bedtime story of Sydney's government, but the city is so prodigously rich it's almost true. Almost.

By the time the *Herald* hit the streets in 1831, Sydney was set in its ways. Phillip's modest town plan had been abandoned by his successors. When irascible Governor Bligh tried to stop army officers building where they liked and fencing off what they wanted, the row hastened his overthrow. Sydney is always said to be marked by its convict origins—it is—but what marks us just as much is the rebellion against Bligh. We know from way back when the crunch comes the powerful of this town—not only the developers—won't worry too much about the law.

Sydney's last chance to be a city to match its harbour was lost with Macquarie. He had plans, but London sent out Commissioner Bigge, that Thatcherite before his time, to stop Macquarie in his tracks. No city squares, no cathedral, no avenues, no viceroy's palace. Meanness triumphed at this crucial point. Sydney was not going to another Imperial city like Dublin or Calcutta: there wasn't the need to dazzle the native population. Redcoats could handle the blacks, and building was left to the merchants.

Not entirely. There were engineers to put in drains and trains, the fire brigade to make sure nothing was built higher than 50 metres in the town, until the AMP at the Quay broke through that ceiling in 1962 and the whole CBD followed. Money won. Money usually does in Sydney. There are rules and norms in the city now, but no absolute ceiling.

And there were rats. *Ratus ratus* brought the bubonic plague to Sydney at the turn of the century, and in its wake the town began to clean itself up. In this city where nearly every planning vision fails before it leaves the drawing board, we developed a modest knack for improvement, planting trees and paving footpaths. Very Sydney. We're still at it with great civic flourish and self-congratulation. Had Macquarie Street been saved from the demolishers it would be one of the great streets—better than anything in New Orleans—instead the remains were 'improved' by Neville Wran for the Bicentenary. George Street, the dark and crooked spine of the city, is being 'improved' right now for the Olympics.

Not that the grand visions of planners for the last century were much good. The muddle of the town—so hated by this paper—was always richer and more fun than their best intentions. There would be no Paddington by now if the planners had had their way, no Surry Hills, no Woolloomooloo and no Rocks. A very Sydney combination of forces saved them—at least for now. First came pig-headed local politicians: slums breed Labor votes. Then the militant Sydney middle classes fought alone or in alliance with communists: the green bans. Then came the money: nowadays suburbs condemned for decades as cesspits of vice and crime are too expensive for governments to muck about with. For the moment, in a few precincts of this city, money is working in the right direction.

The only planners' dream that never dies in Sydney is the vision of a city served by expressways. Nothing has had [such an] impact on this town as cars. For cars we built the Bridge—and who regrets that? Traffic jams on the Bridge gave us North Sydney in the 1960s and as the traffic jams moved north the car gave us Chatswood in the 1990s and now Hornsby. The same is happening south and west. One side of the city was flattened to build expressways into the heart of the city and now—the lessons of the Western Distributor unlearnt—we're flattening stretches of eastern Sydney to do the same again. In Boston they're putting their old freeways underground. We're told we're too poor.

Not poor: this is one of the richest cities on earth. We're mean. The character of this town is marked everywhere by meaness. Powerlines slung through the air are so mean and so Sydney. And those blocks of flats, built hugger mugger and mean, right to the edge of the harbour, are so Sydney standing there brand-new waiting to be the slums of tomorrow. Meanest of all and most like Sydney is its airport. Hong Kong can find $27 billion to flatten a few islands and build an airport for the future. But Sydney has decided to make do with extensions to the old Mascot polo fields. For everyone but the hundreds of thousands who live under the planes, it's a decision that has the winning Sydney virtue of being cheap.

Fear plays a part in this: it takes some political courage to make big civic gestures in Sydney because the country is always ready to punish a government that does. Paul Keating offered about $200 million to bury the Cahill Expressway, money John Fahey's government couldn't touch once the bush decided Keating's cash might be better spent on drought relief. So Canberra kept the money and Sydney looks like having the Cahill for ever. Bob Carr could buy back East Circular Quay tomorrow, but for the fear of the bush's revenge. Already the Olympics are posing problems for Labor because out west they see all this money being spent on Sydney. Even so, Olympic dollars will solve none of the fundamental problems. Exasperating ...

And yet in late October there's a day you can suddenly smell summer coming and forgive the place almost anything. In that burst of heat, houses open themselves again to the air. The suburbs settle into their gardens. Then for a week or so jacarandas—always 'really good this year'—flower that astonishing blue against the town's brown brick. Thunderstorms cross the suburbs. Nights are warm. Under the stairs you search for the last of last year's mosquito coils. The water is still cold at the beach, but the sun is already hot. Sydney is back on the sand again, pleased to find how beautiful it still is: beautiful place, beautiful people.

The sea means escape is always in the air in Sydney, always a possibility, even though we don't, every hot day, down tools and head for the water. A Sydney year doesn't divide neatly into work and holiday: we can be in the surf any day of the week, and weekends here offer what most of the world calls a holiday. Not that we all go to the beach even on the hottest days. There's work to be done and four million of us couldn't find enough space on the sand to spread our towels. The point about Sydney is that the beach is there, always, in our imagination.

Cities are defined by the possibilities they offer. We don't all surf; we don't spend much time on the harbour; not everyone is noshing their nights away in Sydney's stainless steel cafes. The 'What's On' pages in this paper have always been the community noticeboard of Sydney's theatres and galleries. There's a lot happening these days and Sydney is proud of that, but this is a city that's a lot better at knowing what's happening—keeping across the gossip, reading reviews, being really really interested—than actually going. Unless, of course, it's a hit.

Sydney loves winners: horses, shows, writers, painters, football teams, politicians, lovers and crooks. But the long haul of team loyalty isn't for us. When the Swans are on a winning streak we're fans for life—unless they start losing. Sydney is a city of spectators except a few times a year when we play as a city—New Year's Eve and Mardi Gras. What could be more Sydney than few hundred thousand folk down by the harbour to drink and watch the fireworks? Every week this summer there will be four or five fireworks displays somewhere over Sydney—mostly on the harbour which, apart from anything else, is rated the best amphitheatre for fireworks in the world. New Year's Eve is now, via television, a world event. The annual bill for crackers will be $7 million or $8 million. How we love that Chinese fire.

This city will celebrate almost anything that puts on a good show. Patrick White was not alone in fearing a respectable backlash if homosexuals went round 'swinging their handbags' in public. But in the end they won over Sydney by taking off their clothes and marching down Oxford Street. Glitz did the trick. When the police commissioner, the Attorney-General and the Leader of the Opposition gathered in the VIP room to watch the 1997 parade, it wasn't because millions of pink dollars were being spent out there that night, nor were these dignitaries showing political solidarity. They came for the show. So had 700,000 citizens in the streets—including an unhappy little band of preachers. They are with us always.

Fred Nile once said, 'If Jesus wept over Jerusalem, He must be heartbroken over Sydney.' On Saturday nights evangelists gather near Hoyts, preaching sin and redemption as they have on street corners every Saturday night since they came ashore with the prisoners. This paper has often allied itself since with those whose mission it was—and is—to deny the town what it's always wanted: pleasure. Even the name of the place is an elegant little time-bomb for puritans. 'An ugly word, Sydney,' wrote Ruth Park. 'The city was named for a maggot-headed politician ... Yet the name attests the poetic irony of fate. The convict settlement was to be called Albion, but this never took. Instead we got Sydney, a word which is a corruption of St

Denis, in its turn a corruption of the Greek Dionysus. This wild and fatal deity is alive and well in his name city.'

Early on, NSW governments reached a worldly accommodation with the preachers. They passed many strange and cruel laws to keep them happy, while knowing that corruption would allow real life to continue more or less unimpeded. No one could say Macquarie Street hadn't tried—but think of the political mayhem if these laws had actually worked! By small acts of courage, NSW governments sometimes face the puritans and clip a few mad provisions out of the Crimes Act, but it's slow going. The touted sophistication of the town in the last few decades was still mediated by the corruption needed to allow dance clubs, gambling, brothels, booze out of hours and sex in arrangements forbidden by the Bible.

The price of keeping puritan Sydney has been high: turning—who knows how many?—police, magistrates, judges and politicians into crooks. We're not another Lusaka but corruption deeply affects civic life in Sydney, not least because we've known ever since the army was shipping illegal spirits in from Calcutta that the law enforcers here are entangled with the crooks. The royal commissions we hold to expose this every few years—strongly supported by this paper—are part of a long Sydney tradition. They are as theatrical in their way as the latest David Williamson: great characters, earthy dialogue, tears and laughter, strong moral arguments for improvement and then ... not much changes in the real world.

We've just been through it all again, down to the conventional last scenes on the floor of Parliament when the politicians disown the commissioners' hard recommendations and side, instead, with the puritans. Government and Opposition agreed that there would be no change to the age of consent, no let-up in the war against drugs, no 'shooting galleries' to save addicts' lives. The town rated the James Wood show a fabulous success.

We have a lot to be angry about in this town, but anger dissipates so easily here. It's one of the pleasures—and problems—of the place. Fools in Macquarie Street, crooks in the CIB, Goths on the building sites enrage Sydney for a few days at a time, but then comes the weekend: a drink and film on Friday night, sleep, an hour in the surf, lunch with friends in the backyard with good food, a few jokes and that acid gossip we love in this town. If pain persists, there's always the harbour: symbol of the city's great good fortune, still so beautiful it triumphs over most of the worst that's been inflicted here.

All Sydney feels it owns the harbour. It would be perfectly understandable if families living hard in suburbs on the outer rim of the city resented the privileges of the harbour. But that's not how it works: there's no evidence of animosity. Far outnumbering the backpackers at Circular Quay at weekends are Sydney people in for the day to see their city. It's our Opera House even if we never set foot in it. And along the walkways of the Quay and the Botanic Gardens we exercise a right no Australian questions: to get to the water's edge.

The harbour is more beautiful—but less dramatic—than it's been for a century or more because it's no longer a busy port. Trucks have triumphed over trains in Australia, and trucks find it easier to reach Botany Bay. So the working port has relocated, by supreme irony, to the windswept bay Phillip abandoned a couple of hundred years ago. But in a switch that's very, very Sydney, the harbour is now turning its beauty into cash. It always took a small fortune to own a house with lawns running down to one of the bays east of the Bridge; now huge sums are ventured almost anywhere on the harbour for a decent flat with a view of the water. It's a sort of mania loose in the world.

The GDP of small nations is tied up in harbour real estate. In the last decade, six or so billion dollars have been spent buying and selling along the waterfont streets of Sydney. Even in busts, the market in harbour real estate hardly falters. And the *Herald* prospers on the ads.

The inexorable pressure of money is mounting to put bigger buildings on smaller sites where the harbour can be glimpsed. Tourists want hotel rooms with views of what they've flown all this way to see: the harbour. A bit of water is a security prized by Westpac. So the old coal loaders, factories, gas works and docks, decommissioned now, are waiting for apartments to be built in their place. In the name of preserving the heritage, the city is even allowing hundreds of apartments to be built over the water in old—but virtually rebuilt—wharves in Walsh Bay and Woolloomooloo. This is Sydney pioneering a new kind of real estate, subdividing the sea …

The shape of the harbour is being decided for the long haul. Those old industrial sites were easy to clear once the factories outlived their purposes. But the blocks of apartments that are now replacing them along the shoreline, each with dozens or even scores of individual owners, will be all but impossible to shift. We've learnt with relief and at times sorrow—in the case of the State Office Block—that office buildings aren't permanent. Even the big ones come and go. Apartment blocks don't: whatever goes up strataed never comes down.

A bad building on the harbour diminishes the whole city. Imagine how we would feel about this city in the late 1990s if Eero Saarinen had not plucked Joern Utzon's sketch of an opera house out of the discard heap and awarded him the prize. Had we built the Philadephia-designed squeeze box that came second to Utzon's masterpiece, or the little interlinking British boxes that came third, this city and our sense of this city would have been permanently diminished. Utzon was dismissed for the meanest of motives, but even the botched building we got in the end is a triumph—another of those triumphs of good fortune over mean motives that make Sydney.

But for this city and the harbour the winning stroke of luck is that the bush along the northern shore had been occupied all this century by the armed forces of another government: the Commonwealth of Australia. It's been beyond NSW's power to give away. Every square inch of the shore in Hong Kong is built over, and that's exciting in its own way; Istanbul, which might claim an even more spectacular site than Sydney, is city to the waterline. Around Manhattan you're lucky to find a tree. What's uniquely beautiful is that so much of the harbour's shoreline is almost virgin bush. Behind are suburbs bursting at the seams, over the water is a gleaming city but setting the scene is this long line of bush. It's the source, in all lights and weather, of qualities in short supply in this town: innocence and serenity.

But the Commonwealth is shedding the land. Middle Head is destined, if the Department of Defence gets its way, to be subdivided—to raise a few millions to fund the needs of the Commonwealth for perhaps a few hours. The fate of this stretch of the harbour now rests in the hands of a South Australian grazier, the Defence Minister, Ian McLachlan, who I suspect has happy memories of his childhood back on the property when his nurse would read him Norman Lindsay's *The Magic Pudding*. Said Barnacle Bill: 'You have to be as smart as paint to keep this Puddin' in order. He's that artful, lawyers couldn't manage him ... The more you eats the more you gets. Cut-an'-come-again is his name, an' cut-an'-come-again is his nature ...'

In a rage a moment ago, I stopped to stare out the window. From the *Herald*'s perch on the 27th floor I can see to the mountains. The suburbs are softened by hot blue haze. Tonight there should be one of those slow summer sunsets the colour of fire. No sign of the promised thunderstorms. Even the suburbs I spent so many years despising don't seem threatening these days. It looks good. There are still a thousand reasons to rage against Sydney—anywhere we love makes us rage—but no other city here could be so exciting, so funny and alive. Despite everything, this is the place.

> David Marr, 'The irresistible city', *Sydney Morning Herald*,
> 2 December 1997.

Elisabeth Wynhausen

Elisabeth Wynhausen (1946–), journalist, came to Australia as a child with her family.

A remnant of traditional life

A toddler, a sturdy, dimpled child, is playing inside the house, a tenement on Redfern's notorious Eveleigh Street. 'Money,' she says, when I first walk in.

There are beds, but no chairs, in the small, dark rooms downstairs. Such furniture as there is—a rickety chest of drawers and a dresser—is gouged and scratched. Except for a little china cat and a child's clock, on the dresser, there is nothing else—no toys, no books, no pictures and no ornaments.

Young men troop up and down the stairs. People hammer on the battered front door from early in the morning until late at night. Not even those who live there produce a key, instead banging on the door if they want to get in. The noise blends into the general pandemonium, as yet another person starts to shout. The sudden outbursts—furies that subside almost as rapidly as they erupt—add to the sense of discordant life inside and out.

This past summer seemed to sound the death knell for the Block, now the nation's most famous wretched ghetto. The niceties are being observed, perhaps a little late in the piece. Following intervention by the NSW Government, the latest in a long line of reports on the redevelopment of the Block suggests the site could again be used for housing for Aborigines. But by then the few hundred people living there now will have been scattered to the four winds. To record something of their lives before the existing community disappears, I come and go for several weeks, wandering around in the day and spending a few nights in the house on Eveleigh Street.

Piled on top of a cupboard, just inside the front door, are several big plastic garbage bags full of used clothes. More used clothing spills out of bags and cartons in the other rooms. At first sight, the heaps of clothing and bedding resemble the frowzy, forgotten rejects thrown in the back of an old secondhand shop. But Margie, the tenant, vainly tries to instil some kind of order, forever starting to tidy up. At 46, Margie has kept her looks and her bright-eyed, expectant air (as if waiting to see where the next mischief will come from), but says she feels under pressure all the time. That may be why she agrees to let me lodge at her place without worrying about the consequences. The prospect of having a white woman journalist to stay promises a slight diversion from the afflictions of her life. She shares the place with several of her children and grandchildren and whoever else crashes that night. Margie looks after her two grandchildren—her daughter Janice's kids—because Janice has been a junkie since she was in her teens.

'Don't take any notice of her,' Margie says when she first mentions it, but this is difficult: as we walk down Eveleigh Street, with her grand-daughter, adorable, sturdy two-year-old Charmaine, Janice, a haggard woman with pitted skin and caved-in cheeks, sees her mother, and follows in a frenzy. 'Give me some money, Mum ... Mum, give me thirty dollars,' she calls again and again, in a wheedling, childish voice, as her own daughter calls out to her 'Hallo, Mum, hallo Mum ...', anxiously tugging at her mother's tracksuit pants. Janice pays no attention to the little girl.

'Don't take any notice,' Margie says again, as we walk along the street, like deaf people, mother and child still calling out.

Janice is as neglectful of her son. A spindly seven-year-old who is anaemic and looks too small for his age, the boy mucks up to get attention but gets money from Margie instead. 'Gimme me that money back,' she yells next morning when he says he won't go to school. Other children in Redfern Primary's red baseball caps are skylarking around outside, waiting for the bus.

'Shouldn't you be in school?' I say to a nine-year-old who spends all day on the street and Margie leaps in to shut me up, almost as if it is asking for trouble to let on that I've noticed anyone else, even a kid who plays truant day in and day out. The same boy is out there again the following week.

The other boy always out on the street is a big 13- or 14-year-old whose mother died of an overdose and whose father hanged himself. I first see him with another boy, on the roof of a derelict building, hurling condom water bombs at a woman picking up the dirty needles left lying around the shooting galleries on Caroline Lane. She screams a few warnings and heaves a halfbrick up towards them.

A group of men watch from the concrete deck under the Aboriginal Housing Company building on the corner of Eveleigh Street. Most will be there all day and probably the next. One or two make disapproving noises and shake their heads before opening another bottle of beer. They want it understood that in their day they had to go to school.

'This is the nineties,' says one man, adopting the mournful tone Sydney broadcaster Alan Jones adopts to talk about the youth of today.

There's a constant disjunction between the real, the symbolic and the imagined worlds of the Block. In the narrow kitchen of Margie's house, Fender, a freckled, middle-aged man with a paunch, is pacing up and down, talking about prehistory in a loud, insistent voice.

'We were the first blood and we sent youse [the whites] out. Now youse are back. You alienated your Aboriginality ...'

His fantasy places Aborigines at the apex of human life and himself at the apex of Aboriginal life—a suggestive sort of grandiloquence in an urban fringe-dweller (and smalltime drug dealer) who lives among the people at the very bottom of the heap. 'I am the last of the first blood,' he says, continuing his monologue though two more visitors have just walked in.

The constant coming-and-going is part of the fractious sociability of life in this house and this street. No doubt it's a remnant of traditional life. But the remnants can only be stretched so far—Fender is one of the many locals who speak as if they've arranged their lives in the interstices of white contempt. The crazy talk and inflated rhetoric, both common on the Block, add to my impression that people are constantly shadow-boxing with grotesque images of themselves—images that surrounded them even before the damaged community was demonised by those intent on erasing it.

Elisabeth Wynhausen, 'Block out', *Australian Magazine*,
14–15 June 1997.

Leonie Stevens

Leonie Stevens (1962–) is a novelist and short-story writer. The Phoenician Club is now closed. It was a couple of streets away from the Block.

Does this for stress release

'Where are we going?' I asked George, looking around at one of the most godforsaken parts of Sydney. Broadway was a wound, an eruption of noise and filth. I straightened my dress and messed up my hair. 'You got me out of bed for this?'

George led me to the traffic lights, then gestured across the road at the Phoenician Club.

'Wrestling!'

I laughed. 'What? You're kidding, right?'

'You'll love this, Siren. I guarantee ya. Course it wouldn't be as good as the old days—Mario Milano, Spiros Arion. Remember Tiger Singh? Beautiful Brutus? Haystacks Calhoon?'

I laughed. I certainly did remember Haystacks. That's what we used to call George behind his back.

'Ah, those were the days! D'ya remember the Brain Buster?' The lights changed, and we started to cross Broadway. 'And what about the old Texas Polly? Yep, sure is a lethal one.'

I noticed he said 'is', and imagined George the grown man acting like George the youth, dropping his four-year-old niece onto her head. But the adult George probably dropped fully grown men, and I didn't want to think about it too much.

'I don't know,' I told him. 'I'm not really in the mood for simulated violence—'

George laughed. 'Forget that intellectual crap. Nothing more relaxing than some blood and guts, girl. If you learnt that, may be you wouldn't be such an uptight little—' ...

... He sat there sulking until a voluptuous Maria Venuti type with huge hips and flaming red hair approached the ring and climbed the side stairs. She had to bend to get through the ropes, and when she did her cleavage billowed out like buttocks. Whistles went around the hall. She smiled, genuinely pleased.

'Thank you, thank you. I'd like to welcome here you tonight ...' I lost interest and went for the champagne. I nudged the cork, trying hard not to cause a big noise, as she rattled off the stars of tonight's program. The Bloody Baron, Gorgeous Gary. The New South Wales Right. The Butcher Boys. The Brothers. And all the way from Brisbane, the Iron Men. Ha, I'd love to see them get thrashed. I put the heavies on the cork.

It popped at maximum volume and ricocheted off the roof, hitting Ms Billowing Breasts smack on the nose. I couldn't believe it: I wanted to die. Then I wanted to laugh. I had to bend down and climb halfway under the table to control myself. George bent down too, and we looked at each other sideways, amongst other people's legs.

'You right, Siren?'

'Never better, George.'

He laughed like Santa. 'Suit yourself.'

'Pass my drink, huh?'

He passed me down a glass of hard-earned champagne and I listened to an introduction of the first combatants. From Germany, the Bloody Baron. From Sydney, Gorgeous Gary. I waited until the bell went off before I came up from under the table.

Two guys were in the ring. One wore a balaclava, the other a permanently startled expression. They circled each other for a long time, then went for a dual neck hold. The one in the balaclava—the Bloody Baron, I assumed—yelled out in a lousy German accent he'd probably learnt from *Hogan's Heroes*. Gorgeous Gary seemed to be trying hard. His clean blond hair and shiny boots didn't help him when the Bloody Baron hit him with a suplex. Splat, down to the canvas. The Bloody Baron pinned him for a count of two, but Gorgeous Gary humped and broke free.

The noise level was intense. Everyone was shouting, including me. I can't remember what I was yelling, especially after the third champagne, but it was probably something like, 'Ahhhh, get the bastard ... gaaaaaarn ... ahhh, get him ... gaaaaarn, pin him!' It was just like watching the WWF with Vic and the mob from the Lodge, only better, because I could yell my head off and no-one banged the wall.

The match ended with the Bloody Baron trouncing young Gary. It was obviously arranged, but Gary looked really upset, like he'd copped it harder than they agreed on. Still that's what he got for being the good guy. He slipped out of the ring while the Baron was still parading around, revelling in his victory.

'I know that bloke,' said George to me, indicating the Baron. 'He's an accountant from Balmain. Educated man, does this for stress release.'

Leonie Stevens, from *Big Man's Barbie: Ten Days that Shook My Booty*, Vintage, Milson's Point, NSW, 1996.

Sources

Anderson, Jessica, 'A good place to bring up children', from Anderson, *The Impersonators*, Macmillan, South Melbourne, 1980.

Australian Engineering and Building News, 'Relieving the harbour from pollution', from 'The drainage of Sydney', *Australian Engineering and Building News*, vol. 1, no. 2, 1 August 1879.

Bandmann, Daniel, 'A class of vampires', from Bandmann, *An Actor's Tour*, Brentano, New York, 1886.

Barnes, Sid, 'A rent collector at seven', from Barnes, *It Isn't Cricket*, Collins, Sydney, 1953.

Beaver, Bruce, 'Manly it was', from Beaver, 'The village', in *Headlands*, University of Queensland Press, Brisbane, 1986.

Bilson, Gay, 'The Mardi Gras Opera Gastronomique', from Bilson, 'Opera Gastronomique', *Oz Arts*, Issue 6, 1993.

Brewer, F.G., 'The rowdy denizens of Blackwattle Swamp', quoted in *A Century of Journalism: The Sydney Morning Herald and Its Record of Australian Life 1831–1931*, written and published by John Fairfax & Sons, Sydney, 1931.

Brown, Allan, 'The stones of Sydney', from Brown, 'The stonemason', in *The Sleeping City: The Story of Rookwood Necropolis* (ed. David H. Weston), Society of Australian Genealogists with Friends of Rookwood Inc. and Hale & Iremonger, Sydney, 1989.

Bulletin, 'Taking pleasure madly', 9 January 1881.

Cambridge, Ada, 'Cultivated minds rubbing together', from Cambridge, *Thirty Years in Australia*, Methuen, London, 1903.

Campion, Edmund, 'An easy mark for developers', from Campion, *A Place in the City*, Penguin, Melbourne, 1994.

Cappiello, Rosa R., 'Slaves of the dollar', from Cappiello, *Oh Lucky Country*, University of Queensland Press, St Lucia, Qld, 1984.

Catt, C.C., 'Graffito spy' in *State of the Art: The Mood of Contemporary Australia in Short Stories* (ed. Frank Moorhouse), Penguin, Melbourne, 1983.

Chidley, W.J., 'In my lonely cell', from *The Confessions of William James Chidley* (ed. Sally McInerney), University of Queensland Press, Brisbane, 1977.

Chisholm, Caroline, 'Scenes of immorality beyond comprehension', from *Radical in Bonnet and Shawl: Four Political Lectures by Caroline Chisholm* (ed. John Moran), Preferential Publications, Ashgrove, Qld, 1994.

Daily Telegraph (Sydney), 'Troopers charged right and left', 20 September 1890.

Darwin, Charles, 'A fine town', from Darwin, *The Voyage of the Beagle*, J.M. Dent, London, 1959.

Deakin, Alfred, 'Carefully posed for effect', from Deakin, *The Federal Story*, Robertson & Mullens, Melbourne, 1944.

Dilke, Charles, 'No trace of convict blood', from Dilke, *Greater Britain: A Record of Travel in English Speaking Countries During 1866 and 1867*, Macmillan, London, 1868.

Dixon, Adrian, 'Sydney's gayest bars', from Dixon, 'Adrian finds his Avalon', in *Being Different* (ed. Gary Wotherspoon), Hale & Iremonger, Sydney, 1986.

Elliott, Sumner Locke, 'The man with 1000 voices', from Elliott, *Radio Days*, Imprint, Sydney, 1993; 'Would the bridge hold?', from Elliott, *Water Under the Bridge*, reprinted by permission of Pan Macmillan Australia Pty Ltd. Copyright © Sumner Locke Elliott 1977; 'Overpaid, oversexed, and over here', from Elliott, *Edens Lost*, Penguin, Melbourne, 1974.

Ellis, Havelock, 'No good preaching', from Ellis, diaries, 1875, Mitchell Library, Sydney.

Empire, 'Orange v. Green', 29 March 1871.

Express, 'The garden palace', 24 April 1880.

Falkiner, Suzanne, 'The Prince of Wales gets drunk', Barbara Street quoted in *Ethel* (ed. Suzanne Falkiner), Macmillan, Sydney, 1996.

Farrelly, Midget, 'A beat-up paddle board', from *This Surfing Life: Midget Farrelly as told to Craig McGregor*, Rigby, Adelaide, 1965.

Female convict, 'Our kangaroo rats are like mutton', in *Historical Records of New South Wales* (ed. F.M. Bladen), vol. 2, Lansdown Slattery & Co., Mona Vale, NSW, 1978.

Fiaschi, Thomas, 'Wines ordered by medical men', from 'The various wines used in sickness and convalescence. Lecture to the members of the Australian Trained Nurses' Association, by Dr Thomas Fiaschi, on June 27th, 1906', *Australasian Nurses' Journal*, 15 November 1906.

Foster, David, 'A Balmain wake for Martin Luther King', from Foster, *The Glade within the Grove*, Random House, Sydney, 1996.

Fowler, Frank, 'Sydney carries the palm', from Fowler, *Southern Lights and Shadows*, Sampson Low, London, 1859.

Froude, James, 'The most venomous of his whole detested race', from Froude, *Oceana; or, England and Her Colonies*, Longmans Green, London, 1886.

Garner, Helen, 'Our ride to Sydney', from Garner, *Monkey Grip*, Penguin, Melbourne, 1978.

Gill, Lydia, 'Sargent's', from Gill, *My Town: Sydney in the 1930s*, State Library of New South Wales Press, Sydney, 1993.

Godley, Charlotte, 'All Sydney swarms with bugs', from Godley, *Letters from Early New Zealand 1850–53* (ed. John R. Godley), Whitcombe & Tombs, Christchurch, 1951.

Griffith, George, 'That whistle again', from Griffith, *In an Unknown Prison Land*, London, 1900.

Guinness, Daphne, 'Truly posh', from Guinness, 'Spectrum', *Sydney Morning Herald*, 10 September 1994.

Harrower, Elizabeth, 'Another heartless band', from Harrower, *The Watchtower*, Macmillan, Melbourne, 1966.

Harvey, Sandra, and Lindsay Simpson, 'The clubhouse was his castle', from Harvey and Simpson, *Brothers in Arms*, Allen & Unwin, Sydney, 1989.

Hazzard, Shirley, 'Refinement was a frail construction', from Hazzard, *Transit of Venus*, Penguin, Melbourne, 1981.

Hewett, Dorothy, 'Embracing the working class', from Hewett, *Wild Card*, McPhee Gribble, Melbourne, 1990.

Hood, John, 'Gin palaces and pot-houses', from Hood, *Australia and the East*, John Murray, London, 1843.

Horne, Donald, 'A fifty-mile stretch of suburbs' and 'The university's main rebel', from Horne, *The Education of Young Donald*, Penguin, Melbourne, 1988.

Hunter, Governor, 'Abandon'd and profligate manners', from letter to London, 1 June 1797, *Historical Records of Australia* (ed. F.M. Bladen), vol. 4, Lansdown Slattery & Co., Mona Vale, NSW, 1979.

Innocents, 'Unseemly pleasure' from *The Innocents in Sydney*. 'Written by The Innocent/The Prodigal/The Town Crier.' Sydney, 1878.

Ireland, David, 'The study of drinkers', from Ireland, *The Glass Canoe*, Macmillan, South Melbourne, 1976.

James, Clive, 'Praying it would end', from James, *Unreliable Memoirs*, Jonathan Cape, London, 1980.

Johnston, George (1764–1823), 'How the rising was suppressed', letter to Lieutenant-Colonel Paterson, *Historical Records of New South Wales* (ed. F.M. Bladen), vol. 5, Lansdown Slattery & Co., Mona Vale, NSW, 1979.

Johnston, George (1912–70), 'A cocky, callous place' and 'A very short white dress', from Johnston, *Clean Straw for Nothing*, Collins, London, 1969.

Kelly, Archbishop, 'On mixed bathing and alcohol' (from 'Archbishop Kelly's Pastoral Letter, Lent, 1914'), in *Documents in Australian Catholic History*, vol. 2 (ed. Patrick O'Farrell), Geoffrey Chapman, London, 1969.

Keneally, Thomas, 'Down on the mark', from Keneally, *Homebush Boy*, William Heinemann Australia, Port Melbourne, 1995.

Kingsmill, John, 'The Bondi tram' and 'The gab was a family investment', from Kingsmill, *Australia Street: A Boy's-eye View of the 1920s and 1930s*, Hale & Iremonger, Sydney, 1991.

Langford, Ruby, *Don't Take Your Love to Town*, Penguin, Melbourne, 1988.

Lawrence, D.H., 'The bathing suburb', from Lawrence, *Kangaroo* (first published 1922), Penguin, Melbourne, 1976.

Lawson, Henry, 'Board and residence' from *The Stories of Henry Lawson* (ed. Cecil Mann), Angus & Robertson, Sydney, 1964.

Leichhardt, Ludwig, 'You can buy any article', from *The Letters of F.W. Ludwig Leichhardt* (ed. M. Aurousseau), Vol. 2, Hakluyt Society/ Cambridge University Press, London, 1968.

Lindsay, Jack, 'Annie, Betsy, and Bondi', in *The Roaring Twenties* (republished as *Life Rarely Tells: An Autobiography in Three Volumes*, Penguin, Melbourne, 1982).

Lower, Lennie, 'Lower away for the landing', from *The Best of Lennie Lower* (selected by Cyril Pearl and Wep), Lansdowne, Melbourne, 1963; 'The earnestly genteel' from Lower, *Here's Luck*, Angus & Robertson, Sydney, 1938.

Macquarie, Governor, 'No gaming, drunkenness, swearing or fighting', *Sydney Gazette*, 8 October 1810.

Malaspina, Alessandro, 'The climate is variable in the greatest degree', from Robert J. King, *The Secret History of the Convict Colony: Alexandro* [sic] *Malaspina's Report on the British Settlement in New South Wales*, Allen & Unwin, Sydney, 1990.

Male convict, 'The clothes are all wore out', 9 April 1790, in *Historical Records of New South Wales* (ed. F.M. Bladen), vol. 2, Lansdown Slattery & Co., Mona Vale, NSW, 1978.

Malouf, David, 'City of water, light, and air', in *Australian Opera News*, 27, Summer Season 1994.

Marr, David, 'The irresistible city', *Sydney Morning Herald*, 2 December 1997.

Martin, Keith, 'The second Moratorium', from Martin, 'Moratorium march', in *Nation* (ed. Ken Inglis), Melbourne University Press, Melbourne, 1970.

McDonald, Roger, 'Dolphins came in close', from McDonald, *The Slap*, reprinted by permission of Pan Macmillan Australia Pty Ltd. Copyright © Roger McDonald 1996.

Meredith, Louisa Anne, 'Wool, wool, wool', from Meredith, *Notes and Sketches of New South Wales*, John Murray, London, 1844.

Missionaries to the Directors of [London Missionary] Society, London, 1799, in *Historical Records of New South Wales*, vol. 3 (ed. F.M. Bladen), Lansdown Slattery & Co., Mona Vale, NSW, 1978.

Molloy, Margaret, 'I never lifted me head', from Molloy, *A Century of Sydney's Flying Sailors*, Sydney Flying Squadron, Sydney, 1991.

Moran, H.M., 'A Crimean veteran at the street corner', 'The ancient imper-
    sonal dead', and 'War comes to Balmain', from Moran, *Beyond the Hill
    Lies China*, Peter Davies, London, 1945.

Murdoch, Keith, 'The Sydney spirit would not prevail', letter to Andrew
    Fisher, Andrew Fisher Papers, National Library of Australia.

Nathan, Isaac, 'A temple to French cookery', from Nathan, 'The café restau-
    rant', *Illustrated Sydney News*, 11 February 1854.

Nathan [?], Isaac, 'This favourite place of resort', from *The Empire*, c. 1860.

Nelson, Penelope, 'Micky's girls' and 'The Matrons' Ball', from Nelson,
    Penny Dreadful, Random House, Sydney, 1995.

Norton, John, 'Marvellous Melba', from Norton, 'An open letter to Madame
    Melba', *Truth*, 27 March 1903.

Nugent, John, 'A place of resort for low strumpets', from Inspector Nugent,
    'Registry of Flash Men', *Register of Sydney Police Establishments* 1838–51,
    Police Inspector General's Office, NSW State Archives.

Oz, 'A gas turn', February 1966.

Papaellinas, George, 'The welder', from Papaellinas, *Ikons: A Collection of
    Stories*, Penguin, Melbourne, 1986.

Paterson, Banjo, 'Concerning a dog fight', *Bulletin*, 18 May 1895.

Péron, François, 'A sort of coffee house', from Péron, *Voyage to the South-
    ern Hemisphere*, 1807.

Phelan, Nancy, 'Something dangerous and slimy', from Phelan, *A Kingdom
    by the Sea*, Angus & Robertson, Sydney, 1969.

Phillip, Governor, 'The Governor's vineyard', from Phillip's diary (n.d.; c.
    1788?), cited by Philip Norrie, *Vineyards of Sydney*, Horowitz Grahame,
    Sydney, 1990.

Polding, Bede, 'The refuse of other callings', letter, 28 January 1838, from
    The Letters of John Bede Polding OSB, vol. 1, 1819–43, Sisters of the Good
    Samaritan, Glebe, NSW, 1994.

Pringle, John, 'The three winds', from Pringle, *Australian Accent*, Chatto &
    Windus, London, 1958.

Rees, Lloyd, 'A skyline of coral pink', from Rees, *The Small Treasures of a
    Lifetime: Some Memories of Australian Art and Artists*, Angus & Robert-
    son, Sydney, 1988.

Roseville Chase Garden Club, 'Our Christmas meeting' (Ralph H. Law), from
    Journal of the Roseville Chase Garden Club, January 1968.

Roydhouse, Thomas R., and H.J. Taperell, 'The new Labour politician', in
    Roydhouse and Taperell, *The Labour Party in New South Wales: A History
    of its Formation and Legislative Career Together with Biographies of the
    Members and the Complete Text of the Trade Disputes Conciliation and
    Arbitration Act, 1892*, Edwards, Dunlop & Co. Ltd, Sydney, 1892.

Select Committee on the Aborigines, 'All over small pox like', Minutes of
    Evidence taken before the Select Committee [of the New South Wales
    Legislative Council] on the Aborigines, 1845.

Shepherd, Thomas, 'A delightful situation' (1826), quoted in Bernard Smith, *Documents on Art and Taste in Australia*, Oxford University Press, Melbourne, 1975.

Simmons, Joseph, 'The finest views of any spot', *Sydney Gazette*, 23 February 1841.

Slessor, Kenneth, 'Come to Sydney!' from Slessor, *Collected Poems* (ed. Dennis Haskell and Geoffrey Dutton), Angus & Robertson, Sydney, 1994; 'Five bells', in *Collected Poems*, Sirius Books, Sydney, 1964.

Smith, Neddy, 'I ripped the red phone off the wall', from Smith, *Neddy: The Life and Crimes of Arthur Stanley Smith*, Kerr Publishing, Balmain, NSW, 1993.

Smyth, Arthur Bowes (also known as Bowes Smyth), 'Dissipation ashore', from diary, 6 February 1788, Mitchell Library, Sydney.

Stead, Christina, 'The great sub-tropical moon', from Stead, *Seven Poor Men of Sydney* (first published 1934), Sirius Books, Sydney, 1990.

Stevens, Leonie, 'Does this for stress release', from Stevens, *Big Man's Barbie: Ten Days that Shook My Booty*, Vintage, Milson's Point, NSW, 1996.

Stewart, Meg, 'Artists and bohemians of Circular Quay', from Stewart, *Second Half: Autobiography of My Mother*, Penguin, Melbourne, 1988.

Stone, Louis, 'Saturday night at the corner', from Stone, *Jonah* (first published 1911), Endeavour Press, Sydney, 1935.

Streeton, Arthur, 'Steamers whistle and flute', from *Letters from Smike: The Letters of Arthur Streeton* (ed. Ann Galbally and Ann Gray), Oxford University Press, Melbourne, 1989.

Sunday Telegraph, 'Centipedes used in fight against funnel-web spiders', 4 February 1951.

Suttor, George, 'Horror and consternation', letter to Sir Joseph Banks, *Historical Records of New South Wales Wales* (ed. F.M. Bladen), vol. 5, Lansdown Slattery & Co., Mona Vale, NSW, 1979.

Sydney Gazette, 'The amateurs of cricket', 8 January 1804; 'The Church militant', 3 September 1832; 'Fifteen years in the regiment', 9 April 1833; 'A glorious turn-out', 31 March 1842.

Sydney Mail, 'A most determined attempt', 14 March 1868; 'Ungentlemanly conduct' from 'The English eleven v. the eleven of New South Wales. Second day—Saturday, 8 February', 15 February 1879; 'Carbine coming like a locomotive', 27 April 1879.

Sydney Morning Herald, 'Hanging the Mount Rennie rapists', from 'The Mount Rennie outrage', 8 January 1886; 'That floating hell', from 'The great protest meeting', 12 June 1849.

Tench, Watkin, 'Every delicacy was requisite', from Tench, *Sydney's First Four Years*, Library of Australian History, Sydney, 1979.

Tomasetti, Glen, 'My Sydney', in *Expressway: Invitation Stories by Australian Writers from a Painting by Jeffrey Smart* (ed. Helen Daniel), Penguin, Melbourne, 1989.

Trollope, Anthony, 'The very best cabs in the world', from Trollope, *Australia and New Zealand*, Vol. 1, Dawson's of Pall Mall, 1873.

Tucker, James, 'A straggling range of cottages', from Tucker, *Ralph Rashleigh* (first published 1827), Angus & Robertson, Sydney, 1975.

Tyrrell, James, 'A great place for boys', from Tyrrell, *Old Books, Old Friends, Old Sydney*, Angus & Robertson, Sydney, 1952.

Watling, Thomas, 'Sympathetic glooms of twilight glimmering', from Watling, *Letters from an Exile at Botany Bay*, Penrith, Scotland, c. 1794, cited by Bernard Smith, *Documents on Art and Taste in Australia*, Oxford University Press, Melbourne, 1975.

White, Patrick, 'One of the lowest places on earth', from *Patrick White Letters* (ed. David Marr), Random House, Sydney, 1994.

'With kind treatment they are tractable': *Sydney Morning Herald*, 22 November 1890; *Daily Telegraph*, 22 and 27 November 1890; *News*, 27 November 1890; *Exchange*, 5 December 1890.

Wynhausen, Elisabeth, 'A remnant of traditional life', from Wynhausen, 'Block out', *Australian Magazine*, 14–15 June 1997.

The editor and publisher would like to thank copyright holders for permission to reproduce copyright material. Every effort has been made to trace the original source of all material contained in this book. Where the attempt has been unsuccessful the editor and publisher would be pleased to hear from the author or publisher concerned to rectify any omission.

Index